UNVANQUISHED

UNVANQUISHED

Cuba's Resistance to Fidel Castro

ENRIQUE ENCINOSA

Pureplay Press
Los Angeles

Please direct all correspondence to info@pureplaypress.com or Pureplay Press, 11353 Missouri Ave., Los Angeles, CA 90025.

Cataloguing-in-Publication Data
Encinosa, Enrique.
     Unvanquished : Cuba's resistance to Fidel Castro / Enrique Encinosa. — 1st ed.
          p. cm.
          Includes bibliographical references and indices.
ISBN 0-9714366-6-5
1. Cuba — History — Revolution, 1959- 2. Castro, Fidel, 1926- 3. United States — Central Intelligence Agency. 4. Exiles — United States — Political activity. 5. Cuban Americans — United States — Politics and government. I. Title
972.91063—dc22

Library of Congress Control Number: 2003113574

Cover photos: top row and bottom right, guerrillas in the Escambray, early 1960's; bottom left, Cuban commando training in Florida, late 1960's

Photo credits: *Bohemia*; Orlando Bosch collection; Laida Arcia Carro; John Suarez; *Carta de Cuba*; www.free-biscet.org

Author photo: Fernando Castells

Cover and book design by Wakeford Gong

Printed in the United States

Our wine is bitter, but it is our wine.

—Jose Marti

This book is dedicated to my mother and father, who taught me the joy, pain and duty of being Cuban.

EDITOR'S NOTE

Early in 2003, the forty-fifth year of his rule over Cuba, Fidel Castro launched a series of repressive actions that opened quite a number of eyes throughout the world. For most of the last half-century, especially among intellectuals, Castro's regime has enjoyed a vogue far out of proportion to its merits.

Even today, one who expresses clear dislike for Castro is liable to meet with a stern rebuke, such as: "Well, then, you must be for Batista." Castro's predecessor Fulgencio Batista, a tyrant of the old school, has been gone since 1959; but his ghost has been carefully maintained by Cuba's present ruler, and by that ruler's many friends. In America, where anachronisms form quickly, "the corrupt Batista regime" has long been a farcical phrase—as if a liberal Democrat, responding to criticism of the party, were to say, "Well, then, you must be for Eisenhower." Still, people have said it quite often, and with levity nowhere near.

It's notable that advocates of Castro's regime have long been obliged to make outdated references. They invoke U.S. efforts to overthrow Castro—efforts, never more than halfhearted, that American officials halted more than forty years ago. Likewise for those assassination attempts by the CIA, the eternal exploding cigars, which have really become quite stale. For decades, the only means of justifying Castro's policies and explaining their manifest shortcomings has been to blame the U.S. embargo—a measure that lives far more in Castro's and others' rhetoric than it does in Cuba's reality, as Enrique Encinosa's narrative lucidly shows.

The recent crackdown has made plenty of true unbelievers, especially in Europe, from where Castro's regime has been subjected to a barrage of criticism. In April 2003, as condemnations fell on Havana, the run of Western analysts—trying hard to absorb a dreadful situation—speculated that Castro might be using America's highly visible war against Iraq as camouflage for his own campaign. Other observers more astute, however, suggested that Castro wanted all the attention the crackdown gave him.[1] With everyone watching U.S. forces on their way to Baghdad, Castro must have felt excluded from the limelight; and his over-the-top cruelty in sentencing and executing dissidents must have been his way of crying out to the world: "Hey! Don't forget about me!"

Castro's career, at every turn, has betrayed an unnatural lust for attention. More perhaps than with any leader in modern history, his regime has consisted of one public-relations gambit after another. At all times and places, political programs are conceived as public gestures. With Castro, the notable thing is the degree to which PR has lived for its own sake. Castro may have made his living as a communist, but Madison Avenue has had much to learn from the man in the green fatigues. He has virtually turned "the guerrilla" into a commercial trademark. He has made Che Guevara's profile as common as the Marlboro Man. Caricatures and myths he invented—like the "Miami Mafia" or the "kid-napping" of Elian Gonzalez—have become part of our political imagery.

The present work—by a man who has now written four histories of Castro's Cuba, two in Spanish and two in English—passes a fresh lens over apparently settled history. In a striking departure from the usual journalistic practice of putting Castro at center stage, Encinosa lets people, events and situations speak for themselves. Much of the history he relates is new. If not for Encinosa's attentive gaze, it might have perished along with its living witnesses. And much familiar matter emerges in a more revealing light. Quite different from what one reads in standard accounts, this history has the pure savor of experience. Under the author's crisp and undistracted pen, time-honored fallacies fall neatly by the wayside; and what remains is the anguish of Cuba's experience, along with the heroism with which that anguish has been met.

A word of caution is in order. Encinosa's work—even while being the product of extensive thought and careful documentation—is, regrettably, vulnerable to dismissal on the charge that many of its sources dwell in Miami. The Cuban community of that city, thanks largely to Castro's PR, has become a kind of outcast. In the rather pointed phrase of one observer, Miami is today "the most hated city in the world."[2] Perhaps the emerging truth of Castro's regime will prompt a better understanding of the people who have fled from it.

In the meantime, a special virtue of Encinosa's text is that, without polemical effort, it shows the relation between two inseparable things: the experience of Cuba's exiles, and

---

[1] See Mark Falcoff, "Castro's Gambit," *Commentary*, June 2003. See also Jaime Suchlicki, "Crackdown Reflects Castro's Fears, Not U.S. Actions," *The Miami Herald*, April 15, 2003.

[2] Adolfo Rivero Caro, a columnist for Miami's *El Nuevo Herald*

a half-century of repression on "the isle of Doctor Castro."[3] The exiles have come from all groups of society. Cuban Miami is a city of artists and scholars, restaurateurs and storeowners, ex-communists and former members of Castro's armed forces, environmentalists, chess masters, musicians, pastry chefs, radio broadcasters and other working people whom Castro's rule deprived of livelihoods, families, and hopes for a better future. The Cubans in exile also happen to have an uncommonly close bond with their country of origin. When someone in Cuba falls victim to tyranny, someone else, in Miami or New York or Madrid or Paris, is going to weep—and that's the heart of the story Encinosa tells in this mature and satisfying work.

David Landau
Los Angeles, February 2004

---

[3] The title of a work on Cuba by French writers Denis Rousseau and Corinne Cumerlato, *L'île du docteur Castro,* Éditions Stock, 2000

CONTENTS

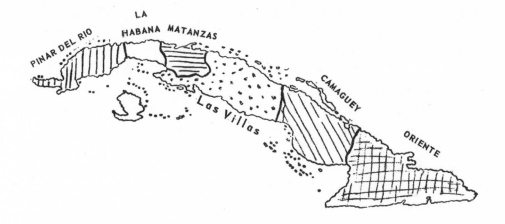

GLOSSARY

of frequently used terms

In advance of the narrative, a few clarifications are offered with regard to names and phrases that might otherwise be confusing to the reader.

"The island." Cubans refer to their country as "the island." The reference is colloquial, for—as one sees above—Cuba is an archipelago. This illustration, taken from an old grade-school textbook, shows the classical six-province division of Cuba that prevailed when Castro seized power in 1959. In 1978, the regime subdivided four of the provinces (and made the western extension of Las Villas, the Zapata peninsula, part of Matanzas) to yield fourteen provinces in all. The classical division, which had lasted for a century, is still the way many Cubans tend to see their country; and it is especially suitable for following the events described in this book. The large island below La Habana (or Havana) province is the former Isle of Pines—now the Isle of Youth.

To give some rough idea of location and scale, the capital city of Havana, in the center of La Habana's northern coast, is about one hundred miles south of Key West, Florida. Cuba's length, measuring from the westernmost tip of Pinar del Rio through the center of "the island" to the easternmost part of Oriente, is about seven hundred miles.

Escambray. After Havana, the most critical geographic reference in the following story is the region of the Escambray. Bounded by the cities of Cienfuegos, Santa Clara and Sancti Spiritus, and by the Caribbean Sea, the Escambray is a hilly and in places mountainous area that comprises some 1,700 square miles in the southern center of the former Las Villas province. The Escambray was a vital theater in the relatively brief liberation war against Batista in 1958, and it was the epicenter of a much more protracted war of resistance against Castro during the early and middle 1960's.

Guerrilla. This word denotes a "band of rebel warriors." Since 1959, all *guerrillas* in Cuba have been fighting against the regime; so in this narrative, *guerrilla* almost always refers to anti-Castro soldiers and armies.

Rebel Army / Rebel. The Rebel Army was the force under Castro's command that defeated Batista's regulars (or the Cuban Army) in 1958. After coming to power, Castro kept the "rebel" name for his army and other key institutions: "Rebel Radio," "Rebel TV," and the like. In 1959, a new crop of rebels sprang up to fight against Castro's regime. In this narrative—and in contradistinction to the regime's rhetoric—the term "rebel" predominantly refers to Castro's opponents.

Resister / Resistance / Underground. Here again, popular usage—following Castro's lead—has blurred reality. For the last forty-five years, virtually all resistance in Cuba has been against Castro's regime. In Cuban settings, these terms refer to anti-Castro actors and activities.

Militia. This is a name for the supplemental army under Castro's command, made up of both men and women.

CDR / Committees for the Defense of the Revolution. An extension of Castro's State Security, this huge network of neighborhood spy groups covers almost every city, town and street in Cuba.

Brigade 2506 is the U.S.-trained force of Cubans that fought against Castro's regime at the Bay of Pigs in 1961. "Brigade" denotes members or veterans of this anti-Castro force.

Plantados. "Staunch ones" or long-term political prisoners under Castro, these are men and women who have refused all efforts by the regime to "rehabilitate" them. The plantados tend to be people serving sentences of fifteen, twenty or thirty years.

Comandante, or "commander," is a term equally used for pro-Castro and anti-Castro military officers.

Spanish-language names and words. Some confusion is unavoidable around proper names, in that Spanish last names consist of the father's family name plus the mother's maiden name. The latter is grammatically dispensable and is often (but not always) dropped, along with unused middle names. For example: Fidel Castro is short for Fidel Alejandro Castro Ruz, and the name is found in indices under Castro.

In this text, Spanish-language names and words are given without Spanish accent markings.

UNVANQUISHED

CHAPTER I.

A NATION IN FRENZY

A caravan of limousines and cars entered Havana's Columbia Military Camp before the New Year arrived.

It was an oddly mixed crowd, gathered together on that last night of 1958: high-ranking officers in khakis, their chests covered with ribbons; women in cocktail dresses; partygoers in dark suits. All had been hastily summoned, offered a berth on a departing flight. As they crowded together in a building next to the runway, two large planes were readied for departure.

A few in the crowd, forewarned, carried small suitcases or overnight bags. Most had only the clothing on their backs. Fulgencio Batista, elegantly attired, surrounded by his family, moved somberly among them.

For three turbulent decades Batista had been the nation's chief hero and villain. He was a former army sergeant who had risen to power during a revolution, had become a constitutional president, had left office and then seized control in a bloodless coup. Once, he had been a hero for conducting the cleanest elections in Cuba's history and for instituting progressive laws. A generation later, his uncontained lust for power had made him an epitome of corruption.

Now, he was about to leave Cuba for good.

Only hours earlier, insurgent forces had attacked Santa Clara, an important city in central Cuba. For weeks, rumor—a notorious witness—had had it that former president Carlos Prio, whom the army had overthrown seven years before, was preparing a coup for early January.

Roberto Martin Perez, a young sales executive, was at the airfield with his father, a colonel in the police. "One moment I was dancing with my wife at a New Year's party at a hotel and moments later I was driving my father toward Columbia Military Camp. What I saw there stunned me. Colonels and generals were peeking through blindfold curtains, worried that enlisted men might mutiny at their flight. Grown men with ribbons on their chests showed fear on their faces, and women were crying…. You could feel the fear filling the room."

Within hours a plane had taken off, carrying Batista, his family and some cronies. A second plane taxied down the runway and headed north to New Orleans.

A dark era in Cuban history had ended. A darker one was about to begin.

❉ ❉ ❉

Havana awoke to the sound of clacking car-horns and scattered gunfire. Cuban flags and hastily scribbled political banners hung from balconies as crowds clustered on city streets. Small mobs armed with sledgehammers destroyed parking meters, symbols of Batista's regime.

From their hiding places, members of the resistance emerged wearing armbands and packing guns. Cruising in cars, they took control of police stations, public buildings and media centers.

Images of battle flickered across every television screen in Cuba. Young survivors of the clandestine war were interviewed. A man stripped off his shirt to show torture scars on his chest and back. Newscasters announced that a caravan of rebel forces was on its way.

The whole island was in a state of frenzy. In Santa Clara and Cienfuegos, rebels from three different factions prepared convoys to race toward Havana. Bearded guerrillas in berets, cowboy hats or captured army helmets, perhaps wearing religious adornments, bearing bullet-filled bandoleers and an assortment of weapons, made up ragged convoys. Mobs engulfed them in every town as women kissed the bearded faces, handing out platters of food and pastries.

Andres Cuevas, then a young boy living in a town along Cuba's Central Highway, remembered the heady moment as rebel troops passed by on their victorious march to Havana. Cuevas: "The convoy was a long line of jeeps, military and civilian trucks and even a couple of school buses. One of the bearded guerrilla fighters wore a Stetson with white roses adorning the hatband. He cut a dashing figure. Another one, riding a motor-cycle, stopped in front of my house and asked if he could use the telephone. He was a young boy, clean-shaven, with long blond hair down to his shoulders. Two revolvers hung from his military belt and a carbine was slung over his shoulder. From my house he called his parents in Havana and told them he would see them the following day. When he hung up the phone, he was so happy he wept. We gave him a roasted pork sandwich and a soft drink."

Not all was joy, however. Batista's flight had stranded thousands of soldiers and officers. Unlike the makers of earlier coups, the new rulers of Cuba were set on destroying the military's command structure and replacing it with their own.

Jose Berberena, then a young army sergeant, received the news of the triumphant rebellion while stationed in Oriente Province, on Cuba's eastern tip. Berberena: "I was not a follower of Batista. I was a soldier. My father had been in the military for years and he had not been a follower of Presidents Grau, Prio or Batista. He had been, as I was, a soldier of the republic. When I was told Batista had left, it mattered little to me. I thought, in a very naive way, that the army would continue to exist as I knew it. When I realized we had to surrender, I shattered my rifle against a tree-trunk."

* * *

A provisional government crumbled quickly with the arrival of rebel forces in the capital.

The largest anti-Batista organization was the 26th of July Movement, led by Fidel Castro. The 26th of July Movement had drawn political support from Cuba's Orthodox Party and from trade unions, while his guerrilla force, the Rebel Army, was largely sustained by the farmworkers of Cuba's easternmost province, Oriente. Smaller units also operated in the central and western provinces, Las Villas and Pinar del Rio.

The Revolutionary Student Directorate or DRE, led by Faure Chomon, drew most of its support from university and high-school students. After a spectacular but doomed attempt to assassinate Batista, the DRE had fielded a small guerrilla force in Las Villas province and a clandestine movement in urban centers; but the idealistic group had sustained heavy casualties, losing most of its top leadership in the war.

A third organization was the Second National Front of Escambray, led by twenty-four-year-old, Spanish-born Eloy Gutierrez Menoyo. The II Front was composed of students, laborers and farmers, with a guerrilla force of several hundred men in the Escambray mountains of central Cuba. The combined guerrilla forces of all three organizations added up to no more than two thousand men spread across four mountain regions, a number that increased somewhat in the last month of fighting.

Fidel Castro was by far the best-known of the rebel leaders, having created an image that transcended Cuba's borders. As early as February 1957, a leading U.S. newspaper had portrayed him as a liberator;[1] and the young fighter, a true master of public relations, had cultivated the image of a latter-day Robin Hood, persuading journalists from far and wide to visit his encampment in the hills of eastern Cuba.

A charismatic leader from head to toe, Castro mesmerized listeners with his gift for flowery rhetoric. Mobs gathered around Castro during his march to Havana, cheering him in an outpouring of adulation. He entered the capital atop a captured army tank, surrounded by bearded, scruffy-looking rebels. He smiled to all, promising free elections and justice for every Cuban. Other rebel leaders wanted to share power with Castro; but while every Cuban knew Fidel Castro, the public had almost no knowledge of Menoyo, Chomon and others who had played important roles in the war. The DRE and the II Front decided to avoid a confrontation that would have resulted in an armed struggle among competing factions, and they acquiesced to Fidel's leadership.

The war against Batista, also known as the Cuban revolution, had had little to do with socialism or communism for the vast majority of those who had fought it. Rather, its goals were to bring an end to official corruption, to establish a democratic government, and to implement social reforms in Cuba's countryside. Nowhere in the Castro regime's early decrees, in the "Manifesto of the Sierra Maestra" or in printed material of the time, can one find favorable allusions to Marxism.

Scholars and other observers have spilled much ink over whether Fidel Castro found his way to communism by political circumstances or by design. Rafael Diaz-Balart, Castro's former brother-in-law and one of his first political adversaries, has voiced strong opinions on the matter. Diaz-Balart: "Fidel is not a communist. Fidel is simply for himself. During his student days he admired Mussolini and quoted Hitler. If he had gained power twenty years earlier, he would have worn a swastika. Two centuries ago, he would have crowned himself emperor."

The PSP or Popular Socialist Party, as the Communist Party was known in Cuba, had not backed Castro until the final months of the struggle. Indeed, the communists had worked with Batista. Some party leaders, like Carlos Rafael Rodriguez, had served as Batista counsellors.

Ricardo Bofill, then a PSP member and later one of Fidel's best-known opponents, explained the PSP's support of Castro in the last few months of the liberation war. Bofill: "The PSP did not take Fidel seriously at first. They saw him as a local thug, one of the leftovers of the student political gangster groups of the late forties, as an instigator. The

---

[1] See the three-part series by Herbert L. Matthews in *The New York Times*, February 24–26, 1957.

PSP was full of sharp, quick minds, but they underestimated Fidel. The man in the PSP who understood Fidel's potential was Anibal Escalante, a lawyer who had strong links to the KGB. Anibal was the one who insisted we support Fidel. It was Anibal who sent Carlos Rafael Rodriguez to the Sierra Maestra to talk to Castro. It was Anibal who channeled PSP resources and recruits to the 26th of July Movement and forced the PSP to break with Batista."

At the time of the revolution's triumph, only a few leaders of the 26th of July were communists. Raul Castro, Fidel's youngest brother, had attended a communist youth conference in Prague in 1953. Ernesto "Che" Guevara, a committed Marxist from Argentina, had worked with the Jacobo Arbenz government in Guatemala in 1954. A few young guerrilla officers were alumni of the PSP youth groups; and Comandante Felix Torres could boast a lifetime of participation in PSP activities.

Fidel installed a government with Manuel Urrutia, a famous judge, as president and Jose Miro Cardona, an attorney from a distinguished family, as prime minister. By placing men of democratic beliefs in positions of power, Castro was able to portray his administration as moderate, palatable to all classes of Cubans, and free of radical associations.

Ricardo Bofill: "Actually a parallel government was created, the one that was really to move Cuba quickly toward Marxism. This group gathered constantly at Castro's beach house in Cojimar. Fidel met there with top leaders of the PSP. Anibal Escalante was the key man. Carlos Rafael Rodriguez was at every meeting and Blas Roca attended often."

PSP members got leading positions in provincial governments. Once in office they purged their departments, replacing key people with PSP supporters. Although the 26th of July was Castro's public party, the PSP was the political force he actually used.

Ricardo Vazquez, a veteran resistance fighter yet in his teens, was a provincial director of the newly formed 26th of July Party in Las Villas province. He quickly became aware of the PSP takeover. Vazquez: "We were upset and felt Fidel was unaware of the problem. We placed the blame on Felix Torres, who was doing as he pleased. Men who had fought against Batista were being fired from jobs, replaced by PSP people who had no merit. We made a report to Castro, and his answer was to destroy the 26th of July Movement in Las Villas. The PSP did as they pleased."

* * *

The days of triumph grew stained with blood. From its very first day, the regime ran

"revolutionary tribunals" that meted out death sentences to hundreds of Batista collaborators.

The firing-squad death of police colonel Cornelio Rojas was repeatedly played on
national television. The gruesome black-and-white film showed the executed man's hat
flying off his head as bullets slammed into his skull, scattering brain matter on the execution wall. The last image was a close-up of the dead man's face, eyes staring open, the top
half of his head sheared by bullets.

Screenings of this spectacle, and others like it, were accompanied by statements to
the effect that justice was being served by the execution of Batista "henchmen." At
rallies, mobs grew accustomed to chant: "To the wall!" At least 858 executions occurred
in 1959.[2]

Elicer Grave de Peralta was a guerrilla commander in the 26th of July Movement. On
the morning Batista fled, he was ordered to occupy Sagua La Grande, a city on Cuba's
northern coast. Grave de Peralta: "I was dismayed. Batista supporters were being held in
cramped quarters without toilet facilities. I decided to move them to a bigger place. As I
started to escort the prisoners out, I was confronted by a mob.... They wanted to lynch
the prisoners. I refused to turn the prisoners over and ordered my men to disperse the
mob. Yet the situation was not defused. Every day someone came to my headquarters to
lodge a complaint against one of the prisoners, and most were unjustified."

A memorable event was the televised prosecution of Major Jesus Sosa Blanco at the
Havana Sports Palace. Sosa Blanco stood handcuffed in front of a microphone, while
peanut and soft-drink vendors walked among the audience. Men and women in the stands
interrupted the court proceedings with loud comments, while others puffed on cigars,
talking or just taking things in.

Some witnesses could not identify the defendant even though he was clearly visible,
handcuffed and wearing prison garb. Other witnesses confused Sosa Blanco with Merob
Sosa, another Batista officer who had escaped to exile. The proceedings mattered little,
for the outcome had been foreordained. Sosa Blanco was executed at La Cabana Fortress
on February 18, 1959.[3]

Public trials and executions fed the blood-lust of a crazed society. Children traded
postcards with images of the rebel commanders or drawings of epic battles. People put
signs on their porches proclaiming, "This is your home, Fidel." Hundreds of hours of TV
airtime were filled with documentaries of the recent struggle. Magazines devoted entire

[2] The author's research for Radio Marti, 1992
[3] Bethel, *The Losers*, pp. 112–13

issues to tales of the war, first-person narratives of Batista's torture chambers or interviews with rebel leaders. Fidel Castro appeared in posters as a young, Christlike figure. Every day plaques were unveiled, rallies announced, proclamations decreed, streets or schools renamed.

Jorge Valls, a DRE veteran, returned from exile in Mexico to find a nation on the edge of collective hysteria. "Several of my professors had lived in Europe during the time of the rise of fascism. I had studied the process and I saw this process in the flesh in 1959 Cuba—the uniforms, the berets, the flags.... The revolution proclaimed itself democratic, but democratic principles were violated from the first day with mass executions and sham trials. Nothing mitigated. Castro demanded executions in public, and the masses echoed his cries. Castro admitted he had lied to the people, cynically telling them he had done so for their own welfare, and the masses cheered him. The whole nation became shrouded in a collective shame."

Several dozen pilots, gunners and mechanics from Batista's air force were brought to trial for firing on Castro's guerrillas. When the court acquitted them, an enraged Castro annulled the verdict and demanded a new trial.

Francisco Chappi was a twenty-four-year-old lieutenant pilot facing a grim destiny. Chappi: "Originally we were accused of bombing and strafing open towns. During our trial it was proven that stray artillery shells fired by the army, not aerial bombings, had killed eight civilians. Our acquittal made headlines in every newspaper in Cuba. Felix Pena, a major in the Rebel Army who had presided over our first trial and had been instrumental in acquitting us, died mysteriously. The government claimed it was a suicide, but we felt he was murdered. We never attended our second trial, for we were not allowed. This time there was no defense, only prosecution. All the officers, I among them, got thirty-year prison terms. Aerial gunners received twenty-year sentences, while mechanics, guilty of tuning engines, got two years."

With the masses, Castro manipulated cleverly. The first laws of his government were designed to win popular support. Salaries were increased, rents lowered, electrical and telephone rates reduced. Among those who had actually fought the liberation war, however, the Air Force trial and other events had sown doubts about the new government. Amid the chanting mobs, rallies and banners, a few Cubans were preparing for a new struggle.

CHAPTER II.

REBEL AGAINST REBEL

Opposition to Castro had started as soon as his regime had reached power. Ironically, one of the first resistance movements came from Fidel's former brother-in-law: attorney and former congressman Rafael Diaz-Balart. The movement was called "The White Rose," in allusion to a poem by Cuba's nineteenth-century patriot, Jose Marti. The White Rose was perceived and portrayed as a pro-Batista group, which damaged its credibility with the public; but the group did manage to carry out a few acts of sabotage, provide some weapons to resistance units and spread some written materials throughout Cuba.

A second group, the MRD or Movement of Democratic Recuperation, was made up of former military personnel and political activists. Eighteen men, including American Austin Young and Englishman Peter Lawton, were taken captive during a small guerrilla attack. All were condemned to lengthy prison terms.

Castro's government had quickly moved to seize media, confiscating television Channel Twelve and several radio stations. Journalists who had been fervent backers of Castro questioned his regime publicly. When the debate grew heated, Castro declared: "There are two types of people: those who read *Diario de La Marina,* and those who believe in our revolution." By May 1960, that newspaper had also been expropriated.[1]

Discontent began to spread in the Rebel Army itself. On July 1, 1959, Comandante Pedro Luis Diaz-Lanz, head of the new Air Force, arrived on U.S. shores and asked for political asylum. He charged Castro with delivering Cuba to the Soviet Bloc. Several weeks later, Diaz-Lanz returned to Cuba by flying a plane over Havana.

Gelasio Castillo, an electrician, saw Diaz-Lanz's plane above the city. "The plane was flying low and fast, dropping leaflets. A soldier ran out of a cafeteria near my house and

[1] Bethel, *The Losers,* p. 182

started firing his carbine at the plane. The plane disappeared and the man kept firing until he had emptied the clip. Several people in Havana were wounded by stray or falling bullets. The following day, Castro's press accused Diaz-Lanz of bombing civilians, which was false. Those people were wounded by others who had tried to shoot the plane down."

In October 1959, several other planes dropped weapons, leaflets and even a home-made bomb, aimed at the Punta Alegre Sugar Mill.[2] Sponsored by the MRD and White Rose, the raids—originating in Florida—received widespread attention as Castro's PR machine accused the United States of sponsoring piracy in the air.

* * *

As radical new laws came into being and the parallel government at Cojimar Beach worked to establish a communist society, dissent grew from within Castro's ranks. In a televised address, Castro purged President Manuel Urrutia, who then sought asylum in an embassy.

Ricardo Vazquez: "I watched the Urrutia-Castro confrontation on television. Urrutia was not invited to the press conference. Fidel talked for four hours. After the broadcast ended, I knew Urrutia was finished and I realized Castro himself was part of the plot. I was only a teenager but I had been active in the resistance and I knew the time had come to fight once more."

Other former guerrillas felt doubts about the changes that were rapidly altering life in Cuba. Juan Rodriguez Mesa was a patrol chief in the newly formed military police. When he visited Comandante Camilo Cienfuegos, one of Castro's top men, Rodriguez Mesa was perturbed by what he saw.

Juan Rodriguez Mesa: "When I entered the office I noticed that half of the wall was covered by a huge photograph of Jesus Menendez, a well-known communist labor leader who had died. Of all the great men of Cuba, he had to pick a communist. It did not feel right. A couple of months later I quit the military and by the end of the year I was meeting with a resistance group."

Armando Zaldivar was a medical officer in the Rebel Army. Zaldivar: "At the Military Hospital in Havana we held what were called Revolutionary Instruction Seminars.... Che Guevara spoke to us and did not mince words. He told us that as doctors we had a responsibility to spread socialist ideas to the people, that we had to destroy the basis of a capitalist society. Raul Castro told us the promised free elections would never take place.

[2] Ruiz, *Diario de una traicion 1959* (section for October)

I realized I had to leave the army, for I could not take part in a betrayal of my people. The revolution I had waged stood for democracy and suffrage, not serving the interests of the Soviets."

* * *

A massive conspiracy was in the works when MRD contacted Eloy Gutierrez Menoyo and the II Front, proposing an alliance to overthrow Castro.

The one who answered MRD's call was Gutierrez Menoyo's comrade William Morgan, a tough-looking character from Ohio who spoke chopped-up Spanish. Cuban publications of the time portrayed Morgan as a combat veteran of the Second World War; but the truth was rather to be found in the records of a military court martial and of the Chillicothe, Ohio, penitentiary.[3]

Morgan had been a fire-eater in a circus, a collector for a small-time mobster, a felon and a weapons smuggler. He was also tough as nails, an expert in judo and an alumnus of the U.S. armed forces. In 1958 he had joined the guerrilla forces fighting against Batista in the Escambray mountains. By the time of the revolution's triumph he was celebrated by Castro as well as by the regime's leading image-makers, notably Herbert L. Matthews of *The New York Times*.

Morgan met in secret with MRD members at the Moulin Rouge Hotel in Miami Beach. The MRD was getting some support from Dominican dictator Rafael Leonidas Trujillo, whose country Castro's forces had already tried to attack. MRD was planning to launch an attack against several key positions in central Cuba as the start of a guerrilla campaign.

Gutierrez Menoyo and Morgan agreed to work with MRD. They then gave details of the so-called Trinidad Conspiracy to Castro's agents, and more than a hundred men and women in Cuba were arrested by State Security. Whether Gutierrez Menoyo and Morgan had intended to betray the conspiracy from the start or decided to do so because they had been trapped has been a matter of frequent debate. Either way, the conspirators were ensnared, and when Trujillo sent an airplane full of weapons for the uprising, it was captured.

Fidel capped his triumph with a televised performance in which he spent several hours narrating the espionage plot as Gutierrez Menoyo and Morgan sat on the floor near his chair. Castro extolled both men and praised their cunning in the espionage game. Soon

[3] Weyl, *Estrella roja sobre Cuba*, p. 260

enough, they would both be out of Castro's affections in a bad way.

Interestingly enough, another person of prominence in this episode was U.S. Ambassador Phillip Bonsal. Bonsal had held private interviews with Cuban foreign minister Raul Roa, telling him of the plot and its timetable; he had also provided information on a plot to kill Castro.[4]

* * *

Two months after the Trinidad Conspiracy, another signal event occurred as Comandante Huber Matos, leader of military forces in Camaguey province, abruptly fell from grace.

Matos, a former schoolteacher, was one of the regime's best-known soldiers. In the liberation war he had secured Cuba's second city, Santiago, for the rebels. He had entered Havana in the lead tank with Fidel. His face appeared in the postcard series of the revolution. In October 1959, however, he wrote Castro a letter announcing his resignation as military commander of Camaguey. The letter complained of communist infiltration at all levels of the government. Castro reacted to the letter by ordering the arrest of Matos and his staff.

Camilo Cienfuegos, the comandante who rivaled Fidel in popularity, came to Camaguey ahead of Castro. Camilo seemed friendly and concerned; but when Fidel arrived, the situation changed. Jose Dionisio Suarez was one of the young lieutenants involved in what Castro termed a conspiracy against the revolution.

Jose Dionisio Suarez: "Fidel arrives, with Ramiro Valdes and a bunch of others. Fidel meets with several of the captains.... When Fidel comes out of the meeting, he puts his left arm around Camilo's shoulders and says, 'Let's turn him over to the people.' Camilo and Fidel go out to the balcony of the headquarters building and speak to the mob outside. Huber tries to stand up and walk toward the balcony to answer Fidel's remarks. Ramiro pushes him and says, 'You are not going anywhere.' Then Huber drops his face into his hands and we hear a sob. That was a scream of impotence."

Matos and all his staff were put on trial and condemned to twenty years in jail. His punishment signified a stern warning that dissent would not be tolerated. The impact of Matos's arrest and trial stunned many at different levels of the regime.

Hiram Gonzalez was a first lieutenant in the Rebel Army. Gonzalez: "The Matos

[4] State Department Telegrams 294 and 360, dated August 3 and 11, 1959, in *Foreign Relations of the United States, 1958–1960*

Affair was a milestone for me. It began to open my eyes to the sad reality of what was happening in Cuba. A few days later I had a talk with labor leader Pedro Aponte and he told me the new government did not want strikes in the factories because the government was now going to mediate with management on the workers' behalf. The idea seemed preposterous to me, for I had always believed in the right of labor to organize and strike."

Within a week after Matos's arrest, the government announced that Camilo Cienfuegos had disappeared while traveling in a Cessna airplane from Camaguey to Havana. A massive search was launched, but no traces found.

A number of questions have not been answered: Was the plane sabotaged? Was Camilo killed because Fidel Castro feared his growing popularity? Did Camilo side with Huber Matos and enrage Castro?

Conspiracy theorists have pointed out that within weeks of Camilo's disappearance, Cristino Naranjo, Cienfuegos's most trusted adjutant, was machine-gunned at the entrance to a military base. Manuel Beaton, who killed Naranjo, claimed a case of mistaken identity.

Several months later, Beaton himself died in front of a firing squad after being accused of leading an anti-Castro guerrilla unit in Oriente province. Another key figure, a traffic controller at the Camaguey air base, died in a reported suicide.

On the other hand, many maintain that Camilo really perished in an airplane accident somewhere north of Cuba's main island.

Jose Dionisio Suarez: "I don't believe Camilo's death had anything to do with the death of Cristino Naranjo. Beaton and Naranjo had an old feud, but legend has linked both deaths.... If the plane left no trace, that is not unusual. A plane doing maneuvers near the seawall in Havana fell into the water, and many saw it happen. Ships went to the rescue and found nothing, not even an oil slick."

Andres Nazario Sargen, a veteran comandante of the II Front, saw Castro during the days of Camilo's disappearance.

Nazario Sargen: "He was very upset. He said that Camilo had disappeared two days before and no one had told him.... In those days many of our men were irresponsible and airplane accidents happened constantly. We were lax in maintenance. Raul Castro had a helicopter accident. Diocles Torralba went down in a Sea Fury and survived. Jose Abrahantes's brother died in an accident. I think Camilo also died in an accident."

Others, however, considered Camilo's disappearance to be a watershed event.

Elicer Grave de Peralta: "The arrest of Matos and the death of Camilo were indications that Cuba was headed towards a dictatorship; so I went to see Comandante Diego Paneque and we started to plot once more."

CHAPTER III.

ARMED RESISTANCE

Anti-Castro organizations sprouted in 1960, and underground networks spread throughout the island.

It has typically been asserted that the CIA created these clandestine movements;
but in fact these groups, rather than being U.S. inventions, were copies of the clandestine
organizations that had thrived in Cuba for decades. The existence of a Soviet-backed
regime next to America created ripples of fear in the U.S. government. As resistance
groups formed in Cuba, U.S. agents offered weapons and technical assistance. In that
manner, many of the groups did come to depend on U.S. support.

Each movement had a secretary general, or leader on a national level who supervised
a group of directors including a military commander, a supply officer, a treasurer and a
propaganda chief. The national leaders supervised chains of command that extended
from province coordinators down to regional and municipal levels. The networks of the
larger groups had thousands of supporters across the six provinces, while smaller groups
worked at regional levels with limited resources.

The largest resistance group was the Movement of Revolutionary Recuperation
(MRR), founded by a group of former guerrillas including a young engineer named Rogelio
Gonzalez and former officers Manuel Artime and Jorge Sotus. The youth wing of the
MRR, comprising university and high-school students, created a splinter group that took
up the hallowed name Revolutionary Student Directorate (DRE). Led by Alberto Muller,
Manuel Salvat and Luis Fernandez Rocha, these students launched a memorable anti-
communist protest in Cuba.

In February 1960, U.S.S.R. Deputy Premier Anastas Mikoyan arrived in Havana to
observe the rapid process of Cuba's Sovietization. The Castro government received him

with fanfare, and he was visibly delighted at what he saw. At one point he placed a flower wreath at the statue of the nation's hero, Jose Marti. Within hours, Cuban students carrying picket signs and a second wreath of flowers confronted Castro's police in a Havana park. Sixteen students were arrested and held before being released on minor charges.

The MRP, or Revolutionary People's Movement, was a clandestine organization led by Manuel Ray, an engineer who had briefly been a minister in Castro's government. Ray had also been a top leader in the clandestine resistance against Batista. Being a public figure made difficulties for him when he went underground. After some months in hiding, Ray left Cuba for the United States.

One of the largest of the new rebel organizations was the 30th of November Movement, led by labor leader (and Rebel Army lieutenant) David Salvador, Hiram Gonzalez and several top union trade officials.

Hiram Gonzalez: "We met at David Salvador's house. He had just returned from a trip to France representing the revolutionary government. Until then I had wondered if Fidel was just caught up in the politics of different factions. David said, 'I've been at those private meetings. I have heard Fidel talk. The country is being sold out.' I sat there stunned. I felt hollow and lonely. Everything I had fought for was being betrayed, given away. I had fought one dictator to replace him with another. It was time to fight once more. I was twenty-two years old and about to start fighting my second war and this time I'd be fighting men who had been on my side."

The prime recruiting ground for the 30th of November was the massive CTC or Confederation of Cuban Workers, an umbrella organization that joined together 33 labor federations and 2,490 local labor syndicates.[1] With David Salvador's connections, a national resistance network involving hundreds of men and women sprang up in a few months. Hiram Gonzalez became the organization's first military commander.

Other, smaller movements included the MIRR (Insurrectionist Movement of Revolutionary Recuperation), led by Orlando Bosch; Unidad Revolucionaria (Revolutionary Unity), led by Rafael Diaz Hanscom; the Christian Democrat Movement (MDC), led by Jose Ignacio Rasco; and Democratic Rescue, with members of the old Partido Autentico (Authentic Party), led by former prime minister Tony Varona. Laureano Batista was a founding member of the MDC.

Laureano Batista: "We tried to create a public conscience but the government was closing off all avenues of free expression, all means of communication to the masses.

[1] Bethel, *The Losers*, p. 37

Because of this, underground activity started before the population was aware of why we fought. We knew that as soon as the last independent newspaper was shut down, serious political work at the public level would be impossible; but we had to go underground too quickly."

Francisco Verdecia was a member of the urban resistance units in the 30th of November. Verdecia: "The government had control of the TV and radio stations, the newspapers, everything. Political parties were abolished and we had no legal way to challenge the system. Our only option was to fight as the French had fought the Nazis—by armed resistance."

The first weapons obtained by these groups were the same as those used against Batista. Orlando Bosch, a pediatrician who had led resistance units of the 26th of July Movement, was procuring arms for the anti-Castro resistance even as he still served, in early 1960, as governor of Las Villas province.

Orlando Bosch: "As governor I had a lot of leeway, enough to be able to obtain some weapons that were used to start the guerrilla uprisings in the Escambray Mountains. These weapons included a .30 caliber machine gun, Garand rifles, M-1 carbines and Dominican-made San Cristobal carbines."

Explosives were harder to find, but rebels could fabricate them.

Hiram Gonzalez: "At the time, in 1960, it was still easy to obtain certain chemicals. Red minium, used in the manufacture of paints, is a very effective explosive when mixed nine-to-one with aluminum dust. In a can with a detonator, it makes a bomb strong enough to open up a hole in a cement-block wall. I had my men visit every hardware store and building supply house in Havana, buying up chemicals. We stored more than a ton of chemicals in the basement of a church and within a few weeks I had three clandestine bomb factories."

The underground networks began to strike. In January 1960, Captain Manuel Borjas, an officer in Castro's army, was wounded in an assassination attempt. In February, bombs went off in government offices. During three days of March, twenty-five arsons in Matanzas province damaged the sugar crop, Cuba's main source of income. In July, rebels machine-gunned the car of Jose Pardo Llada, a prominent pro-Castro radio broadcaster. (Pardo Llada, who survived the attack, later left Cuba and denounced Castro.) Balbino Diaz and Roberto Cruz were executed for the attempt on the broadcaster, and eleven others were jailed as part of the conspiracy.[2]

---

[2] Ruiz, *Diario de una traicion 1960*, pp. 87–99

Bombs exploded nightly. Buildings were set on fire. Underground fighters ambushed police in the darkness of the night.

Hiram Gonzalez: "Our bombs were not aimed at killing or mutilating civilians. We had as our purpose the destruction of the economy, the disruption of the government structure and the demoralization of the system. We were doing to Castro what he had done to Batista."

Humberto Lopez, a young veteran of the resistance against Batista, joined the MRR. "We burned down a Commerce Ministry records warehouse in Havana. Three of us went there by car; two entered the building while one man stayed in the car with an M-3 submachine gun. Only one guard covered the perimeter of the two-story structure. Timing him, we moved into the building, cracking a glass in an office door. Once inside the warehouse, my companion and I moved quickly from room to room. We had small vials of pure phosphorous mixed with water that ignites a few seconds after being exposed to air. We broke the vials on cabinets and on boxes of files. Hundreds of boxes jammed together in racks ignited. As we left the building undetected, the second-floor fire was well under way. Within minutes the whole building was a ball of flame and smoke. Our driver was nervous, inexperienced. Instead of driving away smoothly, he took off like a bullet down those narrow streets of Old Havana. After a couple of blocks, we attracted the attention of a militiaman walking a beat. As our vehicle moved toward him, the militiaman went down on one knee and raised a snub-nosed machine gun. We opened up with the M-3 and a handgun. As we passed by him, he fell under our gunfire."

* * *

Castro was building up his forces. Aside from his newly created army, which had 32,000 men, a national militia boasted 200,000 men and women by the end of 1960.[3] Intelligence agents from different Soviet Bloc nations trained Cuban State Security officers to pursue and eliminate the emerging opposition.

Between January 1959 and May 1960, the Eisenhower administration made nine formal diplomatic approaches to Cuba and sixteen informal ones, asking to negotiate political differences. Castro's government ignored all twenty-five requests.[4]

In summer 1960, the CIA contacted several anti-Castro resistance units. The MRR and DRE gained the CIA's preference, while other movements were denied help or re-

[3] Higgins, *The Perfect Failure,* p. 70
[4] Carbonell, *And the Russians Stayed,* p. 96

ceived only a little. Resistance leaders, facing the growing repressive machinery of a Soviet regime, knew they could not muster by themselves the supplies or finances they needed to oppose the regime, so uneasy deals resulted between clandestine groups and the CIA.

Laureano Batista: "Resistance groups fell into a psychological dependence on the United States.... The CIA liked to provide high-tech gadgets, but I did not want chemical detonators that could not be improvised in Cuba. I wanted dynamite and simple mechanisms that could be detonated with a clock and battery, but they did not want this. They wanted the underground groups to use their system of detonators so they could maintain control. This created a real dependency—an image that the movement with the most sophisticated equipment was the most powerful. They never understood our type of warfare. The Americans did not have the faintest notion of how a clandestine movement worked, despite the tons of books, studies and operations they sponsored. They had not faced this situation inside their own borders. They had their expert who had spent three years inside France in the Second World War; but during those three years, that man did not see the workings of the structure that moved him inside France to safety houses, providing food and transportation. He never knew who brought him or took him, how people were recruited and reported up a chain of command. It was not the American style of war."

The work of an underground organization depended on people with experience, on weapons, safety houses, transportation, logistics and funds. Many of the newly formed groups lacked strength in all areas.

Tomas "Tommy" Fernandez Travieso was a teenager when he started transporting weapons and vehicles for the DRE. Fernandez Travieso: "We had to go and pick up a car that had been stranded on a busy Havana street. We should have left the car. It had bullet holes in its chassis, but we needed cars, so Virgilio Campaneria and I went to get it. Virgilio carried a grenade plus his pistol.... We expected to be surrounded by police, but for some miraculous reason they had not spotted the vehicle."

Safety houses were scarce. It was dangerous to harbor a member of the resistance. Jose Enrique Dausa, a Havana lawyer, came up with a solution. Dausa: "When Cubans began fleeing the country, the government passed a law saying uninhabited houses of people living in exile would be confiscated. My law office set up leasing agreements and we placed resistance supporters, couples or singles, in houses and apartments. In this way we maintained a reasonable number of safety houses."

Cubans continued to flee the country. By the end of 1960, exiles in the United States had surpassed the 100,000 mark.[5] As tensions between the U.S. and Cuba increased, the CIA began recruiting exiles for infiltration teams and an invasion force to topple Castro's regime.

Meanwhile, in the mountains of Cuba, a full-fledged guerrilla war was ready to break out.

---

[5] Fermoselle, *The Evolution of the Cuban Military, 1492–1986,* p. 273

CHAPTER IV.

GUERRILLAS IN THE ESCAMBRAY

Las Villas province was the ideal ground for launching a guerrilla campaign.

Smack in the center of the island, Las Villas offered a strategic location for dividing Cuba. The area had been heavily pro–II Front during the struggle against Batista, and the movement had been left out of the power loop at the triumph of the revolution. Resentment toward the government grew as Castro's agrarian reforms forced farmworkers to join cooperatives, while four hundred private farms in the province were confiscated during the first half of 1959.[1]

The Cuban *campesinos,* country folk of the hill regions, were fierce individualists who resented forced work on state farms, who mistrusted the power of politicians and detested the confiscation of private lands. Agapito Rivera was a farmworker in his early twenties when he joined the anti-Castro guerrillas.

Agapito Rivera: "I was poor, extremely poor. I had nothing except the hope of some day having something. Then I saw Castro was confiscating properties from those who did have something. This meant Castro was closing the only door I had to improve my life. I had had my hope stolen from me—and I had to fight to try to recapture it."

By summer 1960, approximately two hundred guerrillas were active in the Escambray mountains of Las Villas province. Some groups had sponsors in the cities, while others formed spontaneously.

Sinesio Walsh, a former captain in the 26th of July Movement, established a camp in the Nuevo Mundo region of the mountains. Thanks to Orlando Bosch, governor of Las Villas, Walsh received a cache of weapons large enough to supply several dozen fighters. Other small units joined the camp.

---

[1] See Ruiz, *Diario de una traicion 1959* for a more extensive account of this process.

Jose Berberena, the former Cuban army sergeant, was one of the new arrivals. Berberena: "Three of us came together. Two had been in the regular army and the other had fought with the Rebel Army. Now we depended on each other. The three of us drove to Manicaragua, a small town. In a cafeteria we met a contact that drove us in a jeep toward a meeting place. On the side of a hill, a scout on horseback waited for us. We arrived at the camp at two in the morning. Sinesio Walsh was in his thirties, a smiling, impassioned man. He asked me if I had had experience and I told him I had been in the regular army. He had been a captain fighting for the other side but now he said, 'I don't care about the past. Here we are all Cubans fighting communism.' Sinesio ordered food for us and I sat on the ground to eat rice and beans from a metal container. I felt like a frog in water."

Dr. Armando Zaldivar, the former Rebel Army medical officer, was now one of the key men in the MRR. After a meeting with Rogelio Gonzalez, the young engineer who had returned to Cuba to lead the underground movement, Zaldivar was sent to Las Villas to contact Walsh.

Armando Zaldivar: "We discussed establishing a supply route with airdrops from the United States. Returning to Havana, I prepared a trip back to the mountains. There were four of us. Plinio Prieto was a former schoolteacher who had been an officer in the war against Batista. He had returned from exile to become the coordinator of all the airdrops from the United States and command the guerrilla units. We had a radio transmitter. We linked up with guerrillas who were to lead us to Walsh's camp, but found that a firefight had taken place and a lieutenant in the militia had been killed. Troops had massed in the region, and we spent several days dodging enemy patrols. In a farm-field we exchanged gunfire and one of our men was captured. The airdrop of weapons landed in an area controlled by militia forces. We tried to get back to the city but ran into a roadblock. Plinio and I were in a cab and we tried to bluff our way past the roadblock, but an officer saw Plinio's torn shoes and realized where we had been. While we were being detained, the second cab drove by with our radio man in it."[2]

The situation turned disastrous. Jose Berberena, Sinesio Walsh and many others were trapped in a thick noose of enemy soldiers. Walsh and Berberena were captured in a cave after three days of skirmishing with militia forces. Dozens of guerrillas—including Porfirio Ramirez, a well-known student leader and former Rebel Army officer—were captured by Castro's troops.

[2] For Zaldivar's whole narrative, see Chapter Five of the author's *Cuba: The Unfinished Revolution*.

The imprisoned rebels were taken to an interrogation center in the Escambray Mountains. Jose Berberena: "After our capture, Comandante Piti Fajardo, one of Fidel's top men, showed up. He cursed at Sinesio, telling him he would be executed. Sinesio, exhausted, did not answer. Fajardo was not telling us anything we did not know."

Armando Zaldivar: "At Topes de Collantes, where I was interrogated, the night air is very cold. I was stripped naked and interrogated as I shivered. Then I was told I was going to be executed. While I waited to face the firing squad, I remembered the televised execution of Cornelio Rojas. The television image kept running through my head. I saw that firing squad in my mind and I saw myself jerking, my brain exploding, my body falling. Finally the soldiers came to get me. My hands were tied. I began walking. I was twenty-six and I was going to die. My armpits and the backs of my knees were sweating. The firing squad was standing in line. I really don't know how many soldiers were there—perhaps a half-dozen. It was night. Reflector lights illuminated the spot where I stood. I felt sweat on my body but I was calm. Rifles pointed at me. Orders were being shouted but I do not remember them. It was almost over. I don't know how to describe the feeling, but I could feel the fingers curling around the triggers, I could feel the trigger pressure to the microsecond. There were flashes of light but I did not fall. I was shot with blanks.... They told me the next time would be real, and then they did the same thing again."

Captured guerrillas were tried at the city of Santa Clara on October 12, 1960. Five, including Sinesio Walsh, Plinio Prieto and Porfirio Ramirez, were sentenced to death by firing squad. The rest, including Zaldivar and Berberena, got long prison terms. Ricardo Vazquez, the teenage resistance fighter, was in Santa Clara during the trial.

Ricardo Vazquez: "Porfirio Ramirez was from Santa Clara. He was a handsome young man who had been a captain in the anti-Batista guerrilla forces and president of the University Students Federation in Las Villas. When he was captured, his mother had asked for clemency. Castro had promised that Porfirio would not be executed—but everything indicated he would face a firing squad. Two public demonstrations took place in Santa Clara on behalf of Porfirio. The first was organized by students and broken up by State Security officers armed with lead pipes. The second had many women dressed in widow's black. The police stopped them."

The five guerrillas were executed at a target range at La Campana military camp. Their deaths did not deter the uprisings. By year's end, insurgents in the Escambray region numbered around eight hundred, skillfully organized by Evelio Duque, a former lieutenant in the Rebel Army. Duque had been sent to the Escambray by the urban underground, whose leaders had promised weapons drops and given him the hard task of creating a command. Within a few weeks he had combined all guerrilla groups into eight basic units. One of the units was under the command of Osvaldo Ramirez, a former captain in the II Front against Batista.

Evelio Duque: "Organizing the guerrilla groups under one command was very difficult. Several groups had been sending messages, dispatching men, appointing field commanders—and that made for confusion. People were playing politics while we were in danger."

In late 1960, two weapons shipments reached the guerrillas in Las Villas. Both caches arrived by boat: one on the northern coast of the province and the other in the south. One shipment consisted of thirty M-3 submachine guns and five Browning automatic rifles, with ammo. The second shipment included a few mortars, automatic weapons and ammunition.[3] Agapito Rivera: "We were never able to use the mortars. When the shipment came in, it was divided up and the hiding place for the mortars was discovered. But we did have the BAR's and the Garand rifles."

Six attempts to supply the guerrillas by air were made, but all six weapons drops fell into Castro's hands. Armando Alberty was a Cuban exile pilot flying airdrops for the CIA. Alberty: "I flew four or five of the missions, and it was a headache. If the people receiving the drop on the ground did not know how to measure distances, calculate wind velocity or the inertia of the weight, then that made the drop very difficult. The guerrillas did not know how to make these calculations. Besides, the drops were in mountainous regions, where parachutes could easily disappear behind hills and foliage. It was a logistics nightmare."

The communications system of the guerrillas was primitive. Couriers on foot or horseback had to carry a message to a town in Las Villas, from where the message went to Havana via a clandestine courier riding a car or bus. In Havana, a radio operator called "Augusto," a.k.a. Ramon Ruiz Sanchez, transmitted the messages to a CIA operator in Miami. The time consumed in passing information made the task of coordinating airdrops almost impossibly difficult.

Despite such problems, guerrilla activity was flourishing across Cuba. Small units appeared in all the provinces, while the main opposition force kept fighting in the Escambray mountains. At the end of November a guerrilla squad caught a military jeep in a deadly crossfire. Among those who perished was Piti Fajardo, one of Castro's top military commanders and the man who had tormented Sinesio Walsh.

With rebellion rapidly spreading, Castro could not ignore the Escambray guerrillas.

---

[3] From interviews with Agapito Rivera and Ramon Ramos (see "Interview Sources" at the back of the book)

They had to be eliminated before any invasion force from the U.S. might arrive. A massive military operation was planned for January 1961.

CHAPTER V.

URBAN WAR, EXILE WARRIORS

As guerrilla war increased, underground units in the cities also grew to considerable strength.

In Havana, the Communist Party offices were set ablaze by saboteurs. Eleven bombs at key locations produced a massive blackout in the capital. Explosions damaged Havana's capitol building, aqueduct and electrical power lines. Four government warehouses in Matanzas were struck by arson. So were trucks in Santa Clara and an office building in Camaguey. Fighters belonging to the 30th of November Movement blew up a refinery in Havana in a daring attack that did real damage to the regime.

Hiram Gonzalez: "My brother, Tony Gonzalez, was an engineer working in the control department at the recently confiscated Shell refinery. I made arrangements for Tony to leave the country as soon as he left work, several hours before the bomb was to explode. Things were slow at the airport and his plane left only an hour before the explosion. The fire raged for eight or nine days, destroying thousands of gallons of government fuel."

The anti-Castro rebels included women and teenagers. Pedro Solares joined the DRE at age thirteen.

Pedro Solares: "My job was to distribute 'Trinchera,' a clandestine, mimeographed publication. We put the papers on rooftops and let the wind scatter them to the street below. I expected to receive some urban guerrilla training, but my contact told me that no one under sixteen was allowed to participate in military operations."

Polita Grau, the niece of former Cuban president Ramon Grau San Martin, led a network of women in the resistance unit of Rescate Revolucionario Democratico (Revolutionary Democratic Rescue).

Polita Grau: "We had very brave women in the underground. One that I will never forget was Maria Nunez de Beato, an aristocratic woman in her late sixties. In spite of her age, she became the provincial coordinator for Matanzas, where she set up a very efficient group. Her women agents helped hide and feed guerrilla groups operating against Castro in that region. My most trusted friend was Nenita Carames, who always volunteered for the most dangerous work. Albertina O'Farrill was outstanding. She developed first-rate contacts in many embassies in Havana. Albertina looked like a party girl but was really a very valuable agent. We used these embassy contacts to smuggle information and arrange asylum for many underground fighters fleeing from Castro's police."

Indeed, the role of women in the resistance and the guerrilla supply lines can be seen in the notable fact that during the 1960's, an estimated one thousand women got stiff sentences in Castro's political prisons.[1]

The urban resistance had a very steep casualty rate, as well as high attrition. The commander of the 30th of November Movement, Hiram Gonzalez, after nine months of living clandestinely in Havana, was arrested by State Security on December 30, 1960. Within ninety days, Gonzalez's two successors would also fall captive to Castro's secret police, whose efficiency was proving more than a match for many of the new rebel organizations.

Apart from his military and State Security personnel, Castro had also created the Committees for the Defense of the Revolution (CDR). These neighborhood spy groups gave information to State Security about any suspicious meetings in their neighborhoods, about new people moving in, and even about packages being brought to private homes. The massive exodus toward Miami limited underground members in their ability to obtain funding, vehicles and security houses. Every day they had fewer resources and suffered more arrests.

Cuban prisons were filling up, and firing squads did not rest. By the end of 1960—two years in power—Castro's government had executed some two thousand Cubans and had put some 15,200 persons into political prison.[2]

Francisco Chappi, convicted in the second Air Force trial of 1959, went to the Isle of Pines prison in the south of Cuba. Chappi: "The [main part of the] prison was a group of

---

[1] Interview with Polita Grau, 1986. At least two women's prisons in the country, Manto Negro (Black Cloak) and Nuevo Amanecer (New Dawn), were dedicated almost exclusively to women political prisoners. At their peak during the sixties, each held several hundred women. Research data point to at least eleven executions of women political prisoners, including one who was pregnant.

[2] Bethel, *The Losers*, p. 178

[four] circular buildings several stories high. In the center of each circular was a court-yard. The donut-shaped buildings were almost empty when we arrived. Within two years, the circulars held more than six thousand men, the elite of the anti-Castro leadership imprisoned by the regime.... The food portions became smaller and often inedible. There were maggots in the rice and more than once we found hairy pieces of rodents in the stew. Anything more than a few spoons of dried macaroni was considered a feast."

Francisco Verdecia was a political prisoner at La Cabana Fortress in Havana. Verdecia: "I saw my friends given quick trials and sent to face a firing squad. At Armando Bernal's trial, the guards did not even allow him to embrace his small son for the last time."

Hiram Gonzalez had also gone to prison at La Cabana. Gonzalez: "Bienvenido Infante had been my friend since childhood. He slept on the bunk above me at La Cabana. On the day of his trial and execution he washed, shaved smoothly and dressed as elegantly as he could under the circumstances. He looked like a man ready to party. 'I want to die looking good,' he told me.... Bienvenido walked out surrounded by the firing squad. He turned and looked toward us. His hand went up in the air. He waved at me and I waved back—a last goodbye. A couple of minutes later, as tears rolled down my face, I heard the sound of gunfire. I had lost another friend."

The same week Infante was executed, another firing squad claimed the life of William Morgan, the American who had fought against Batista and gained Castro's praise. The Ohio-born ex-con, having found in Cuba a reason for living and dying, had redeemed his ideals by turning against another dictatorship. William Alexander Morgan died on March 10, 1961, after being shot in both legs and forced to kneel before his executioners.

* * *

While the underground and guerrillas fought inside Cuba, exile groups in Miami were having problems with the U.S. government in coordinating infiltration teams and preparing an invasion. The CIA set up Station JM-Wave, a gigantic operation involving hundreds of exiles and U.S. advisors, with a huge apparatus and sizeable resources committed to a war against Castro.

Some organizations received help, while many others did not. Manuel Ray's MRP, for example, was denied assistance on grounds that it was "Fidelism without Fidel." For some reason, U.S. intelligence agencies had concluded that the MRP was politically unreliable. Not until 1961 did it receive assistance.

In June 1960, five anti-Castro organizations came together to form the Revolutionary Democratic Front (FRD). Somewhat later, under the aegis of the United States, the

Cuban Revolutionary Council took shape, including in its ranks the FRD, MRR, DRE and MRP. Leading the council was Dr. Jose Miro Cardona, who had served as the first prime minister of the revolutionary government. Friction existed among the Cuban leaders of the council. Laureano Batista was a staff officer in the organization.

Laureano Batista: "There were two factions. One only wanted American aid, while the other wanted U.S. leadership. Everyone was for the same goal—fighting communism—but some wanted the initiative and planning to come from the American side, and others from the exile side."

Heavy recruitment took place and hundreds of exiles went to secret camps in Guatemala and Nicaragua to train for an invasion. Manel Menendez Pou was one of the young men joining Assault Brigade 2506, the U.S.-sponsored invasion force.

Menendez Pou: "Signing up was easy—an application and a medical exam that a corpse could pass. Then we waited for orders to ship out to Guatemala. In my case, it took a month and a half."

At base camps in Guatemala, arguments developed between different factions. Some men left the camps and others were detained for mutiny. In a report to U.S. President-elect John F. Kennedy, CIA director Allen Dulles complained that it was impossible to create a Cuban government-in-exile that could unify 184 different organizations.[3]

The harmonious blending of all Cuban groups was a pipe dream. Anti-Castro organizations varied from the conservative "White Rose" to former anti-Batista groups like the MRP or the 30th of November Movement. Political influences came from the Orthodox Party, the Autentico Party and Catholic youth organizations. Ideologies ranged from Christian Democrat to Social Democrat, conservative to anarchist. Many of the men now fighting on the same side had recently been enemies, and grudges were hard to forget. Despite such problems, the invasion force continued to train.

Covert operations proceeded at different levels. Some groups worked directly under CIA sponsorship, receiving money, weapons and specialized training for key operatives. Other groups, not under direct sponsorship, got some equipment and other limited assistance.

Laureano Batista: "The CIA gave independent groups some weapons, but no craft or fuel. Those things the group had to provide on its own. On the way back from an operation, one was supposed to dump the weapons at sea. The CIA did not want in Miami any weapons or explosives it could not control. Of course no one threw any weapons away. They were hidden in Miami or in the Keys."

Other Cuban exiles worked directly for the CIA in special units. The highest casualty

---

[3] Higgins, *The Perfect Failure*, p. 68

rate was in the infiltration teams that penetrated Cuba for months at a time, carrying out military or intelligence operations. These men were carried to shore by the CIA's exile naval-marine unit, which had at its disposal several large transport ships and a number of light, well-armed smaller craft. Apart from infiltration and naval forces, the Cuban CIA unit had two commando platoons totaling about fifty men, and a frogman squad of about twenty.

Jose Basulto, an engineering student, joined the infiltration teams. Basulto: "The options for anyone fighting Castro were very limited, and the one that offered the best weaponry and resources was the CIA. We did not feel like mercenaries or employees of the Americans. We did what we did because we were Cubans and we loved our country. We did not realize the United States visualized the Cuban process as a chess game between the Soviets and themselves...."

Alvaro Cosculluela received instruction from the CIA on how to be a radio operator, and how to command an infiltration squad. Cosculluela: "Some of the classes were interesting. Training included maritime and land radio reception, explosives, light weapons, coding and decoding, surveillance, survival. They taught us what to eat in the woods, how to cook food without being spotted, how to confuse dogs that follow you in the wild. For the radio-operator classes you were stuck alone or with another radioman in a house, and you had to spend months in that house, without ever leaving. A supply officer brought food and cigarettes, but you could not leave. They did this to get you used to spending time alone and prepare you for the boredom of being isolated for weeks. Instructors dropped in and gave us lessons, and I spent many hours reading technical manuals. Even my parents did not know what I was doing because they received postcards, signed by me, from different places in the United States, telling them about fictitious jobs."

Five men usually formed an infiltration team, but in some instances it was three, or a man could even infiltrate alone. Radio operators used Collins transmitters and the weapons of choice were M-3 submachine guns with silencers.

Jose Basulto returned to Cuba legally, registering as a student at Oriente University while setting up his radio to transmit intelligence data and coordinate weapons shipments. He was not alone. Alberto Muller, a DRE student leader, returned to set up guerrilla operations in Oriente province. MRR chief Rogelio Gonzalez, known in the underground as "Francisco," was already hiding in Havana. Dozens of Cubans were returning to help prepare for the invasion.

CHAPTER VI.

THE GREAT OFFENSIVE

In December, Castro's troops arrived at towns around the Escambray mountains. From every corner of Cuba, the regime had mobilized a force of sixty thousand militiamen in Las Villas province. The government used five hundred trucks, dozens of jeeps and light-armor vehicles in the massive operation. Trainloads of ammunition and weapons arrived at the station in Santa Clara and State Security teams received reinforcements for their interrogation and intelligence units.

On New Year's Day, the operation started. All entrance roads and highways into the Escambray region were sealed off with roadblocks. All cars and trucks were searched and suspects arrested. The roadblocks would remain in place for three months.

Every farmer "suspected" of harboring or supporting guerrillas was arrested and his properties confiscated. These suspects were forcibly evacuated to concentration camps in other provinces, in a dragnet operation that eventually displaced more than thirty thousand people from Las Villas. Three decades later, many survivors of the dragnet, and many descendants, remained in the "captive towns" of Pinar del Rio, long after the guerrillas of Las Villas had ceased to exist.

In farms throughout the region, militia squads were bivouacked to spy on the farmers and ambush or engage any guerrilla unit looking for food. A map of the region had been divided into squares, with ten battalions assigned to each square. Whenever a guerrilla unit was spotted, all ten battalions—more than five thousand men—were moved to that place, encircling it in three rings. The guerrilla squad would find itself heavily outnumbered, trapped in a triple ring of troops. The guerrillas might break out by shooting their way through the rings at their weakest points; or they might spend days or weeks hiding in caves while the militia tired of searching.[1]

Evelio Duque: "When the offensive started I had a number of well-armed and several hundred poorly armed men.... I organized the guerrillas into separate units, but from the beginning we were trapped in a noose of troops. After a few encounters, all units began running low on ammunition and we had no supply lines to provide us with bullets for our weapons. In every firefight we were outnumbered 30 to one, 50 to one, 100 to one. Because the whole region was overflowing with Castro's troops, it was impossible to communicate among our units. We had no medicines to cure our wounded, no food to eat. We were chased all over the mountains by so many troops that it was impossible to rest, to sleep. We did not sleep or eat for days, while they rotated fresh troops to engage us in battle."

Julio Lara, a former Rebel Army officer, was a guerrilla captain in the Escambray. Lara: "We were outnumbered all the time. We exchanged gunfire on a daily basis, or several times a day. We were constantly on the move. When they spotted us, they opened fire with mortars. I was pinned down by a mortar attack and I saw one of my men torn apart. His blood and pieces of skin splattered on me. He just disappeared. Another of my men lost an arm. We lost five that day. I was wounded in the foot during a skirmish. Even wounded, without food and totally exhausted, we kept moving, dodging ambushes, escaping their dragnets."

Felipe Villamil, a former Escambray guerrilla, was stunned at the deployment of troops. Villamil: "I climbed a tree and saw a long black line of trucks and jeeps on the roads heading toward us.... All we could do was defend ourselves and hide. Our only hope was to survive for a few weeks until they tired of tracking us down. I survived the sweep by hiding in a small farm with another guerrilla. We spent all day hiding in a lake, in tall grass, with water up to our chest. At night we came out, ate food the farmer provided, and slept. We hid out for forty-five days while the militia swept the area."

Guillermo Perez Calzada, a former guerrilla officer, recalled being caught inside a "cerco," the innermost enemy ring. Perez Calzada: "Julio Emilio Carretero and I hid inside the thick foliage of a lemon tree for eight days. At night we crawled through pasture grass to a water pond to drink. During the day we broiled inside our hideout. We had no food. Hunger gnawed at us. We were weak. Every day we sat, hour after hour,

---

[1] This information comes from interviews with former guerrillas and ex-members of Castro's armed forces. The concept of the triple ring appears to have been designed by Soviets and taught to Cuban troops. Although some guerrillas have claimed that Soviet officers directed field operations against them, no credible testimony exists to this effect.

crowded in that clump of leaves, staring at each other without talking, melting in the heat while militia troops ate and chatted a few yards away from our hideout."

Victor Gamez, a guerrilla lieutenant, had plenty of experience breaking through the enemy rings. Gamez: "One of the times we were surrounded, we were close to the ring of troops when we noticed that every time a helicopter flew overhead, the militia soldiers looked up to the sky and cheered. We timed it and moved through the ring without being spotted, as they looked up. We used to walk backwards in muddy areas, to leave a false trail. The farmers helped us. A couple of children, sons of one of our supporters, guided us out of a dangerous ambush. Castro's men did not suspect that the two farm boys, not even teenagers, were serving as scouts and took us past a ring of troops. In another tight situation, we stampeded cows and steers and ran among them to escape through enemy lines."

As militia units moved deeper into the Escambray, a plethora of skirmishes and small battles broke out. A militia squad was wiped out by an ambush in San Ambrosio. Militia troops destroyed guerrilla units near Pico Tuerto and Matas de Cafe. Every day the noose grew tighter.

Perez Calzada: "We left one firefight and stumbled into another one. We were fighting skirmishes on a daily basis, and sometimes more than one a day. We could not fight head-on for we were always outnumbered. We fought like this for weeks; and the worst thing was that our ammunition was very low. Any one of us with a handful of bullets could consider himself lucky. We always waited to fire at point-blank range, so we wouldn't waste our ammo...."

Victor Gamez: "We won some battles. When we attacked a militia camp at El Jovero we inflicted many casualties on the enemy; but we also lost some good men. A few days later we had a battle in San Blas, where the militia fired mortar shells against us. We lost one man there and others were wounded. By the time I was captured, in a long day of fighting near Topes de Collantes, the three men with me and I had a total of three bullets left."

Julio Lara: "During those weeks, we lived on survival instinct. We saw many men die. We were so tired, so hungry.... Six of us finally arrived at a cave where a river began. We had to enter through the river and move deep inside the mountain through the water. Inside the cave it was very dark and there were holes and cliffs where a man could fall and never be seen again. There were bats and the stench of bat waste, which was very strong. Inside we found Evelio Duque and eight of our people. We stayed there for several days. We used a bucket with a rope to draw water from the underground river. We tore bark from tree roots on the sides and ceilings of the cave to cook what little food we had. One had to spend most of the day in the same spot, without moving, for fear of falling down an underground cliff, or being smeared with excrement. Castro's troops came into the cave with torches and an exchange of gunfire took place. I was lightly wounded. One of our men was killed next to me. We had an escape route through the caves and we lost two more men. One fell down a cliff in the dark. We managed to get out of the cave and split up again and continued trying to break through the enemy lines. I had two meals in sixteen days. One of the meals was raw goat, which smelled very bad and was probably spoiled, or partly spoiled. We sliced the meat in very small pieces and salted the tiny pieces as well as we could. My brother and I were both wounded, dehydrated and near collapse, but we were lucky. We were able to escape the troop noose in the Escambray, and later leave Cuba."

Evelio Duque was likewise able to break through the rings and make his way to Havana, then off the island by boat. Fourteen other guerrillas escaped the mountains and reached a coastal area, where a CIA boat picked them up and carried them to Miami. Lara and his brother managed to get asylum at an embassy in Havana. Hundreds of others were killed or captured in the massive assault.

Perez Calzada: "I broke out of the Escambray, crawling through enemy lines, crossing roads barefoot so as not to make noise; but I was captured three days later, while drinking water. I was a dehydrated mass of skin and bones, and I had not eaten in thirteen days. Seven out of the eight men under my command had been killed in those brutal weeks of fighting."

The prisoners were taken for interrogations to Topes de Collantes, where Castro's men subjected them to mock executions and near-drowning experiences.

Victor Gamez: "They tied me up and threw me in a dyke. They pulled me up just as I was losing consciousness and swallowing water, and they tried to interrogate me as I vomited. They did this several times."[2]

In March 1961, Fidel Castro announced that the "Escambray bandits" had been eliminated. Newsreels showed scores of captured peasant farmers being led to prison. Castro's media launched a big campaign, accusing the guerrillas of assassinating schoolteachers and innocent peasants. The guerrillas, with no access to media channels, could not defend themselves. The insurgents did hang government informers active in their areas. In most cases, those executed were local militia members who had served as scouts in the hunt for guerrilla units.

---

[2] Torture of guerrillas, directed by Comandante Felix Torres and Captain Chino Figueredo, was common (from interviews with former guerrillas, 1987–1999).

Even after the government's mammoth assault, the Escambray guerrillas were far from finished. Although hundreds had been killed or captured, more than two hundred hardened veterans had survived the bitter weeks of fighting and would unite under a leader who had eluded eleven enemy rings: Osvaldo Ramirez.

* * *

While most of the government's repressive efforts focused on the Escambray mountains during the first months of 1961, the resistance movement was active throughout Cuba.

The highlands of Pinar del Rio, on Cuba's western tip, had several small guerrilla units, led by former Rebel Army captains Bernardo Corrales and Clodomiro Miranda as well as by a former U.S. Army paratrooper, Francisco "Machete" Robaina. About a dozen small units probably numbered around one hundred men.

In the Jaruco and Guines areas of Havana province—not an area that favored guerrillas—two units comprising some fifty men were operating. Matanzas province, between Havana and Las Villas, had two dozen insurgent units organized by Erelio Pena. When Pena left Cuba, the command of some two hundred guerrillas fell to Pichi Catala, a stocky former Rebel Army lieutenant.

Ramon Ramos was a twenty-seven-year-old farmer who became a guerrilla captain. Ramos: "At first I was coordinating groups, hiding guerrilla units in different farms, getting them food, medicine, supplies. Then I became a guerrilla. On my first day as an insurgent, our group was spotted. I knew the area and we left a false trail, so enemy troops would think we were hiding out on a hill. Instead we went to a spot about eight kilometers away and rested. The following day, they bombed the hill and hundreds of troops combed the area, looking for us. We could see it all from where we were hiding."

Many of the Matanzas guerrillas also fought in neighboring Las Villas. Apart from the large nucleus active in the Escambray mountains, two other guerrilla fronts had opened. About one hundred guerrillas were active on the northern coast under the command of Marti Campos, a former lieutenant in the Rebel Army.

Ramon Ramos: "I was with Marti Campos for almost four years, for our guerrillas moved between Matanzas and Las Villas provinces constantly. He was an excellent shot and a very good friend."

In the hills and farmlands along the province's other coast, the "Southern Front" had several small units under the command of a former Rebel Army sergeant named Carlos Gonzalez Garnica.

Another hundred guerrillas operated in the farmlands of Camaguey province, led by former rebel officer Arnoldo Martinez and a daring eighteen-year-old youth named Manolo Lopez.

In Oriente, the easternmost province, insurgent units were dispersed in different mountain regions, each for the most part fighting its own war. Meanwhile, the DRE and the 30th of November Movement were planning to stage revolts in the province that would coincide with the expected invasion.

CHAPTER VII.

BAD CHOICE, ONLY CHOICE

In Washington, officials of the Eisenhower and then the Kennedy administrations were distressed to observe the speed with which Castro moved toward the Soviet Bloc. Following the $100 million cooperation agreement it signed with the Soviet Union in February 1960, Cuba concluded treaties with East Germany and Poland.[1] On October 13, 1960, Law 890 provided for the expropriation of 380 corporations that mostly belonged to Cuban citizens: banks, sugar mills, factories and other enterprises.[2]

As the regime continued to seize private properties and the exile community bulged with daily arrivals, the United States continued to train Brigade 2506.

The CIA's chosen leader among Cubans was a former medical student named Manuel Artime. Once a lieutenant in the Rebel Army, Artime had gone on to co-found the MRR. A man of good organizational ability and a certain charisma, he was named civilian commander of the invasion force.

Finding a Cuban military man to lead the strike force had not been easy. First to hold the command had been Manuel F. Goudie, a retired Cuban Army colonel with no links to Castro or Batista. Goudie antagonized U.S. advisors by asking that an airfield for the invasion be set up in Cozumel, Mexico. The ex-colonel argued that the airfields in Guatemala would be too far away from Cuba to support the invasion once it was under way.

Manuel F. Goudie: "It did not make sense. A plane leaving Guatemala would use up so much fuel that by the time it arrived at the battle zone in Cuba, it could only fly over the area for a short time before having to return to Guatemala to refuel. The planes allotted for the invasion were heavy bombers, leftovers from the Second World War. I

---

[1] Carbonell, *And the Russians Stayed,* pp. 95–96
[2] Ibid.

pointed out that Castro had some T-33 jet fighter planes and Sea Fury combat planes, which could outspeed, outgun and outmaneuver the Brigade planes; and the Brigade planes had no tailguns to protect themselves, making them easy targets. They ignored me, so I resigned."

Eduardo Martin Helena, a former colonel with an unblemished reputation, succeeded Goudie, but also resigned after a few weeks of arguing with his advisors. Oscar Carol, who headed the Guatemala unit of Brigade 2506, also resigned. After weeks of arguments, the post of Brigade commander fell to a twenty-nine-year-old former Cuban Army captain, Jose "Pepe" San Roman. He had trained as an officer in the United States, had served a prison term for conspiracy to overthrow Batista's regime, and was considered a solid professional in the military field.

In the camps, political friction persisted. Some complained that the U.S. was calling all the shots and not listening to Cubans. More than a dozen mutineers were incarcerated in the remote region of El Peten, accessible only by helicopter.[3]

The nearly 1,500 men in Brigade 2506 were Cubans from all social strata and with diverse backgrounds. Only 135 had served in the military. The biggest group was made up of high-school and university students, numbering 240. Average age was 29; the youngest soldier was 16 and the oldest 61.[4]

Brigade members had mixed emotions about working with the United States. The history of Cuba and the Caribbean basin had been tainted by U.S. interventions. In the past, Cuban commentators had denounced various facets of the U.S. presence as encroachments on their national sovereignty. In the present day, however, Castro's alliance with the Soviets left the exiles feeling they had little choice but to accept U.S. support in contesting his regime.

＊　＊　＊

In offices at the White House and the Pentagon, decisions were taken that modified the invasion plan. The first option, conceived by planners in the outgoing Eisenhower administration, had posited a landing near the city of Trinidad in southern Cuba, close to the Escambray region. That way, the force would have a fighting chance to join with the guerrillas and set up a zone where the insurgents could receive airdrops and extend their control. This invasion would be seconded by another incursion in Oriente province; by air

[3] Johnson, *The Bay of Pigs*, p. 61
[4] Ibid., p. 98

strikes sufficient to destroy Castro's planes on the ground; and by a campaign of sabotage in Havana and other cities whose goal would be to produce mass confusion leading to Castro's collapse.

Instead of the Trinidad region, planners in the new Kennedy administration chose another area for the attack: the Bay of Pigs and Zapata swamp, a relatively desolate area further to the west. Proponents of this plan argued that, once taken, the area would be easy to defend, as it had only one entrance road, which could easily be blocked. This plan depended on the invasion force having dominion of the air. The Brigade's Cuban pilots were outstandingly qualified. According to a report, six of them had a higher level of proficiency in combat flying than their own U.S. instructors.[5]

A CIA report stated: "Surprise is essential to the success of the mission.... [T]he possibilities of obtaining surprise are 85 to 15.... Loss of the surprise factor could mean the destruction of part, or the totality of the invasion force."[6]

Setting aside the problems of air bases too far from the field of battle, and of slow-moving planes with no tailguns, planners accepted the Bay of Pigs scenario without doing a feasibility study of the terrain—and also without preparing a worst-case evacuation plan.[7]

Months after the fact, U.S. Army Chief of Staff General Earle Wheeler acknowledged to his colleague, General Maxwell Taylor, that planners assumed survivors would simply melt into the swamps and become guerrillas in the event the invasion failed.[8] In fact, the swamps of the region were poor terrain for a guerrilla unit. From time to time insurgents had hidden there, but only as a last resort—in small numbers, for brief periods of time, to avoid Castro's massive dragnets.

Pentagon planners and CIA officials did not correctly assess the strength of Castro's military. With a regular army of 32,000 men and a militia of 200,000 men and women, it was a huge fighting force that was also receiving ample material support from the Soviet Bloc. In March 1961, the Cubans received shipments including 104,000 light weapons, 80 anti-aircraft cannons and 55 tanks. Two to three hundred Soviet military personnel were serving as advisors to the armed forces, and fifty combat pilots were being trained in Czechoslovakia.[9]

Planning aside, the most crucial actor in the invasion was the new U.S. President.

[5] Interview with Eduardo Lambert, 1992
[6] Ibid.
[7] Aguilar Leon, ed., *Operation Zapata*, p. 208
[8] Ibid.
[9] Higgins, *The Perfect Failure*, p. 90

John F. Kennedy told U.N. Ambassador Adlai Stevenson that rather than arm Cuban exiles, he would prefer to confront Castro through the politics of the Organization of American States.[10] Kennedy, plainly, was not comfortable with the pending invasion.

* * *

By year's end 1960, infiltration teams were entering Cuba, establishing contacts with clandestine groups, setting up radio communications and providing intelligence data to assist planning for the invasion. Most infiltrators, like nineteen-year-old Felix Rodriguez, landed at night on rubber rafts. A few, like Jose Basulto, entered legally.

Jose Basulto: "I went back to Cuba and told them I had studied in the United States but did not like it, and was returning to my homeland because I liked the revolution. I went to Santiago de Cuba, registered at the University of Oriente, and began leading what seemed to be a normal life. A radio was delivered to me, and I set up an operation that would bring ten tons of weapons into Cuba: five for a guerrilla uprising in the Sierra Maestra mountains, and five for the underground."

Most of the men in the infiltration teams would be captured, killed in combat or executed.

[10] Ibid., p. 60

CHAPTER VIII.

INVASION

By March 1961, Cuba was fully at war. While Castro's militia forces swept through the Escambray to rout out guerrillas, underground units in the cities stepped up their activities.

Havana's leading department store, El Encanto, lately confiscated by the government, was set ablaze. On the same night, in faraway Santiago de Cuba, two stores were consumed by fire. Almost daily, bombs exploded in urban centers and government buildings, and industrial machinery was sabotaged. Humberto Lopez, in an urban unit of the MRR, anxiously awaited the invasion.

Humberto Lopez: "We were ready. Teams had been assigned to attack all the police stations in Havana, take over public buildings, disrupt communications, sabotage transportation systems. All we needed was the order to go ahead."

DRE leader Alberto Muller had returned from the United States clandestinely, moving a group of his men to the Sierra Maestra mountains, where he waited for an airdrop of weapons to start a guerrilla operation.

Alberto Muller: "We had done a lot of work in that region and we were hoping to receive enough weapons to equip several hundred men. The men were ready but we needed the weapons."

Five of the ten tons of weapons requested by Jose Basulto were destined for Muller's unit.

Jose Basulto: "I asked for weapons and they gave me the date of arrival as April 19. This was ridiculous, as the bombing of the airfields was on the fifteenth and the invasion landed two days later. We needed the weapons a few days before the invasion, not a few days after. I was almost trapped in roadblocks as I headed for the drop site."

Castro's troops were on full alert. Francisco Chappi, a political prisoner, saw something extraordinary at the huge maximum-security facility on the Isle of Pines.

Francisco Chappi: "On the same day the air raids started, tarpaulin-covered trucks loaded with cases of dynamite arrived at the circular buildings. Soldiers with jackhammers began drilling holes in the columns and foundations of the structure. Primacord wire was attached to the explosives. Incredible as it may seem, every building was being prepared to blow up. If the invasion succeeded, the prison was to be reduced to rubble—a mass grave for six thousand men. We sat in the circulars, behind our iron bars, watching men in olive-green fatigues preparing our slaughter, unable to fight."[1]

* * *

Two ships, with two invasion forces, were making for Cuba. The bulk of the Brigade was headed toward the Bay of Pigs, while a second unit of 150 men, led by former Rebel Army officer Nino Diaz, was on its way to Oriente province. Jose Antonio Ortiz, a native of Oriente, was a member of Diaz's unit.

Jose Antonio Ortiz: "Most of the men in my unit were from Oriente and knew the region well. Most of us had been students, like Jorge Mas Canosa, Tony Calatayud and myself. A few, like Nino Diaz and Jose Dionisio Suarez, had guerrilla experience."

The unit for Oriente was supposed to land on the fourteenth, hours before air raids started—a diversionary tactic to make Castro believe that the invasion was coming on the eastern tip of Cuba. As that force approached the designated landing zone, they found it teeming with Castro's troops and illuminated by reflector lights. Next day, as they looked for another place to land, they were spotted.

Jose Antonio Ortiz: "We were seen by an observation plane from Castro's air force. We later found out that we were to be bombed, but the airplane that was to attack us was sabotaged by a sergeant in Castro's air force who was a member of the MRR. The following day we crossed paths with an enemy patrol boat. Then the order came from Washington to forget our invasion in Oriente and head for the Bay of Pigs. When we arrived, the battle was over."

* * *

[1] Other former prisoners at the Isle of Pines have testified that an emplacement of explosives similar to TNT, very much like the incident described by Chappi, occurred several months after the Bay of Pigs.

On the morning of April 15, eight B-26 bombers of Brigade 2506 entered Cuban air space. At the last minute, for no clear reason, two key air bases were cancelled as targets.

Painted with Castro's air force insignias, the low-flying planes attacked Columbia Military Camp and bases at San Antonio and Santiago de Cuba, covering the airfields with explosions, fires and clouds of dust. Anti-aircraft fire made a mortal hit on one of the planes, which fell into the sea near Havana; pilot Daniel Fernandez Mon and navigator Gaston Perez were killed. Two other Brigade bombers were damaged and made emergency landings in the United States, one plane in Key West, the other at a Miami airport. As a cover-up, the U.S. government issued a statement saying the planes had been piloted by deserters from the Cuban military. Castro contested the statement and angrily accused the U.S. of aggression.

The plan to destroy Castro's air force on the ground had been only partly successful. Although most of his small air force had been damaged, Castro still had a T-33 jet and several Sea Furies, quite enough to outspeed the slow-moving Brigade bombers.

✳   ✳   ✳

On the morning of April 17, paratroopers of Brigade 2506, led by former military cadet Alejandro Del Valle, jumped onto Cuban soil. A few kilometers to the south, hundreds of men in camouflage uniforms approached the beaches at Giron and Playa Larga in sixteen-foot landing craft. A coastal radio observation post notified Castro's militia forces in Cienfuegos, where Battalion 339 responded to the call.

Tony Salgado was a squad leader in Brigade 2506. Salgado: "The battalion from Cienfuegos moved down a road that the paratroopers had not yet sealed off. We caught them in a crossfire with our .30 caliber machine guns, killing and wounding dozens of them, but they fought back very well, very bravely. The night lit up with tracer rounds; the sound of gunfire was deafening, constant. Screams of the wounded intermingled with sounds of explosions. It was a brutal battle. The sun came up and in the light of the morning we fought on, sometimes so close that we could hear their squad leaders shouting orders to each other. At ten o'clock in the morning I volunteered to lead my squad on a flanking maneuver against one of their point units. I crawled up as close as I could and lobbed a grenade in their direction. There was a flash followed by a scream. As I turned toward my men, a bullet entered my chest, pierced my lung and went out the back. I opened my mouth and it felt sticky, coated with blood. I felt light and calm. Everything was white. In my only moment of anguish, I asked God to let me see my wife and three children one last time. Reality came rushing back. Pain burned through me. I felt as if a hot iron had been pushed through my body."

More militia forces arrived. At Covadonga the paratroopers of the Brigade halted the advance of a militia battalion. The fighting was so intense that the Brigade used up two days' allotment of ammunition on the first day of battle.[2]

By afternoon, Castro had moved almost thirty thousand men to the combat area. The roads leading toward the Bay of Pigs were jammed with trucks, jeeps and tanks carrying army and militia troops.

At 3 p.m., two Brigade 2506 planes strafed and bombed one of the convoys. Fire and explosions covered the field, littering the highway with dead and wounded. A T-33 plane shot down both Brigade planes before they could return to Guatemala. One of the planes had run out of ammunition and neither had tailguns to defend against the attacking fighter.[3]

Eduardo Moya, an ambulance driver for Castro's ground forces, witnessed the strafing of the Brigade planes. Moya: "I saw it from a distance at first, big balls of flame and smoke rising up from the highway. I remember looking at the black smoke and thinking, it's just like a movie—and when we were close it all looked very real. There must have been thirty or forty dead and more than a hundred wounded. Trucks were on fire and the whole road was covered with broken glass, pieces of metal. The air smelled of burnt tires and burnt flesh. I saw a shoe standing in the road with a foot sheared off at the ankle, and I vomited. I placed six of the badly wounded in the ambulance and headed for the hospital. Two of the six died on the way; then I went back and picked up more. That's all I did for two days and nights."

Castro's planes, now in control of the air, flew over the battle zone and bombed the *Houston* and *Rio Escondido,* the two main supply ships of the invading force. The situation turned desperate for Brigade 2506. Without supplies, ammunition or food, they could not hold the beachhead. As night fell, Castro's troops commenced a sustained mortar and artillery barrage against the Brigade's positions. While Jose San Roman radioed for help, squad leaders of the assault Brigade scrounged for ammunition, redistributing the weapons of the dead or wounded among those who were still fit to fight.

San Roman's plea for help fell on deaf ears. Admiral Arleigh Burke, who was in Washington D.C. as the invasion hit the south coast of Cuba, proposed that U.S. Navy jet fighters be sent to establish air supremacy. He asked that Navy ships in the area be used

---

[2] Aguilar Leon, ed., *Operation Zapata,* p. 187
[3] Johnson, *The Bay of Pigs,* pp. 124–25

to lay an artillery barrage over the beach, halting Castro's troops in their advance, and that several hundred Marines be sent in to supply and reinforce the Brigade's assault. His requests were denied.[4] Burke later stated that the operation should have had a naval commander on the spot to make decisions rather than oblige combatants to refer everything to the Pentagon and the CIA.[5]

*   *   *

While men fiercely fought each other on a Cuban beach, press releases in the United States announced the imminent collapse of Castro's government. The CIA had hired the Madison Avenue firm of Lem Jones to handle its PR for the invasion.[6]

U.S. media were well clued-in to what was happening. On the night the Brigade approached the Bay of Pigs, an editor at *The New York Times* called the desk editor of *Revolucion* in Havana to follow the progress of the landings.[7]

In Cuba many people were listening to Radio Swan, a CIA station broadcasting from Swan Island, hundreds of miles to the south. The station was giving out patently false information.

Julian Garcia, a member of the MDC's resistance units, was in Colon, Matanzas province, when the invasion started. Garcia: "I was listening to the broadcast when Radio Swan issued a news flash that the city of Colon was in the hands of the invasion force. I was in Colon, and the city was full of militia troops heading south to fight the Brigade."

*   *   *

Throughout Cuba, State Security and police units were making arrests by the thousands. All people suspected of being involved with resistance units—including all relatives of clandestine warriors, former military men, politicians who had failed to favor Castro, priests and journalists—became prisoners. When jails overflowed, theaters and public buildings were used to hold detainees.

Jorge Chappi, a member of the resistance, was taken to Havana's Blanquita Theater. Chappi: "Five thousand people were locked inside that theater, tight as sardines in a can. They had set up large reflectors that were never turned off. Our only drinking water was from the toilets, and an epidemic broke out. A woman gave birth inside the theater and a

---

[4] Wise and Ross, *The Invisible Government*, p. 71
[5] Aguilar Leon, ed., *Operation Zapata*, p. 115
[6] Wise and Ross, *The Invisible Government*, p. 29
[7] Franqui, *Family Portrait with Fidel*, p. 121

man died of a stroke. It was hot and we could not bathe. There was an uprising on the fourth day and a lieutenant fired his machine gun, killing two and wounding others."

State Security took casualties in the massive raids. Resistance fighters Marcial Arufe and Olga Fernandez, husband and wife, used three handguns to fend off a police squad that had found their hideout. Six of Castro's men died, as did the recently married couple. A brother of Arufe, Miguel, was arrested and sentenced to prison for being the brother of a resistance leader.[8]

While thousands were hunted down and arrested, clandestine fighters waited for orders that never came.

Humberto Lopez: "My first reaction was: what should I do now? I went to my section leader, telling him that I wanted to fight in support of the invaders, but he just shook his head sadly. The chain of command was frozen."

At La Cabana Fortress and elsewhere, firing squads continued to kill without letup. Those who died at the wall included two Americans, Howard Anderson and August McNair. Fifteen top resistance leaders were executed in the three days the invasion lasted. Rogelio Gonzalez, known as "Francisco," was one of the martyrs.

Jose Basulto: "I saw him shortly before he fell into enemy hands. He was a very brave man, but he was under a lot of stress. He feared the Americans were playing political games with us, and he knew his time was running out."

Manuel Puig was another resistance leader killed by a firing squad in that bloody week. His brother Rino was serving a fifteen-year prison sentence for conspiracy to overthrow the regime.

Rino Puig: "My brother and I were very close and his death affected me deeply. The government tried to use his death to weaken me, but it made me stronger."

Two other men who faced firing squads were Virgilio Campaneria and Alberto Tapia Ruano, architecture students who had become DRE leaders. They had been arrested with Tomas "Tommy" Fernandez Travieso in March. Although Travieso was not executed because he was a minor, he received a twenty-year sentence and was placed in a death-row cell with his two friends.

Tommy Fernandez Travieso: "Nine of us were in that room. While we waited for the executions to start, some prayed, others wrote letters to their relatives, some even joked. There was an awesome inner calm. Virgilio looked at my worn-out shoes and said, 'Let's trade, Tommy, so you can take a good pair of shoes to prison....' I was feeling bad. I was with all these men who were going to die, and I was not, and I had to be witness to their last

[8] Interview with Tito Rodriguez-Oltman, former member of the resistance, Miami, 1992

moments. I had red eyes, and one of the men came and said to me, 'Look, don't worry about our dying. This will be over quickly.' Virgilio answered, 'Leave him alone. He's the only one among us who will not have to face the firing squad.' There were three rusted metal gates that our jailers had to open before they reached our cell. And every time a man was to be executed, we could hear the gates open, one by one. The door to our cell opened, a name was called out, and they took the man away and the gates closed, creaking, one by one. Then we heard the shooting of the squad, followed by the sound of a pistol shot.... Virgilio was the third. I counted two pistol shots. Tapia wanted to die beside his friend. He said, 'I hope I'm next'—and he was. He went away smiling. They all died bravely—and after it was all over came silence, and I was left alone in that room for the rest of the night."

*   *   *

At the Bay of Pigs, Castro launched a full-scale assault on Brigade 2506 positions. At the Rotonda, twenty tanks and 2,000 of Castro's troops attacked a position defended by 370 men. The youngest member of Brigade 2506, sixteen-year-old Felipe Rodon, died as he fired a .57 recoilless shell at an advancing tank. The shell blew up the tank but Rodon was so close that his own shrapnel killed him. Another teenager, Gilberto Hernandez, lost an eye in the first moments of the battle. He continued fighting until a militia grenade took his life.

Brigade planes kept arriving from Guatemala. A bombing-and-strafing run on militia positions destroyed a convoy.

Mario Perez was a militia lieutenant in the front lines. Perez: "When the plane bombed the convoy, the truck in front of me exploded. I jumped off my jeep. A bus that had been used to transport troops was in flames. Men were jumping out the windows. They were from Battalion 123. Their driver was dead. Seven or eight men died in that bus, roasted by the flames. One man was on the ground, near a ditch. His kneecap had been blown away. I went to him and he looked at me and said: 'I have no complaints, comrade, I'm still alive.' "

Castro's air force pursued the slower Brigade 2506 planes. Eduardo Whitehouse was a Brigade pilot. Whitehouse: "I was flying low and saw below me, in the water, what looked like a large school of fish. I was actually seeing bullets fired at me from a T-33. They missed my plane and hit the water below. I was flying so low, the T-33 couldn't get a fix on me. If I had been higher, I would have been downed for sure."

Armando Alberty, who had flown airdrops over the Escambray mountains, was now over the Bay of Pigs. Alberty: "I was very low over the water when one of Castro's Sea Furies came diving down from up high. It was very tough for him to measure how low I was flying. He wanted to dive, go under me, and come in for a second sweep. But since I was flying so low, he had no chance to maneuver. His plane hit the water, bounced over the sea and exploded."

Castro's air force freely pounded Brigade 2506 positions and attacked the supply ships. Juan Luis Cosculluela, a naval officer, was in command of the ship "Blagar" when one of Castro's planes attacked.

Juan Luis Cosculluela: "It was a big B-26 bomber, like the ones in our own Brigade. He made two passes at us. We had six combat stations and the .50 caliber machine guns laid down a heavy barrage, but he kept coming, like a kamikaze. One of our crew manning a .50 was Reinaldo Silva, who was 22 or 23 at the time. Silva's was the only gun not firing.... The other .50's ran out of ammo. The plane came back and dropped two rockets. When I saw the plane moving closer and the rockets coming toward us, I threw myself on the deck, landing on men who were already crawling or lying flat. Then Silva began to fire, face to face with the incoming plane. I heard explosions. I thought the torpedo rockets had hit us but they missed us. It was the other plane that exploded almost above us, and pieces of burning debris fell on our deck. When I looked up, Silva was screaming: 'I got him!' "

*   *   *

Four P-51 Mustang fighter planes arrived in Guatemala on April 18 but the Cuban pilots were not allowed to use them, as they had not had any practice flights. Brigade crews were exhausted, having flown missions nonstop for a day and a half. Some of the American instructors offered to fly in place of the Cubans. In the end, half of the Brigade's twenty-four B-26 bombers would be shot down; ten exile pilots and four U.S. advisors would lose their lives.[9]

The dead Americans—Thomas Willard Ray, Riley Shamburger, Leo Francis Baker and Wade Gray—would be a subject of controversy in the invasion's jumbled aftermath. Their own government would label them "mercenaries," denying official recognition of their service or valor. Widow and dependent benefits did not come to their families via a military pension fund, but rather through the law offices of Alex Carlson, a Miami attorney representing the "corporation" that had employed the four men. As late as 1963, Attorney General Robert Kennedy, the President's brother, was publicly denying that any American had died at the Bay of Pigs.[10]

[9] Wise and Ross, *The Invisible Government*, p. 75
[10] Ibid., pp. 78–85

The daughter of Thomas Willard Ray, Janet Ray, would spend twenty years making requests through diplomatic and political channels until the Castro government, in 1979, surrendered the remains of the downed American pilot, who was buried with honors in Alabama.

*   *   *

Along several miles of swamp and beaches, Cubans continued to fight each other, exchanging mortar shells and light-weapons fire.

Mario Perez: "The Brigade started losing ground that afternoon. They didn't have the firepower to resist us. We outnumbered them; my unit took four prisoners. They were all men in their twenties, very tired and haggard-looking. They had been fighting for a day and a half and were exhausted. By late afternoon, they were falling back toward the beach and some isolated pockets had been surrounded."

Some sixty Brigade 2506 men had been killed and many others wounded. Tony Salgado, with a bullet wound in his chest, had spent the day at an improvised hospital on the beach.

Tony Salgado: "By the end of the second day, we all realized the situation was hopeless. Fighting had been fierce. The man who had replaced me as squad leader had also been wounded. Word came down that the Brigade was to disband into small groups and try to escape as best we could, or make our way to the Escambray mountains. During that last day the CIA informed the Brigade commander that the agency would evacuate the headquarters staff to safety. Jose San Roman declined. 'Either we all leave,' he said, 'or we all die here. I will not leave my men.' I consider Pepe San Roman a hero, one of the bravest men I've known."

On April 19, the last Brigade 2506 lines at the Bay of Pigs crumbled. In Oriente, Alberto Muller and many of his DRE men had been arrested unarmed, waiting for weapons that never arrived. Jose Basulto, now hiding from State Security, received a coded message urging an uprising. In a coded message of his own, Basulto answered angrily: "Uprising now impossible. Most patriots in jail. Thanks for your damned invasion. Closing transmission."[11]

---

[11] Interviews with Jose Basulto, Miami, 1991–1993

CHAPTER IX.

BITTER AFTERMATH

Sporadic gunfire was still heard along the beaches as the remnants of Brigade 2506 dispersed and tried to pass through enemy lines or fade into the swamps.

Vicente Leon, a Brigade officer, used the last bullet in his pistol to kill himself rather than face capture. Amado Gayol also took out his gun to end his life, but Erneido Oliva, a Brigade commander, talked him out of suicide.[1] Oliva, who would become a brigadier general in the U.S. armed forces, organized a group of survivors. Gathering whatever weapons, ammunition and food he could find, Oliva ordered all serviceable vehicles and equipment destroyed so they would not fall into enemy hands.

Tony Salgado, dressed only in military pajamas, his chest wound plugged by a bandage, still refused to surrender. Salgado: "I found myself alone in the Zapata swamp. I didn't know where I was headed. Above, helicopters cruised on patrol, looking for us. I heard scattered gunfire.... At night I sat alone in the darkness, too tired to walk. I leaned on a large boulder and I could feel small animals moving in the darkness. One touched me. I kicked out. Dozens of crabs were moving toward me in the night, attracted by the smell of my blood. I could feel the little pinhead eyes staring at me in the darkness. I could hear clicking of little claws opening and closing. I was going to be eaten alive. I managed to climb on the boulder. I spent the night moving a branch with one arm, keeping the crabs away. I sat on the rock and cursed and cried...."

Salgado was captured the following morning and taken to a temporary detention center at the Bay of Pigs.

Enrique Ruiz-Williams was among the wounded Brigade members being held prisoner at some cottage cabins at Giron Beach. Wounded, barely able to move, Ruiz-Williams

[1] Johnson, *The Bay of Pigs*, p. 171

looked up to find Fidel Castro staring at him. Fidel had arrived to look at the newly captured prisoners. Ruiz-Williams attempted to reach for a hidden pistol, but he was too weak to make it. Castro did not seem bothered.[2]

Tired, hungry and exhausted from days of fighting without rest, hundreds of Brigade survivors were being captured, one by one, in the swamps. Erneido Oliva was picked up after he had gone four days without water. Jose San Roman lasted a week in the swamps; Manuel Artime was taken after a dozen days.

Eduardo Lambert, a Brigade paratrooper, led Castro's forces on a two-week chase through Las Villas province. Dressed in worker's garb taken from a clothesline, armed only with a .45 Ithaca pistol, Lambert escaped a score of tight situations, shooting his way through enemy lines. By the time of his capture, Lambert had killed five militiamen and wounded two others in four separate incidents.

Lambert: "I ate roots, any kind that didn't taste bitter, and I chewed on pieces of sugar cane. The inside of my mouth and my gums were cut and bleeding. Sugar cane is very tough…. I had climbed a tree. The militia were sweeping the area looking for me, and they passed below me, firing their weapons into the sugar cane field, chopping down the canes, thinking I was in there. When they came back, one man saw me. The militia pointed their rifles up the tree. I had no possible escape."

* * *

On the morning of April 20 a group of 179 captured Brigade prisoners, including wounded men, were jammed into an airtight semi-trailer for transportation to Havana.

Tony Salgado: "It was dark inside the truck. As we began moving, prisoners were falling, bumping into each other. It was hot, very hot, until it became an oven. Sweat poured from us. With every mile, it became harder to breathe. Men banged on the truck walls, screaming. Someone vomited. Then more began vomiting. One man prayed aloud. Others were screaming. The floor was slick with vomit. Some men used their belts to try to open small holes in the wood walls, to breathe. A few holes were made, but it was not enough. One man died, then another. Condensation from our bodies formed on the ceiling above us, then dripped down. Another man died and the stronger men began to move the weaker ones, pressing their faces to the holes, trying to keep them alive. Our hands and feet were swollen. When we arrived in Havana and the doors opened, we were

[2] Ibid., p. 177

a lump of dehydrated bodies covered in vomit and sweat. Nine men had died in the truck and a tenth died afterward."

Other Brigade 2506 men endured equally wretched fates. Although thirty Brigade members managed to make it away from the beaches in a launch to open sea, where a U.S. ship rescued them, another launch with twenty-two more men was lost. On the second day, those men survived heavy rains; by the fourth day, they had been reduced to drinking their own urine. Without food or water, baked by the sun, several died, their bodies jerking in spasms, a greenish pus coming from their eyeballs. Paratroop commander Alejandro Del Valle died with his hand tapping SOS signals in Morse code on the side of the boat. On their fifteenth day at sea, a passing cargo ship found them. Ten had died, and all twelve survivors had to be hospitalized for severe burns and dehydration.[3]

* * *

Almost one hundred Brigade 2506 members had died at the Bay of Pigs, and more than one thousand had been captured. Castro's government acknowledged 155 of its military personnel killed in battle, while the CIA claimed that Castro's forces had taken 1,800 casualties during the fighting.[4]

Mario Perez, a lieutenant in Castro's army, stated his disagreement with both estimates. "Castro's figures claim that the Police Battalion lost 17 men. Not true—I saw 25 or 26 bodies stretched out on the ground after the battle. Every officer in the Police Battalion was wounded in the fighting. The Cadet Battalion from the Militia School also had high casualties; more than twenty killed and thirty or forty wounded. There were hundreds of wounded. I visited the hospitals and the sights were gruesome. Quite a few died in hospital. The Brigade fought well, but could not win. Many people still supported Castro, and we outnumbered them at the beach twenty to one. I think Castro's troops probably had about two hundred and some killed and five or six hundred wounded."

* * *

At the base camps in Guatemala, survivors of Brigade 2506 expressed rage and frustration. Rogelio Helu, a young veteran of the MDC resistance groups, arrived at the

---

[3] Ibid., pp. 195–202
[4] Aguilar Leon, ed., *Operation Zapata,* p. 91

training camp too late to take part in the invasion. He was with more than a hundred late arrivals when Cuban exile leader Tony Varona visited them.

Rogelio Helu: "We were told we would be part of the next invasion force, but we already knew about the disaster. We made it clear we did not trust them, or those who were now training us."

The exile community accused their leaders of "sellout" or "betrayal." In retrospect, the exile leaders appear to have been simply naive rather than ill-intentioned. They put too much faith in promises by U.S. officials—promises the Kennedy administration did not keep. A sign of their misplaced trust is that many men from their own families had been in the swamps. Aside from having to bear the hard verdict of history—the realization that they had been used and abandoned—Tony Varona had a son, a brother and a nephew seized by Castro's forces, while Jose Miro Cardona's son was also captured.

* * *

Fidel Castro hugely relished his hour of victory. Proclaiming that the "forces of imperialism" had been destroyed, his media paraded images of militia forces escorting prisoners, of downed invasion planes, and of the leader himself bestriding the beaches at the Bay of Pigs.

To create a myth of invincibility and to portray the invaders as mercenaries or social parasites, Castro's TV broadcasters interrogated Brigade 2506 captives before nation-wide audiences. Some Brigade members had been soldiers in Batista's army; others were scions of wealthy families; still others were men whose spirits had been exhausted by days of fighting and surviving in the swamps. Withal, some of the televised captives were able to project a certain dignity.

Carlos De Varona, son of exile leader Tony Varona, managed to question his on-air interrogators. "If you have so much support," he said, "why don't you have free elections?"

Fidel Castro questioned Tomas Cruz, a black man. When the Maximum Leader pointed out that Cuban private beaches had been opened to all, including blacks, Cruz nodded sadly.

"I have no hangups about my color and race," the black man answered Castro, "and I did not come to Cuba to swim."

Felipe Rivero, educated in Europe, cleverly debated the interrogators, asserting that Cuba had gone from "one imperialism to another." Of the invasion forces, he said: "We lost for one simple reason. We were one thousand men fighting against five or ten or thirty thousand."

To his interrogators, paratrooper Carlos Onetti gave idealistic answers. "We came to fight against a despot regime—communism—to establish a democratic system in our country, to reestablish the 1940 Constitution, free enterprise and human rights."[5]

After the televised interrogations came a trial. The Cuban government held the prisoners for ransom, imposing prices for their release and return to the United States. The three top leaders were "worth" $500,000 each, while 221 were offered at $100,000 apiece. The remaining 995 went for between $25,000 to $50,000 each. To cap his PR victory, Castro later withdrew the ransom demands, offering to accept shipments of medicines and other products.

President Kennedy sent New York lawyer James B. Donovan to arrange the prisoners' release. In exchange for $53 million in various goods, almost all members of Brigade 2506 were allowed to leave for the United States. Five were executed and another nine kept in prison when the rest of the invasion force was let go.

On Christmas Day 1962, more than eleven hundred survivors of the failed invasion reached the United States. A few days later, in an Orange Bowl filled with exiles, they presented President Kennedy with a Brigade 2506 flag.

"This flag," Kennedy vowed, "will be returned to the Brigade in a free Havana."[6]

The audience cheered. The men of Brigade 2506 declared themselves fit to return to battle. Fifteen years later, angered at jailings of anti-Castro exiles in the U.S., the veterans of Brigade 2506 asked for their flag to be returned.

It came back to them in the mail.

[5] Carbonell, *And the Russians Stayed,* p. 177
[6] *The Washington Post,* December 30, 1962

CHAPTER X.

CAPTURES AND ESCAPES

The defeat of the invasion force at the Bay of Pigs crippled the internal resistance and further legitimized Castro as an international figure. In Latin America and Europe, the image of a "David who slew Goliath" grew to mythic proportions as intellectuals lionized the Cuban regime. In the resistance, men and women continued to risk their lives every day, but they were having doubts.

Humberto Lopez: "We had waited for orders that never arrived. We had hundreds of fighters ready. We could have paralyzed the city of Havana and all of Cuba, blowing up bridges, attacking police stations—but nothing happened. And when it was all over we were left with a bad taste in our mouths. We thought: 'How could so many mistakes be made?' It was incredible. We kept on fighting and help kept coming, but we wondered if we would be betrayed once more."

The Bay of Pigs defeat multiplied the mass exodus, and Cubans left for Miami in record numbers. Whole families took off by the thousands, effectively handing over their homes and other properties to the government. As the legal process for a "freedom flight" took months of paperwork, many made for Florida in boats. During 1961, some 1,801 Cubans took this route in 194 small craft.[1]

The mass exodus hurt the resistance movements. Not only did it drain away the opposition; it also shrank the number of available safe houses and vehicles. Enrique Gonzalez-Pola was a resistance fighter: "I heard talk about large shipments of weapons reaching Cuba.... The amount that came in was, in proportion, much less than what we needed. When weapons were moved around it was just a few pistols, a few rifles, never enough. My group had a British Sten gun and we could not use it. We had no clips."

[1] Ruiz, *Diario de una traicion 1961*, p. 283

Resistance casualties did not let up. Jorge Fundora, a key man in the infiltration teams and supply lines, died before a firing squad. So did Ernesto Perez Morales, the military commander of Revolutionary Democratic Rescue. Carlos Delgado of the 30th of November, after killing a police captain in a shootout, was wounded, captured and executed. Juanin Pereira Varela, a young DRE leader, died in a firefight with Castro's security forces. Enrique Gonzalez-Pola recalled his friend Tony Chao Flores.

Gonzalez-Pola: "Tony was an incredible guy. We called him 'El Americanito' because he was blond. When he was just a teenager, he was fighting against Batista in the Escambray mountains. Tony did not understand fear. If he heard shooting, he moved toward the sound of gunfire. Once, when told that Minister Carlos Rafael Rodriguez was in a restaurant, he barged into the place, pistol in hand, like a cowboy, though he did not find him. He was tough. When we discovered a State Security spy in our organization, it was Tony who took care of the man. Tony lived upstairs from a CDR office and until the last day the local squealers did not suspect him."

In front of the Belot Refinery, Tony lobbed a grenade at a police car and injured three officers. He and Hugo Rodriguez Soria escaped in a bullet-riddled car. That same day, they traded gunfire with militiamen, killing one;[2] and then a third incident occurred.

Enrique Gonzalez-Pola: "There was a shooting right in front of Tony's house. A resistance fighter died and a policeman was wounded. Tony came out of the house, pistol in hand. A police car arrived and Tony opened fire. The police fired back and hit him. Tony went down wounded and they fired at him again. Seventeen bullets hit his legs. One was amputated."

Twenty-two-year-old Tony Chao Flores and Hugo Rodriguez Soria were executed at La Cabana Fortress on Hugo's twenty-third birthday.

Two organizations were working together to eliminate Castro and his council of ministers at a stroke. Alberto Cruz of Revolutionary Democratic Rescue obtained a bazooka and several shells. The MRP (Revolutionary People's Movement) rented an apartment on the eighth floor of a building at Avenida de las Misiones 29, overlooking the Presidential Palace. The plan was to fire several shells at the balcony where Castro and his cabinet were to address a crowd. The assassins would then leave the building in militia dress and lose themselves in the crowd. The plan was discovered and the weapons confiscated by State Security.[3]

Chelo "El Mulatto" Martori, a Matanzas guerrilla, had returned to the urban under-

[2] Interview with Aldo Lopez, former member of the resistance, Miami, 1991
[3] Gonzalez, *Y Fidel creo el punto X,* pp. 85–92

ground to lead high-risk operations. He planned to rescue MRR leader Carlos Bandin from the "belly of the beast," State Security headquarters.

Jose Enrique Dausa was then a leader of the MRR. Dausa: "Bandin was being held at State Security offices on Fifth Avenue. Martori took three cars full of armed men and they parked nearby. Then he walked into the building dressed as an officer, with false documentation ordering the transfer of Bandin to La Cabana Fortress. Martori took Bandin out of the building safely, even kicking him a couple of times to make things look real...."

At La Cabana fortress, Hiram Gonzalez had an eventful visiting day.

Hiram Gonzalez: "A prisoner made me a skirt from a blanket. A wig was smuggled into the prison inside a pillow. A smuggled bra was stuffed with paper. For shoes I used a pair of beach sandals. With a pair of pliers, Israel Abreu clipped a door in the wire fence that separated visitors from political prisoners. I waited for visiting hours to be over. A woman from our organization, who had come to drive me away, applied make-up to my face. I was thin and very clean-shaven, and I walked out."

Two days later Gonzalez was caught in a police dragnet and rearrested. Then, under detention at State Security headquarters, he managed to get a uniform and put it on.

Hiram Gonzalez: "I walked through the maze of offices. Guards walked through the hallways. I saluted, walking as calmly as I could. It took all my strength and willpower to control my fear, to calm my nerves. I even spoke briefly with the gate guard, distracting him so he would not ask me for a countersign. Then I walked away through the gate to the street, and every step I took moved me a few inches away from the main gate. 'This cannot be happening,' I told myself. 'They are going to shoot me in the back. I am going to die.' I kept walking, expecting the bullet to come from behind at any moment—and I escaped."

Gonzalez hid in the trunk of a diplomat's car on his way to asylum. He lived in the embassy of Uruguay until 1963, when he left Cuba for Miami.

* * *

In the Escambray mountains, guerrillas reorganized under the command of Osvaldo Ramirez. A former captain in the anti-Batista guerrilla forces, thirty-seven-year-old Ramirez was a wiry man of some charisma, with a fine natural intelligence and a capacity to organize. Distrusting a chain of command from U.S. officials, whose attempts at supplying guerrillas had failed dismally, Ramirez broke with established structures. He accepted help from any resistance group that provided weapons, but refused to obey orders from remote sources he could not verify. From the guerrilla forces that remained after the early 1961 military offensive, he created the United Revolutionary Front of Escambray (FURE), which quickly spread through Las Villas province. A covert community of several thousand supporters was soon giving help to the guerrilla forces. Enrique Ruano and Jose Antonio Diaz were part of that supply structure.

Enrique Ruano: "It was a large network with limited resources. Storekeepers donated canned foods, shoelaces, boots and blankets. Doctors provided medicines and antibiotics to cure wounds or fungus. People donated money to buy weapons, bullets and anything that was needed. Bullets were bought or stolen. We even paid a militiaman one hundred pesos to report his submachine gun stolen. The supplies were hidden in trucks and taken to farms near guerrilla areas, where scouts picked them up. We provided a lot, but it was tough. The guerrillas numbered in the hundreds, and keeping a small army supplied was not easy."

Jose Antonio Diaz: "With each passing day it was tougher to supply the guerrillas. As rationing started in Cuba and consumer goods became scarce, even finding simple medicines became difficult; but month after month we came up with supplies—a couple of rifles, some ammunition, bags of rice and beans, a few pairs of boots. It is amazing how people helped, despite the fear of prison or a firing squad."

Ramirez established a network of farmworkers who spent nights harboring guerrillas, or serving as scouts, or moving small units through an area, avoiding government patrols. Amador Acosta, later a guerrilla captain, started as a *practico* or scout, moving guerrillas at night.

Acosta: "We knew the area. We knew where a creek could be crossed, or where a small cave could hide six or seven men. We'd played in those woods as kids. We knew every road and dirt trail, while many of the militia were city boys and could not even track. The guerrillas had a whole system of messages. If a guerrilla group approached a farm and saw clothing of a certain color on the clothesline, it could mean 'Stay away.' If a calf was tied to a certain part of a fence, it could mean something else. The *practicos* could move a unit through the woods very fast. At one time I had six different guerrilla squads hiding in an area less than one kilometer long."

By the summer of 1961, Escambray guerrillas were actively striking at militia patrols, capturing and hanging Castro's spies, stopping buses and burning them on the highways, or raiding warehouses of state cooperatives. Jorge Rodriguez Masias was a young guerrilla who had served in the Southern Front of Las Villas.

Jorge Rodriguez Masias: "Six of us went to a hamlet called El Pajarito. We knew that there were a few militiamen there; the plan was to disarm them and take their weapons.

When we arrived, we were surprised to see that several warehouses had recently been built. We disarmed the militia, and when we opened the warehouses we found them stacked to the roofs. It was a regional warehouse for the military, with oil drums, blankets, all sorts of supplies. We set the buildings on fire but were not aware that a battalion of militia was stationed not far away, at the grounds of a brewery on the Central Highway. When we came out of the last warehouse, we saw militia running among us in the smoke. The six of us left in a hurry with the captured weapons. The fires burned for hours."

Guerrillas remained active in every province of Cuba. Pinar del Rio and Havana provinces had a few small groups, barely numbering a hundred men in total. Matanzas had more than two hundred insurgents, and Las Villas boasted three sectors where more than seven hundred men were fighting. Camaguey's flatlands had nearly a hundred active guerrillas, and Oriente had several pockets. Although the regime has offered little data on the subject, it has acknowledged that some forty guerrilla groups with more than six hundred men were active in Oriente following the Bay of Pigs, and that they inflicted sixty-two deaths on Castro's forces.[4]

In the Sierra Maestra, a unit led by former Rebel Army officer Fernando Del Valle Galindo launched an uprising sponsored by the 30th of November Movement. Pedro Fraginals was the supply officer for the operation.

Pedro Fraginals: "It took months to obtain the weapons and ammunition. We transported more than seventy weapons to Oriente, a few at a time. I was detained at a roadblock and attempted to escape, but soldiers fired on us. Esther Castellanos, a very brave woman who accompanied me, was shot in the heel."

Del Valle's unit attacked and took a small army outpost at La Pimienta, but was pursued and overwhelmed by a force of thousands. Del Valle and his second-in-command, Reynaldo Lopez, were executed in Santiago de Cuba. Alberto Muller, then a political prisoner, met the guerrilla and spoke with him the night before he died.

Alberto Muller: "He was very calm. He was a man convinced of the purity of his cause. He had faith in God and his people."

※   ※   ※

From exile, Cubans working with the CIA continued to cross the Florida Straits.

Alvaro Cosculluela: "We members of the infiltration teams went on transport vessels wearing hoods, to protect our identities. On one of my trips, when I climbed aboard,

[4] See the account by Norberto Fuentes in *Nos impusieron la violencia*, published in Cuba by permission of the regime.

I saw my cousin Juan Luis, who was one of the officers of the ship. I passed by and said hello. He recognized my voice and his eyes opened in surprise."

Life in the underground crackled with tension, particularly for CIA radio operators like Cosculluela and Basulto.

Jose Basulto: "An infiltration was hard on the nerves. As soon as they spotted you in an area, a cat-and-mouse game started. You didn't know whom to trust or who might betray you."

Alvaro Cosculluela: "It was tough. A member of the team went off on a mission and was two days late, and all that time we waited and wondered. We slept with one eye open and M-3's cuddled to our bodies."

Jose Enrique Dausa had left the MRR underground in Cuba for exile; then he went back into action, supervising infiltration teams. Dausa: "We had some very daring men. Pepe Santiago had been a guerrilla, and he went on many missions back to Cuba. One time he was walking down a street dressed in a military uniform and saw his own father being arrested. He walked over and talked to the officers, trying to convince them to release the old man to him. He didn't get what he wanted, but he made sure the charges were not serious. It takes guts to do something like that."

The CIA "Cuban Navy" men also lived under stress, cruising the island's coast at night, facing enemy shore fire. Lucas Alberto Ponzoa, a naval officer, served on many hazardous missions.

Lucas Alberto Ponzoa: "One time we went to Las Villas to pick up an infiltration team. It was a tough squad. One of the men in it was Diosdado Mesa, who had been an Escambray guerrilla chief. Castro's people were waiting for us, and they opened up with heavy weapons. We pulled back and tried again. This went on for several days, until we managed to pick up the team."

Alexis Rodriguez Sosa, another experienced veteran, recalled some stormy weather, not all of it from the sea. Rodriguez Sosa: "In the middle of an operation, two boats separated and seven men were lost, adrift in an area of ocean. The Americans in Miami worried about the security of the ships and gave us orders to pull back; but Gaspar Brooks, our captain, refused. We cruised those waters for four days, at high risk, and found the men before Castro's forces did."

Exile organizations, with or without U.S. help, continued to move men and weapons onto the island. The casualty rate kept growing, as Cubans on both sides perished.

CHAPTER XI.

"DON'T WORRY ABOUT ME. I KNOW HOW TO DIE."

A year after the "Great Offensive," Fidel Castro ordered a second massive operation against the troublesome guerrillas. Law 988 backed the military maneuver, decreeing that all captured guerrillas or supporters could be executed on the spot, without trial.

Enrique Ruano: "Before it was implemented, when guerrillas were captured, some were executed and some imprisoned; but when Law 988 was enforced, almost all guerrillas were killed within hours or days after being captured. Very few guerrillas survived Law 988. It was a license to execute without trial. It discouraged people from joining the guerrillas, but it also made the guerrillas fight harder, because they knew death to be inevitable."

Castro's second operation targeted all of Matanzas and Las Villas provinces. In Matanzas, 26,000 militia were mobilized to destroy the guerrillas.[1] Arcadio Peguero was a farmworker turned guerrilla in Matanzas province.

Arcadio Peguero: "The province does not have mountain ranges, so we operated in many flat areas of the countryside. We used some small hills, hid in sugar cane fields, in farms of friendly supporters, in caves dug underneath houses and in the swamps when we had no other choice. At times we split up, each man going his own way and all reuniting days later somewhere else. We hid during the day and attacked at night. For a time, government vehicles didn't travel at night on Matanzas highways, because we peppered them with sniper fire."

Ramon Ramos: "Castro had called us bandits, but in fact we had the support of

---

[1] Carbonell, *And the Russians Stayed*, p. 239

thousands of farmers. We did not steal. We moved from farm to farm, hiding. Our friends fed us and guided us through the region. Could bandits have survived four years, as I did, fighting in the flatlands, without the support of people in the region? We built caves for hiding out. One of them was about forty feet wide and a hundred feet long. It was right next to a creek, where we could take fresh water. The entrance was a wood board covered with grass and dirt. We had ventilation holes and a fan that we operated manually with parts from an old bike. We stockpiled each cave with some food and ammunition so we could hide out for days while the militia walked right above us."

In Las Villas, battalions of militia swept the northern sector of the province.

Agapito Rivera: "We took some losses during the end of 1961 and the beginning of 1962. Captain Tondike, one of the best-known guerrilla leaders, was trapped in a cane field. The militia set fire to all corners of the field to flush him out. Tondike dug a hole in the ground and buried himself alive so the flames would pass over him. They captured him badly burnt, and executed him."

Thousands of other troops massed on the "Southern Front," pushing the guerrilla units back toward the Escambray mountains.

Jorge Rodriguez: "At Hanabanilla, we were chased by large numbers of militia. We stopped, set up a sniping ambush, hit them and fell back. They had a lot of casualties. At Las Cruces the guerrillas of Joaquin Benitez and Arnaldo Villalobos were trapped in a *cerco* [circle]. The militia massed forces between the guerrillas and the Escambray, thinking our men were trying to reach sanctuary in the mountains—but Benitez and Villalobos turned around and attacked the ring of troops at its weakest point, backtracking, heading west. They broke out of the ring, but almost all the men in those two units were wounded. They were in bad shape."

Agapito Rivera: "The guerrillas were seasoned fighters at this stage of the game. Many had survived more than a year of constant fighting. We lacked heavy weapons and we were often short of ammo, but we had highly motivated fighters and we were in excellent shape. Although we missed many meals and our bodies were skin and bones, we could walk miles through hills and cane fields. We knew how to cover our tracks, how to set up an ambush, how to find weak spots and break through a ring of troops. We were not an easy bone to chew."

The Escambray was once again sealed off as masses of Castro's regulars combed the hills and farmlands, searching for insurgents. The forced relocation of farmers and their families continued as thousands of men, women and children were removed from their homes and forced to live in faraway prison towns, so they could not give guerrillas their support.[2]

Acelia Pacheco Anido was a child affected by the relocations. Pacheco Anido: "People were taken to live hundreds of kilometers away from their own homes. It was terrible to see those poor souls riding on donkeys with their children crying. They were not fed properly. The children didn't have clothing or beds. One can't know how horrible it is to see thirty or forty children, some of them one or two years old, without a gulp of milk to drink—children crying, begging for a little sugar—and fathers separated from their families for years. I saw it."

Skirmishing spread and sniping increased daily as militia forces moved into the Escambray. Guerrilla leader Maro Borges was wounded and managed to escape through the militia rings; but in April 1962 Castro's army scored significant victories. Osvaldo Ramirez, commander-in-chief of the insurgents, was hit in an ambush on April 16. Congo Pacheco, the guerrillas' other top commander, was wounded and captured in another skirmish, then died at Santa Clara Hospital. Osvaldo Ramirez, Jr., son of the slain guerrilla, recalled his life in the town of Sancti Spiritus.

Osvaldo Ramirez, Jr.: "I was a young boy. My house was under twenty-four-hour surveillance. Every day, when we left for school, our notebooks were searched. In school we were harassed. Even after my father died in combat, our house was still surrounded by militia and police. I remember my mother telling a soldier who searched our house: 'Osvaldo Ramirez is dead and you still fear him.' "

Ramirez was replaced as guerrilla leader by twenty-three-year-old Tomas San Gil, whose whole family was involved in the struggle. San Gil's mother and sister ran the supply network for the Escambray region. Castro's officers, who seemed to think the insurgents had been virtually annihilated, were surprised at the energy of this youngster who had willy-nilly become the central figure in the stubborn struggle for the Escambray.

✳ ✳ ✳

In the cities, the underground reorganized constantly. Every week, resistance leaders were arrested or executed; and every week, new ones replaced them. In the last months of 1961 and the first months of 1962, urban guerrillas damaged the Ariguanabo textile

---

[2] The captive towns still existed thirty years after the Escambray struggle had ended. An American woman wrote a novel about them; see Margarita Engle, *Singing to Cuba* (Houston: Arte Publico Press, 1993).

mill, burned thirteen buildings under construction for the Cuban National Bank, destroyed a government warehouse at Punta Brava, sabotaged a fertilizer plant in El Cotorro and torched a Havana refinery.[3]

Street protests in Santiago de Cuba and Cardenas drew angry retaliation from Castro's troops. The Cardenas protest, on June 16, 1962, was so large that Castro's officers moved armored cars onto the streets of the city in a massive display of force.[4]

After the Bay of Pigs fiasco, resistance leaders—rather than continuing to suffer in a prolonged war—were restless for a major blow at the regime. Men of the FAL, a clandestine group made up of officers in the regime's forces, met with leaders of the MRR, MRP, DRE and 30th of November to propose a nationwide revolt. Manuel Fernandez Grande was a national leader in the 30th of November.

Manuel Fernandez Grande: "It was going to be a large-scale operation. All the entrances to Havana would be sealed with large vehicle roadblocks. Some police stations had personnel that were going to surrender or join us. Other teams had been assigned to attack other police stations, paralyze industries, direct sniper fire at key locations and occupy radio stations. The problem was that an operation of such size involved many hundreds of men and women—almost impossible to keep secret. State Security had some informants in every organization, but we knew we had to take the risk. It was the only card we could play...."

Maruca Alvarez was a veteran underground fighter. Alvarez: "Other women and I were to dress as nurses and go to hospitals with doctors from our groups. That way, any of our wounded would be cured quickly and moved out of the hospital before police intervened. We couldn't keep Castro's people from finding out. We had six informants in our organization and the uprising involved thousands."

In late August, a few hours before the uprising was to start, Castro's agents began their massive roundup.

Manuel Fernandez Grande: "Despite the massive arrests, all thirteen or fourteen entrances to Havana were temporarily blocked by abandoned cement mixers. A group of our men was going to attack a police station. They had submachine guns that we had stolen from the militia. Early in the morning, as they moved around the neighborhood across from the station, a sergeant came out, crossed the street and went to a cafe, signaling our men to join him. He was on our side. He told them: 'Our district commander, our captain and all our lieutenants have been placed under arrest. I'm the highest

[3] Bethel, *The Losers,* pp. 313–14
[4] Ibid., p. 316

rank left. A .50 caliber machine gun has been placed inside, facing the door, to mow down your team. Get out of here while you still can.' "

Within hours, executions had started. No one knows exactly how many faced firing squads in the next weeks. One source has estimated 460.[5] Two who perished were comandante Francisco Perez Mendez and former Cuban Army Colonel Manuel Alvarez Margolles, the uprising's main leaders.

Maruca Alvarez: "The firing squads at La Cabana Fortress started on the third or fourth of September. Every night they executed six, seven or eight. They killed more than a hundred that month, perhaps as many as two hundred.... When my trial came up, five from my group were given the death penalty. One was Juan Carlos Montes De Oca, whose resistance name was 'Daniel.' He was only twenty-one but he had been fighting against dictatorships from his high-school years. He did not even have a girlfriend. He used to say to me: 'Maruca, as long as my country needs me, I'll be involved.' When he was given the death sentence, he said to us: 'Don't worry about me. I know how to die.' "

As hundreds died, others kept living in the shadow world of the resistance fighter.

*   *   *

One of the most striking concepts of Castro's early rule was the regime's reconstruction of *patria potestad,* which gave the Cuban state absolute power over the destinies of children. At a certain point, Fidel also conceived a program—never carried out, but seriously proposed—to separate families and create cities of youngsters whom the regime could mold without parental interference. Fearing their children would be taken away—perhaps to live in "model" youth centers, perhaps to be sent on "scholarships" to the Soviet Union or satellite nations—many parents opted to move their children to the relative safety of the United States.

Legal exodus for whole families was a tortuous process that often resulted in lengthy separations. So parents shipped their children ahead of themselves, to the temporary care of the Catholic Bureau and other charitable organizations.

Ramon Grau Alsina and his sister Polita Grau—nephew and niece of Cuba's former president Grau San Martin—set up "Operation Peter Pan" (Operacion Pedro Pan) and organized a network to get large numbers of children, as well as adults, out of Cuba.

Ramon Grau established contacts with the Catholic and Protestant churches in Cuba. Polita Grau recruited women in the resistance to be part of the organization.

---

[5] Valladares, *Against All Hope,* p. 158

Executives of KLM and Pan American Airways offered to supply passage, without the government's knowledge. In Miami, Monsignor Bryan Walsh served as liaison with charitable and church organizations.

At Arrealca Printers—which produced all kinds of pamphlets and other papers for the resistance—owner Enrique Arredondo made up false stamps and visa documents which he passed on to Alberto Cruz, a resistance leader in Rescate Revolucionario Democratico. Cruz then provided Ramon and Polita Grau with the documents they needed.

In the U.S., volunteers from charitable organizations placed children in camps at Florida City and Kendall, to the south of Miami. Hundreds more went to orphanages in Kansas, Indiana and other states to wait for their parents. Pedro Solares, a fifteen-year-old member of DRE, became a "Peter Pan" child.

Pedro Solares: "It would be years before I found out the visas were forged. I was one of the thousands helped by Polita and Ramon Grau. I pray that my life be worthy of their sacrifice. Long afterward, I came to see my life as composed of clearly defined segments. One of those segments was the time I spent at the refugee camp for children, even thought it lasted only eight months. The camp had two large sleeping barracks, a mess hall, a roofed picnic area and a huge swimming pool. The people who ran the center treated us well and the food was good—but there's nothing like the warmth a family can offer...."

Polita Grau: "We were active from 1960 to 1962. Our headquarters was our home, in the Miramar sector of Havana. Our large house was directly across the street from the main offices of State Security. That street in Miramar was a busy place. On one side of the street, Cubans were being arrested and tortured by State Security. On the other side of the road, we were busy trying to process as many false visas as we could, running an espionage network and even plotting to eliminate Fidel Castro."

In the three years Operation Peter Pan was active, 14,000 children and some 6,000 adults—including many resistance fighters—were able to leave Cuba under its auspices. In early 1965, Ramon, Polita and other members of their network were arrested by State Security and sentenced to thirty years in jail.[6]

✳ ✳ ✳

In Miami, Jose Basulto, the young engineer who had joined the CIA and twice infil-

---

[6] Interviews with Polita Grau, Miami, 1986–1991

trated the island, was disgruntled. After the Bay of Pigs, Basulto had left the CIA in anger. He worked with another young veteran, Carlos Hernandez, and they came up with a plan to raid a hotel on Havana's shoreline.

The Rosita Hornedo Hotel had been taken over by the Cuban government, which used it to house visiting diplomats and intelligence personnel from Soviet satellite countries. Fidel Castro apparently visited the hotel's dining rooms and meeting halls on an almost daily basis. Basulto and Hernandez got in touch with the DRE. Manuel Salvat offered a crew and volunteered for the mission.

Jose Basulto: "We had a thirty-one-foot boat and a twenty-millimeter Finnish cannon that I bought for $300. We carried a couple of Belgian FN rifles and an M-1 carbine. Our boat had two engines and used a lot of fuel, so we strapped on deck a container with four hundred extra gallons. Near Cuba we refilled the tank and got rid of the container. Our gas filter was damaged, and some fuel spilled on deck. We faced the danger that when we fired the cannon, the spark would set the boat ablaze. We took blankets and soaked them with seawater, hoping it would prevent a fire. That's how we entered Havana. Two hundred yards from the hotel I opened up with the cannon. I aimed at the meeting rooms, the lobby area, and the whole structure of the building. I think it was seventeen or eighteen shells. The military security detail returned our fire. On the way back we were chased by a Castro gunboat but managed to get away. It was a useful operation. It made Castro look bad and showed that a group of young students on their own, without help, could fight for their country. It made front pages all over the world, including *Pravda*…. The Americans were angry that we had done something on our own. I was kept under surveillance for a time."

Basulto's action had been a precursor. In years to come, and despite official U.S. opposition, many more such raids would occur.

CHAPTER XII.

SOVIET MISSILES, U.S. CHANGE OF HEART

Historical circumstances did not favor the anti-Castro cause. From their inception, almost all resistance groups had had to seek assistance from the United States, losing their autonomy in the process.

The Americans, who distrusted the independent leanings of the guerrilla commands, were reluctant to airdrop supplies and often left the insurgents to fend for themselves. They also played the exile groups against each other as a way to exert control. Anti-Castro groups, willy-nilly, became pawns in an international chess game, and they were often kept out of the fight. U.S. Defense Secretary Robert McNamara would come to perceive as "terribly ineffective" those very CIA commando units made up of Cubans who complained they were not getting their chances for action.[1]

Castro, meanwhile, was building the image of his regime as an enemy of "U.S. imperialism"—but Castro had arranged for his country to be the tool of another empire, and his regime pursued imperial ambitions of its own. Cuba had become a Soviet strategic base, a launching pad for political disruption in the Western Hemisphere. Since 1959, Castro had used his nation as a training center for guerrillas from other countries, and he had struck out on his own missions of conquest.

In the most absurd and bloody of these adventures, on July 14, 1959, Castro had sent an army of three hundred men to the Dominican Republic to overthrow Trujillo. The Dominican counter-strike had been joined by a contingent of Cuban exiles. Miguel Sanchez, who had served as a U.S. paratrooper in Korea and had then helped to train Fidel Castro's own guerrilla force in Mexico, was one of the Cubans who fought against Castro's invasion force, as was Roberto Martin Perez.

[1] Blight and Welch, *On the Brink,* p. 249

Martin Perez: "The invasion was crushed. We had several combats in the first few days. We all fought without rest. The invasion had Cubans, Dominicans and other people from the Caribbean and Central America—and Trujillo gave no quarter. Very few of the three hundred survived."

Miguel Sanchez: "Trujillo had announced that any peasant bringing in an invader, dead or alive, would be paid a thousand dollars, which was a lot more than some of those poor farmworkers made in a single year. An old lady came into a base, carrying a severed head in a cloth bag."

Castro's government also supplied and coordinated Marxist guerrillas in Venezuela, Colombia, Guatemala and Nicaragua. Boasting about his help to insurgent factions, Castro promoted his image as a "Robin Hood." For the United States, the Cuban dictator seemed to represent an irksome neighbor in the back yard; that is, until he delivered a nuclear threat.

* * *

Revolutionary Democratic Rescue and the DRE reported the presence of Soviet rockets on Cuban soil. Both organizations sent clandestine reports to Miami, detailing the location of missile bases in Pinar del Rio and Havana.

Polita Grau: "Ofelia Miranda, a woman in our organization, was one of the key people involved in the espionage operation against the missile bases in Pinar del Rio. The reports provided by the resistance were accurate."

The United States, preparing for another confrontation with Castro's forces, had recruited exiles into special "Cuban Units" of the U.S. Army. Trained at Fort Knox and Fort Jackson, several thousand exiles were ready to spearhead an invasion of the island.

Humberto Lopez, recently arrived from Cuba, was one of those who joined up. Lopez: "The worst thing about basic training was the time involved. Morale was high. Our number reached somewhere around five thousand men. We were all volunteers, some as young as seventeen, the oldest in their early thirties."

Through 1962, Castro had beefed up his armed forces in expectation of more trouble from the United States. By October 1962, his once-little air force had grown to include 62 MiG fighters and 22 Ilushin airplanes, backed by a land force of more than 200,000, which included artillery and armored units.[2]

Ramon Luaces was a lieutenant in Castro's militia forces. Luaces: "At the time Castro still had a significant amount of popular support. If the Americans had invaded Cuba, it

[2] Ibid., p. 350

would have been very costly for them. No doubt they would have won, but thousands of American soldiers would have been killed or wounded."

The CIA infiltrated small groups of exiles onto the island. Diosdado Mesa, a former Escambray guerrilla captain, was in one of the CIA teams. Mesa: "A car picked me up and took me to Homestead Air Force Base. The place was packed with troops and airplanes. I was shown to an airplane hangar. The wall of the hangar had a gigantic map of Cuba, made up of many maps from different regions. It was huge and very detailed. When I walked up close and looked, I was surprised. In areas I knew well, the map was missing information, like highways and other details. I realized I was looking at maps from the forties. I told an officer and he ordered all maps taken down and replaced with new ones. I slept in the base that night, and the following day I was on my way to Cuba."

*   *   *

On Monday, October 22, President Kennedy announced to an anxious nation that Soviet nuclear missiles were being set up on Cuban soil. These intermediate-range missiles were capable of striking much of the U.S. eastern seaboard, including Washington, and many areas throughout the hemisphere. Kennedy declared that he would consider any use of those weapons, against any country, as an attack by the Soviet Union on the United States. Kennedy ordered the Soviets to remove their missiles from Cuba and established a naval blockade around the island to prevent further military buildups. The U.S. went to full military alert, and the world found itself in the most dangerous of crises.

As the crisis deepened, Fidel Castro grew infuriated that Cuba had become part of a negotiation in which he was being ignored. Castro came forth with his own statement. He demanded an end to the U.S. blockade, to U.S. support for the exile groups, to U.S. reconnaissance flights over Cuba, and to the two-year-old U.S. economic embargo. He further demanded that America's naval base at Guantanamo in eastern Cuba—a territory Cuba had leased to the U.S. in perpetuity—be closed.[3]

It is highly unlikely that Castro had access to the Soviet missile bases. The Soviets, it seems, were so worried that the Cuban military might try to seize the bases that KGB officers were on full alert against a possible attack from Cuban troops. On October 28, as the crisis wound down, Castro's armed forces surrounded the bases and held their positions until Deputy Premier Anastas Mikoyan could arrive in Havana to negotiate with Castro.[4] Afterward, Soviet leader Nikita Khrushchev stated that Fidel Castro had

[3] Ibid., p. 269

requested a Soviet nuclear attack on the United States. The Cuban regime has denied Khrushchev's claim.[5]

Resolution of the crisis might have included an indication from the United States that it would no longer support exile activity against Castro. Although the U.S. has often averred that no such promise was made, American officials markedly changed their attitude toward the anti-Castro Cubans in the aftermath of the crisis, and the "Cuban Units" of the U.S. Army were disbanded.

Humberto Lopez: "Those wishing to return to civilian life were placed on reserve status, while those who wished to remain went to regular army units to serve out their tours of duty. It was as though a bucket of ice water had been poured on us."

Alvaro Cosculluela: "CIA activities on the island changed. Before, the priorities had been to organize uprisings, arm the resistance, carry out a war against Castro. Now we continued to infiltrate, but the emphasis was on creating networks for intelligence-gathering. The CIA still carried out some commando raids, and they established MRR training camps in Nicaragua and Guatemala, but they were dismantled after a few months of operations."

Nicolas Perez Diaz-Arguelles was a resistance leader in the DRE underground. Perez: "The weapons shipments dried up. We simply continued fighting with what we had left, which was not much."

Coast Guard units in South Florida were increased by 20 percent, to 3,600 men. These units were soon confiscating weapons and boats from independent exile groups, while authorities were arresting those who had taken steps to overthrow Castro. In Washington D.C., former Cuban prime minister Jose Miro Cardona had a heated discussion with Attorney General Robert F. Kennedy—and the U.S. President's brother threatened the exile leader with deportation.[6]

[4] Ibid., p. 56
[5] *The Miami Herald,* September 24, 1990
[6] Carbonell, *And the Russians Stayed,* pp. 246–47

CHAPTER XIII.

OF GLASS AND MEN

Toward the end of 1962, despite massive military operations, insurgent units in the Escambray mountains and other areas of Cuba were still active. Castro's regime therefore created a counter-guerrilla unit, the "Lucha Contra Bandidos"(LCB). Enlisted men in the LCB units were volunteers, most of them farmers—just like the guerrillas—and almost all veterans of military operations in the Escambray or at the Bay of Pigs.

The officer ranks of the LCB were a mixture of battle-hardened officers and prisoners from La Cabana Fortress. Incarcerated men with military backgrounds, awaiting trial for a variety of nonpolitical crimes ranging from fraud to murder, were offered a chance to "rehabilitate" by serving in the LCB—their alternative being stiff prison sentences.[1]

The leaders of the LCB were Comandantes Raul Tomassevich and Lizardo Proenza. Tomassevich, a stocky, balding man, had served time for writing false checks before becoming a revolutionary leader. Proenza, a tough farmer from Oriente, was a veteran of the war against Batista, the two Escambray campaigns and the Bay of Pigs.

The new anti-guerrilla tactic was a swift deployment of thousands, with the LCB manning the first ring of encirclement and militia backing them up in the second and third rings. LCB platoons were also sent on patrols to track and ambush guerrillas. They relied on State Security interrogators to extract information that would allow for pinpointing locations of guerrilla units. The LCB units would then move in, encircling the area and eliminating the insurgents.

LCB units were armed with Belgian FN rifles, of which Cuba had purchased 10,000 at the beginning of the revolution. The FN rifles were superior to the less accurate nine-millimeter CZ submachine guns and the bulky M-52 rifles used by the militia.

[1] Interview with a former LCB officer, Key West, 1986

Enrique Ruano: "No invasion was coming and the men in the hills were receiving very little help. In the first days of January I went to take supplies to Porfirio Guillen's group. Nine of them were hidden in a field near Manicaragua. I brought them several new backpacks, food and a new recruit armed with a San Cristobal carbine. Three days after I visited them, they were surrounded by LCB troops. All of them died except for Israel Pacheco. He escaped wounded, was captured in another battle and executed. So all ten died.... The guerrillas of 1963 were very tough. Many of them had endured two years of constant fighting. They were very hard men."

Amador Acosta: "We could survive on very little food, walk for miles through rough terrain without resting, and we fought hard. When the enemy used tracking dogs, the animals couldn't pick up our scent because we smelled like the forest. We had no soap, and we could not afford to strip down and bathe in a river when areas were saturated with enemy troops, so we didn't bathe very often. We cured our wounds with creoline paste, which is used on horses, and we stitched our own wounds."

Twenty-four-year-old Tomas San Gil, the new leader of the Escambray guerrillas, decided to fight aggressively. Despite the shortage of weapons and ammunition, San Gil ordered a guerrilla offensive against Castro's troops. A bus was set aflame on a Las Villas highway. When troops from Military Unit 1633 responded, the guerrillas opened up with a deadly crossfire, killing four soldiers and wounding five others. A militia jeep was ambushed on the road to Manicaragua. Guerrillas attacked government warehouses and cooperatives, trading gunfire with militia security squads. San Gil's military offensive lasted four weeks. According to Castro's own sources, fifty-four soldiers and militiamen were killed, while thirty-six buildings and two buses were lost to arson.[2]

The LCB countered with all its strength. Dozens of skirmishes took place in the Escambray hills. Chased by thousands of troops, San Gil broke through a ring by crossing a river. His guerrillas reached the farm of Andrea Castro with enemy soldiers in pursuit.

Andrea Castro: "They arrived wet and hungry. They had lost their backpacks crossing the river. All they had were their rifles and ammunition. I collected clean clothing from my farmworkers and gave it to them: pants, shirts, socks. We had some blankets and we cut each blanket into two pieces so they would have enough to go around. We prepared food for them—chicken and rice and fried plantains—and they left a few hours before the militia arrived."

Conchita San Gil, known as "Virginia" in the underground, ran supply lines for the Escambray guerrillas while she was still a teenager. Conchita San Gil: "Every day we had bad news. We never had enough supplies, enough rifles, enough bullets. The resistance

---

[2] See the author's *Escambray: la guerra olvidada* for details on the guerrillas.

offered to take my brother out of the mountains, to Miami, but he refused. He said he would never leave his men. If they could take them all out, he would be the last to leave Cuba."

San Gil was trapped once more in a triple ring near Andrea Castro's farm on the last day of February 1963. Romulo Rodriguez was one of the guerrillas caught in the noose.

Romulo Rodriguez: "The battle started at nine o'clock in the evening and lasted all night. We were surrounded by thousands of the enemy and there were only twenty-six of us. I had an M-2 carbine that had a worn spring and I had to feed each bullet one by one into the chamber. That's how poorly armed we were. The enemy fired flares into the sky and the night lit up like daytime. We tried to break through their lines and we were fighting hand to hand. Tomasito broke through and could have escaped, but he returned to help a group of us who were pinned down. A bullet hit him in the head and he died. Nilo Armando Saavedra, his second in command, was hit in the chest and head and died. I went down a hill and a militiaman appeared in front of me, armed with a 'Checa' [Czech machine gun]. He fired, but his weapon jammed. Only one bullet came out. I was at an angle and the bullet entered my shoulder and lodged next to my spine. Manolo Neira, one of our men, shot the militiaman point-blank, killing him. A few minutes later Manolo was also killed. Thirteen of our men died that night. Robustiano Blanco, who was very badly wounded, escaped, but killed himself several days later rather than suffer any longer. Of the others who escaped, all died over the next two years. I was taken prisoner the following morning. I saw how the enemy carried our men's bodies, tied hands and feet, their corpses dangling from long sticks, like butchered animals."

Andrea Castro: "Militia forces started passing in front of my farm at nine in the morning, and at three in the afternoon they were still coming through. All that night there was gunfire in the hills…. In the morning my farmworkers saw the bodies. One of Tomas's men, a black man from the village of Caracusey, was the last to die. His legs had been shattered; he died cursing at the militia before the helicopters came to pick them up. The bodies were not even given to their relatives for proper burial. Three months later we could still see dried bloodstains on the rocks where the final battle took place."

Las Villas had become a blood-soaked battleground. Juan Felipe Castro and his men died in combat, wiping out an LCB squad in the battle. Chiqui Jaime's guerrilla unit was wiped out by bazooka fire. Rigoberto Tartabull, a guerrilla captain, died in a battle where he faced his own brother, an officer in the LCB.[3]

One after another, the insurgent groups were being eliminated. Raul Garcia was a

---

[3] See *Cazabandido* ("The Hunt for Bandits") by Norberto Fuentes, one of the Castro regime's leading chroniclers, who in the early 1990's chose to go into exile.

young guerrilla in Maro Borges's unit when LCB troops surrounded them at Guasimal, August 15, 1963.

Raul Garcia: "We started fighting around noon. That was a bad time for us. At night it was easier to break through a ring but in the daytime it was very hard. Maro had a Garand rifle and a nine-millimeter pistol. We moved as close to the edge of the ring as we could, trying to slip through it. A militiaman popped up in front of us. Maro shot him with the pistol, and the man went down. Then the firefight started. I was the first wounded. I took three bullets in the legs and went down. A helicopter strafed us. Nineteen rounds hit Elias Borges and he fell next to me. We all thought he was dead, but incredibly he survived. Domingo Garcia, one of our men, emptied two Garand clips at the helicopter. At times the fighting was hand to hand, with rifle butts. Of our twenty-one men, eleven were killed, including one of Maro's brothers, Ismael Borges. Three, including me, were captured wounded. The other seven, including Maro, escaped the ring, but all were wounded. Maro had a chest wound. The LCB had seven killed and ten or eleven wounded. It was a brutal fight and it lasted less than an hour...."

The struggle in Las Villas was not confined to the Escambray hills. The flatland guerrillas to the north and south were also being besieged. Agapito Rivera, one of the highest-ranking guerrilla leaders to survive the clashes, had been fighting in northern Las Villas for over two years. Of his family, two brothers, nine cousins and he himself had joined the guerrillas. Agapito would be the only survivor.

Agapito Rivera: "Raul Castro had run operations against me and could not catch me. Che Guevara failed against me. Proenza tried three times and each time I slipped away. The fourth time was different. I only had two men with me on that day, Mayito Garcia and my brother Francisco. We were surrounded in a cane field. We came out firing, trying to break through. A bullet hit my right arm and we went into another cane field. We bumped into militia troops inside the cane field and fired at point-blank range. My brother was wounded twice and died there. We kept going, although it is very tough leaving behind the corpse of a brother. Mayito was almost cut in half by machine-gun fire when he tried to jump over a picket fence. Another bullet hit my right arm and broke it. I ran on, while chunks of dirt kicked up around me. As I entered a cane field I was hit two more times, in the legs. One bullet hit my femoral artery, but I didn't bleed to death because a blood clot from one of the other wounds blocked the blood flow. It was a miracle. I collapsed inside the cane field. I couldn't use my Browning rifle because my arm was broken. I figured I was going to die, so I sat there waiting for it to be over. I took out a .45 pistol to keep fighting and lit up a cigar stub I had. I waited, all soaked in blood, and they didn't come. I passed out, woke up, passed out again, woke up—and they were carrying me through the cane field. I was thrown to the ground. A soldier spat on me. Another ripped the cigar stub from my mouth. I was yanked up to a sitting position by a hand pulling on my hair. I asked them to finish me off. Then I heard FN rifle gunfire. It was Lizardo Proenza. He had fired his gun at the ground and begun screaming at his own men. 'Cowards, you sons of whores, when he was inside the cane field you didn't want to go in and get him! But now you are all playing macho. Treat him well!' And he saved my life. Proenza came to see me later in the hospital, and he told me he respected me, for I had eluded him many times."

Jose Antonio Diaz, a member of the guerrilla supply lines, recalled an incident in Santa Clara. "There were seventeen of us locked in that jail cell, and nine were guerrillas from Nano Perez's unit. They were fed a last meal of yucca, chopped beef and rice. Then they were taken out one by one, their hands tied as soon as they stepped out. One was a young boy, very young, who was to be executed alongside his father who was also a guerrilla, and the boy's hands shook. The militiaman said to him: 'You going to crack?' The boy, who did not even look old enough to shave, answered: 'Glass cracks. Men die on their feet.' "

On the Southern Front, LCB units with still greater firepower were chopping up the guerrillas. Luis Molina and Miner De La Torre, the main guerrilla chiefs in the area, died fighting. In other provinces, the LCB wiped out small pockets of guerrillas. In Pinar del Rio, the guerrilla units of Francisco "Machete" Robaina, Noel Dominguez and Pedro Celestino Sanchez were destroyed in combat. In Matanzas province, Pichi Catala and Perico Sanchez, two important insurgent commanders, perished in battle.

Arcadio Peguero, a veteran of two years' guerrilla combat in Matanzas, was seriously wounded in an attack on a militia outpost. Peguero: "I took a bullet in the leg and went fourteen days without medical attention. My leg was dark, covered with maggots and an unbearable, foul smell. I was carried on a stretcher by my buddies, who broke through troop rings four or five times. I had my leg amputated by doctors in a clandestine hospital. Later I was arrested and in prison I saw how the militia buried a friend of mine, a guerrilla named Evaristo Boitel. He was a big man and didn't fit in the box, so they sawed off his feet."

Perico Sanchez, a cattleman from Matanzas, had led an insurgent unit for two years. Two of his sons died in battle, two days apart. Sanchez, heartbroken and worn out from fighting, hid in a town of Havana province. Wilfredo Fernandez met Sanchez at Guira de Melena.

Wilfredo Fernandez: "He hid in my house for a few hours. I was twenty-three and he hugged me with feeling, saying I reminded him of his sons. He was tall and thin and looked haggard from suffering. He reminded me of Abraham Lincoln without the beard. He was taken to another house and the following day a long line of police cars entered the town, looking for him. They surrounded him and he escaped. He made it to the edge of town and they machine-gunned him as he jumped a fence. Then they killed him as he lay wounded. His body was taken away in a cloth bag."

The body of Perico Sanchez was taken to Jaguey Grande and displayed on the back of a truck for all to see. The truck, driven by a Castro partisan who happened to be a cousin of Sanchez's, made a morbid stop in front of his parents' house.[4]

In Camaguey province the small guerrilla units were practically annihilated. In Oriente several insurgent groups in the Victoria de las Tunas area were destroyed by the superior firepower of the LCB units. One of the guerrillas killed in Oriente was Racien Guerra, only fifteen years old.

By the end of 1963, fewer than three hundred insurgents remained in all of Cuba, most of them in the Escambray mountains under command of Julio Emilio Carretero, a veteran of four years' guerrilla combat.

The price of victory had not been cheap. According to Norberto Fuentes, a war correspondent on Castro's side, LCB casualties in Las Villas during 1963 numbered 305 men killed in battle.[5]

[4] Interview with Fidel Gonzalez, brother-in-law of Perico Sanchez, Union City, New Jersey, 1987

[5] See Fuentes's *Cazabandido*.

CHAPTER XIV.

GIRL OF ESCAMBRAY

A crushing year for the guerrillas, 1963 also saw the weakening of an already fractured urban underground.

Enrique Gonzalez-Pola: "The situation became more unbearable with each passing day. There were not enough weapons or explosives. Security houses were almost impossible to find. Vehicles were difficult to obtain. The reign of terror had frightened many people. Cubans were being executed every day, others were serving long prison sentences and the lucky ones were leaving the island as in a stampede. Every day the resistance grew smaller."

The government's repressive machinery had gained in sophistication. State Security had refined its interrogation and surveillance methods with hundreds of graduates from the training schools of the Soviet KGB and the East German Stasi.

Infiltration of the anti-Castro resistance was constant. State Security officer Jorge "Mongo" Medina Bringuier joined DRE and quickly became known as a man who could solve problems—obtaining cars, weapons, whatever was needed. When Nicolas Perez Diaz-Arguelles became chief of supply for DRE, Mongo Medina Bringuier was his second-in-command.

Nicolas Perez Diaz-Arguelles: "Medina Bringuier wore glasses. He had a wide waist and a small back. The man who had been his boss in the supply chain, Manuel Sabas, was run over by a car. They probably did it to make it look like an accident, so Mongo would move up the chain of command. When he turned us over, not only did we lose the national leadership of DRE; some high-ranking members of MRP and the 30th of November [Movement] who had contacts with us were also arrested. More than a hundred key people in the resistance were captured. A guerrilla group we sponsored fell into a trap set by Medina Bringuier. Four died and five others were captured. Even my mother and father were arrested in that dragnet. He destroyed the structure of the underground, and it was never the same after."

Medina Bringuier was toasted as a hero of State Security. Soon afterward, ironically, he fled to West Germany as an exile.

The underground was indeed withering away. In a letter to Hiram Gonzalez, a resistance leader of the 30th of November Movement wrote: "I want to make you aware that at this time the organization only has one car, a 1954 Oldsmobile in Oriente. We have no raw materials to work with. Handguns can be counted on the fingers of one hand; same with rifles. Our finances are destroyed. Men are still working and keeping on because they are men."[1]

Resistance fighters died in clashes with State Security. Luis David Rodriguez, military commander of the MRR, was captured while meeting other conspirators in a cafeteria. During transport in a squad car, Rodriguez took out a hidden .38 and shot both policemen in the vehicle. The car crashed and Luis David attempted to escape, but was killed by gunfire from a second squad car.[2]

*   *   *

Thousands of resistance and guerrilla fighters were now political prisoners. Many of these went to the huge confinement facility on the Isle of Pines, south of Cuba's main island.

Francisco Chappi: "Every morning we were awakened at 5:30 a.m. Breakfast consisted of watered coffee and a crusty piece of bread. We were taken out on trucks to work in the citrus fields. We worked about sixty hours a week. Lunch was boiled macaroni and a piece of hard bread; supper a few spoons of rice and peas. If a prisoner slowed down at work, armed guards beat him. A prisoner who went to pick up a hat blown away by the wind was shot in the back and died. After a while, when the circulars at the Isle of Pines were packed with thousands, the only ones taken on forced labor were the new arrivals. I had several asthma attacks, lost weight and survived several beatings."

Jose Berberena: "The sun in the fields was burning hot. We had a very poor diet. Jorge Valls was so thin, his skin so drawn, that the contours of his bones could be seen on his face."

Enrique Ruano: "We were hit with the flat sides of bayonets or stabbed with the

---

[1] Interview with Hiram Gonzalez, Miami, 1988
[2] Interview with Luis David's son, Miami, 1992

sharp tips. We were forced to work in the rain, in the mud, under a hot sun that was a ball of fire. My skin was blistered by the sun, and the only means I had to soothe the burning was to rub toothpaste on the blisters."

To harass political prisoners, guards carried out *requisas* or searches of their living areas at all hours of the day and night.

Roberto Martin Perez: "They jammed the prisoners out in the yard, naked or in their underwear. They beat some prisoners, we fought back, and they used rifle-ends or bayonets on us. In one *requisa* we had sixty men wounded. While we were fighting in the yard, other guards were going through our living quarters, searching for contraband, tearing up our books, throwing our personal belongings on the floor. The full treatment included murder."

Enrique Ruano: "Ernesto Diaz Madruga was late for work formation one morning. Sergeant Porfirio Gonzalez and several guards beat him. Gonzalez drove a bayonet into Ernesto's belly. Three days later he died. He was a good Cuban, a good family man. Porfirio Gonzalez was promoted to lieutenant, and he bragged about killing Ernestico."

Roberto Martin Perez: "It was a rainy day in the work fields and I walked toward Eddie Alvarez Molina, who was to share a piece of nylon with me, as protection from the rain. I was a meter away from him when his head exploded, splattering me with blood. He was killed by a guard for target practice."

Rino Puig: "Men were killed in cold blood. Every political prisoner suffered from beatings, hunger, disease or malnutrition. It was a horrible life, but we held together. No matter how bad things were, we had the power of our convictions."

Despite the tortures, the searches, bad food and living conditions, political prisoners managed to organize for survival.

Francisco Chappi: "When they could no longer take us out to work because there were too many of us, we created study groups inside the prison. The educated prisoners taught others whatever they knew. As time passed we developed an impressive curriculum. A prisoner could learn English, French, German, Italian and even Japanese. He could study history, religion, philosophy or mathematics."

Agapito Rivera: "I was a farm boy without education, but I learned to read and write at a pretty fair level in prison. Political prisoners made chalk out of wall plaster, and they improvised blackboards. You could be totally illiterate and in prison learn to read, write, do basic math, and discuss history and politics. Those who had education did not waste their time. They taught each other foreign languages."

At Isle of Pines the prisoners made a clandestine radio, which they used to listen to exile broadcasts.

Roberto Martin Perez: "It didn't look like a radio. The batteries were made of pencil graphite and bottles of urine treated with ammonia. It had pieces of wood, wire and rubber hoses taken from the infirmary. After using it, we took it apart so it wouldn't be seized in a *requisa*."

Despite the horrors of prison life, inmates had a sense of freedom.

Francisco Chappi: "It sounds strange, but no man in Cuba is more free than a political prisoner in rebellion. Although we were tortured and starved, we did what no citizen in the street could do: we cursed our guards, we screamed out loud our feelings about the dictatorship, and we fought with bare fists against bayonets. The average Cuban in the street lives a life of total compromise in order to survive. We barely survived, but we lived in total defiance."

*　*　*

Women resistance fighters fared no better than men did. In prison they endured torture, squalor and poor food. Like the men, they resisted beyond their limits, refusing to bend to the system.

The role of women in the anti-Castro resistance was significant. Women took part in military campaigns, carried out intelligence operations, served as couriers, transported weapons, hid resistance fighters or worked as links in the supply chain. Benilde Diaz and her daughter Conchita, mother and sister to Tomas San Gil, had supervised supply lines to the Escambray guerrillas.

Zoila Aguila was known as "The Girl of Escambray." Zoila had fought against Batista while still in her teens. In 1961, with her electrician husband Manolo Munso La Guardia, she once more chose the hard life of a guerrilla. Zoila became a guerrilla lieutenant, leading a squad of hardened male veterans on dangerous missions.

Andrea Castro: "The Girl was very brave. Once, when Castro's militia were combing the area, she hid on my farm with her husband. Militiamen were on the farm, camping out in wait for guerrillas who might come to us looking for food. The Girl and Manolo hid in bushes near a corral where I kept pigs. Every day one of my workers, while taking buckets of feed for the pigs, brought them food and water. They hid under the noses of the enemy for fifteen days. When she left and told me which way she was headed, I said, 'Girl, don't go that way, there are a lot of Castro's troops in that area.' She just nodded her head and answered, 'Andrea, I have to go.' They both left. An hour later we heard shooting in the distance. Afterward I found out that she had broken through the ring of troops and joined Carretero and the others."

After losing two children stillborn in the mountains and surviving dozens of skirmishes and battles, Zoila Aguila was captured and sentenced to thirty years in prison, while her husband was executed by a firing squad.

Polita Grau: "Even the guards feared her. She was not afraid to fight anyone, and she fought with an insane anger. Zoila set mattresses on fire."

Nenita Carames: "From Guanabacoa Prison I remember the loudspeakers and a whistle that was imposed as punishment. After 72 hours of that infernal whistle, our eardrums were exploding. The Girl of Escambray shouted that she wanted to go to the washroom, and they allowed her to come out of her cell. Right there she grabbed the electric wires to silence the whistle. She pulled on them with her bare hands. Her body shot through the air and her skin was blackened by the jolt. It was a miracle she didn't die. The authorities were so impressed, they never reconnected the whistle."[3]

Polita Grau: "Life in political prison was brutal. There were about a thousand of us at Guanajay Prison. The lights were never turned off. We covered our eyes with small pieces of cloth to sleep. The food was terrible. We ate dry noodles that often had bugs. I suffered from dysentery, parasites and skin infections on my feet and under my fingernails. From lack of oral hygiene my teeth rotted, until every tooth in my mouth became a black nub over infected, swollen gums. I lost all my teeth in prison. The Girl lost her mind. She had suffered too much. Her husband had been executed, her children stillborn, her guerrilla fighters killed in combat—and then all those years in prison, all that time in constant rebellion, destroyed her sanity. Even though she lost her mind, she never surrendered; she never submitted to the indoctrination."

The Girl of Escambray survived months locked underground in a solitary black hole, as well as beatings, extensive interrogation and psychological torture. When she arrived in exile during the mid-eighties, the former guerrilla officer had become a mentally unstable shell of a woman, disabled but still unvanquished.

Women political prisoners were subject to the same types of harassment as men. The system did not discriminate, wounding both sexes with equal ferocity.

Polita Grau: "When female guards couldn't handle us, male guards were brought in. I have seen young girls beaten severely, their bones broken, their gums bleeding. Doris Delgado had her mouth ripped open by a blow from a rubber hose, her salivary gland receiving permanent damage. Mercy Pena was hit in the chest by a rubber truncheon. Her left breast swelled up, becoming a grotesque ball of black and blue flesh. She was in pain for weeks."

Nenita Carames: " At State Security I was almost mad. I did not eat, did not sleep.

---

[3] Medrano, *Todo lo dieron por Cuba*, p. 181

They took me out at odd times, at night, at dawn, from total darkness to blinding light, from cold to heat. It was an anguishing situation, metal doors slamming, the screams and howls of men being tortured."[4]

Albertina O'Farrill: "During the month and a half I spent at State Security, I didn't know when it was daytime or night. They used to tell me that my mother had been jailed, my husband executed, and that my children in Miami would be assassinated. I spent weeks without bathing or combing my hair."[5]

Manuela Calvo: "On Mother's Day of 1961, as our mothers and sons were visiting us, we were beaten with rubber hoses, and streams of water were turned on us, with pressure so strong it made us roll on the floor."[6]

Esperanza Pena: "During a hunger strike, they started by beating us with twisted coils of electric cable. Teresita Bastanzuri was on the ground, with all her lower ribs broken. Gladys Suarez had both arms broken. Doris Delgado had such a facial cut that when I tried to disinfect the inside of her mouth, water came out of a hole in her cheek."[7]

Teresita Mayans: "There was torture and even sexual extortion. The guards were not able to bribe women political prisoners, but with the nonpolitical women prisoners it was different. There was a Captain Echezabal who offered nonpolitical prisoners extra noodles in exchange for sex. Political prisoners had higher standards."[8]

Cary Roque had been a young TV actress. While still a teenager she had been a resistance fighter against Batista. After the triumph of the revolution she once again joined the resistance. She endured years of incarceration, beatings and tortures, the suicide of her mother and death of her father. Looking back from exile, she reflected on her life as a prisoner.

Cary Roque: "We were a generation that gave its all, fully aware of how justified we were in conspiring against Fidel Castro—and if I had to do it all over again, I would once more do the same. To me, the most important thing in my life has been my country. For my country I lost my mother, my father, my career and my best years of life. I lost the opportunity of being a mother. And for my country I would do it all over again."[9]

※　※　※

[4] Ibid., p. 53
[5] Ibid., p. 48
[6] Ibid., p. 105
[7] Ibid., p. 229
[8] Radio Mambi, Miami, August 18, 1995
[9] Medrano, *Todo lo dieron por Cuba*, p. 262

The clandestine war against Castro was stymied by intractable problems facing the resistance.

The resistance was not able to promote its ideas or build a solid base of internal political support. Castro's government had moved swiftly to control the media and destroy established parties. In a system where the opposition could not project its viewpoints, the only audible voice was the government's.

When the first resistance units were created, Castro still had the overwhelming support of the masses. By the time most people had turned against the system, the guerrillas and organized resistance had bled into oblivion, leaving the Cuban people with no vehicles for rebellion and no avenues for legal political change.

Castro's repressive machinery apart, the resistance continued to suffer divisions that had taken root in the early 1960's when the CIA had played different groups against each other, adding to friction instead of building unity. After 1961 the guerrillas were not supplied except through their own networks, and members of the urban resistance never received the weapons they needed.

*　*　*

With the collapse of resistance in Cuba, anti-Castro groups began to crop up in Miami. Alpha 66 was started by Antonio Veciana and sixty-five other men, many of them former members of the II Front of Escambray. Besides Veciana, the movement included former guerrilla comandante Eloy Gutierrez Menoyo, who had betrayed the Trinidad Conspiracy of 1959; Armando Fleites; Lazaro Asencio; and two brothers, Aurelio and Andres Nazario Sargen. The group advocated guerrilla and urban warfare in Cuba, backed by commando raids.

Commandos L was led by former swimming champion Tony Cuesta, while MIRR, or Insurrectionary Movement of Revolutionary Recuperation, was brought into exile by its leader Orlando Bosch, the rebel governor of Las Villas who had supplied the first Escambray guerrillas.

Orlando Bosch: "We fought with what we could. We manufactured our own bombs right here in Miami—homemade but functional—and we flew small air raids over Cuba with small planes, bombing sugar mills and attacking other installations."

*　*　*

The CIA was not quite finished with the anti-Castro resistance. In 1963 it gave economic and logistical support to its favorite group, the MRR, in setting up training centers in Costa Rica and Nicaragua.

Humberto Lopez: "I received training in the United States. I learned advanced infiltration tactics, teaching methods, communications, survival and covert operations procedures. Four of us left one morning in a plane bound for Costa Rica. Eventually we would be a dozen in number, working as instructors for the covert teams. When we arrived in Costa Rica, the camp did not exist. What existed was a jungle. We worked seventeen-hour days, seven days a week. With explosives and bulldozers we cleared a twenty-three-mile trail through the bush. We built huts and rigged up our own electric power. We built six small camps a couple of miles apart from each other, where teams of five to seven men would be trained in different tasks: infiltration, guerrilla war, commando raids...."

The United States had drastically slowed down weapons shipments to the resistance, and had steered the networks in Cuba away from armed struggle toward intelligence data-gathering. Through 1963 and 1964, the U.S. continued to finance the MRR camps in Central America and carried out CIA commando operations with Cuban exiles. Guadalupe Lima was an officer in the "Comandos Mambises," an elite CIA exile unit.

Guadalupe Lima: "In October 1963 we attacked a large government sawmill, firing on a fourteen-man militia detachment. When the militia retreated, we placed explosive and incendiary charges all over the warehouses, equipment and diesel drums—two hundred pounds of plastic charges. By the time the drums exploded we were running toward the beach, but the explosion was so huge it knocked us down. A cloud rose behind us and became a large mushroom."

These operations were not cakewalks, as Humberto Lopez and a naval unit found when they approached a Cuban beach.

Humberto Lopez: "From behind a finger of land a frigate appeared, giving chase. They were heavily armed, firing at us with a cannon. Geysers of water spurted in the water near us. Our gunners answered with the recoilless rifle. The vessels zigzagged in the water. From the shore, shelling started from quad 20mm cannons. In seconds we were out of range of the shore batteries, but the chase and exchange of gunfire lasted four hours. We managed to lose them before morning."

Then, still mightier forces intervened in Cuba's internal conflict.

CHAPTER XV.

REPLAY IN AFRICA

The assassination of President Kennedy was a heavy blow to the Cuban resistance. For anti-Castro Cubans, the tragedy contained a paradox. Even if Kennedy's policies had foiled the resistance, and even if the President had betrayed his own promises to the anti-Castro fighters, he and his office yet commanded their highest respect. Inmates at the Isle of Pines, learning of the assassination by clandestine radio, were shocked and grieved. The following day, the prisoners' own announcers called for a minute of silence for the fallen leader—and Castro's prison guards cursed and screamed while thousands of inmates stood to attention in Kennedy's memory.[1]

After Kennedy's death, a still heavier blow to the resistance was that CIA sponsorship of covert operations against the Castro regime also came to an end.

Alvaro Cosculluela: "The infiltration teams were still active in '63 and '64. We created large networks on the island, but then American policy concentrated on Vietnam. The last big network in Cuba was led by a very brave man named Esteban Marquez Novo."

Marquez Novo was code-named "The Uncle" because several of his nephews and nieces served as his lieutenants. "The Uncle" started out as a guerrilla in Pinar del Rio province. Arriving in the U.S. in 1960, he was trained by the CIA and returned to Cuba that same year. He organized a large network with more than one thousand supporters in Pinar del Rio, Havana and Matanzas. Realizing that the U.S. had slowed down military activities, Marquez Novo requested and obtained some weapons that he planned to use for a guerrilla uprising without U.S. permission.

[1] Interview with Emilio Adolfo Rivero, a former inmate at the Isle of Pines, Washington, 1990

Before the attacks could be launched, State Security moved in, arresting hundreds of suspected collaborators. Twenty-seven men from Marquez Novo's network would be executed by firing squads, while more than five hundred men and women would receive prison sentences for their part in the network. As for Marquez Novo, he was surrounded by government forces at a farmhouse. Rather than surrender, he set the building ablaze to destroy all papers concerning his network. He fought until the burning building had collapsed on him, then took his own life with a last round of his submachine gun.

*   *   *

Cubans were killing Cubans, and not all the fighting occurred in Cuba. Fidel Castro, in pursuit of worldwide glory, had intervened throughout Latin America and even on the far side of the Atlantic.

Africa in the early 1960's was a continent in turmoil. Soviets and Americans were trying to increase their spheres of influence by meddling in local rivalries. The newly independent Republic of the Congo, smack in the center of Africa's huge land mass, was an ideal springboard from which to spread conflict and grab political opportunities. Rich in resources and lacking stability, the Congo was a magnet for foreign adventurers. Castro began supplying the insurgent soldiers of Pierre Mulele with arms and technical advisors.

In 1962, the U.S. had sent a team of anti-Castro Cubans to fly missions against Mulele's force, the so-called Simbas. The exile pilots, known as the Cuban Volunteer Group (GVC), were mostly veterans of the Bay of Pigs. When Castro launched a full-scale military operation in the Congo under Che Guevara's personal command, a replay of the earlier battle was set in motion.

Ernesto Guevara was an Argentine-born Marxist who had drifted through South and Central America during the early fifties and had played a role in the socialist government of Guatemalan leader Jacobo Arbenz. A doctor by education, Guevara was working as a street photographer in Mexico City when he met Fidel Castro. Following Castro to Cuba in 1956, Che became a guerrilla commander and scrambled to the top of Castro's power structure. After the triumph of the revolution, he ordered hundreds of executions and appointed himself an authority on guerrilla warfare.

A taciturn man with a morbid sense of humor and poor personal hygiene, Guevara was a true believer in Marxism. With his limited experience of war—he had seldom led more than a hundred men in combat, and most of his battles were skirmishes—he committed the mortal sin of buying into his own legend. To his credit, he did have a knack for organization, and he was courageous in battle. In Africa, though, he was a white leader commanding black subordinates—a fervid anti-colonialist who ironically replicated the colonial pattern he so despised.

Che's Congo force consisted of two hundred Cubans, almost all black men who were carefully chosen to blend in with the native population. These men had been battle-tested in the guerrilla war against Batista, at the Bay of Pigs and in the LCB Escambray campaign. The troops had undergone rigorous training at a military base in Pinar del Rio and had then been moved secretly to Africa in small groups.

To check Guevara's force, the CIA sent a Cuban exile commando unit and an advisor named William "Rip" Robertson, a tall man with graying hair, wrinkled clothing and a paperback stuffed in his pants pocket.

Lucas Alberto Ponzoa was a veteran of the CIA units. Ponzoa: "Rip spoke broken Spanish, but we all understood him. At the Bay of Pigs, U.S. advisors were forbidden to land, but Rip was on the beach before anyone else, to make sure the area was clear. When two of our men were lost at sea, Rip stayed in the area and refused to leave until we found them and rescued them. He never let anyone down. In Korea, he had led a unit behind enemy lines. After the Congo, he went on to Vietnam and led a special unit that operated inside VC territory. He was a real-life John Wayne…. One time he told me to go on a mission and I told him I wouldn't have enough fuel to return. He smiled and said, 'Trust me. Go.' When I was running out of fuel on the return trip he appeared in a hydroplane and dropped down two containers of fuel. Rip was a hell of a guy."

The exiles and the ill-trained Congolese army were not the only ones opposing Guevara and the Simbas. A genuine mercenary unit was also in the soup. The men of the Fifth Commando, or the "Wild Geese," were led by "Mad Mike" Hoare, a South African who had fought in Burma during the Second World War. Their mission was to rescue and protect Europeans from the violence that had gripped the Congo. The force of several hundred included veterans of the French Foreign Legion, the British Royal Marines and Belgium's paratroop force. They had been hardened by combat in many wars.

Eduardo Whitehouse, who had survived the air war at the Bay of Pigs, became a CIA pilot in the Congo. Whitehouse: "It was a brutal war. The rebels captured nuns, raped them and cut off their breasts, hacked their faces, dismembered them. I saw dead babies that the Simbas had used for bayonet practice. They had thrown them in the air and pierced them as they came down. Fausto Gomez, one of our pilots, went down in the bush. In a frenzy, they hacked up his body and ate his liver and heart."

Hoare was no fool, and the Fifth Commando troopers were not green recruits. Well-armed with Belgian FN rifles, the Wild Geese moved swiftly about in jeeps with mounted heavy machine guns, making sudden strikes at rebel positions. Hoare's mobile and light-footed attacks, with the Congolese army as a mop-up squad, took Che Guevara by surprise. In four swift strokes the Wild Geese and Cuban exiles occupied Aba, Faradje, Aru and Watsa. While the gun jeeps attacked on the ground, planes piloted by Cuban exiles patrolled the skies, raining destruction down on rebel convoys.

Eduardo Whitehouse: "This was the opposite of Bay of Pigs. We owned the air—and the Simbas made the same mistakes over and over. Often they tried to move their supplies during the day instead of waiting for night, when we would not have spotted them.... All that could be seen afterward was black smoke, dead bodies on the ground, burning brush and soldiers running in all directions."

Guevara tried his best to counter Hoare. Che's forces blew up a bridge near Bukavu and ambushed a Congolese unit in the outskirts of Albertville. His campaign, however, was hampered by the uneducated Simbas, who lacked basic discipline and tactical knowledge. The constant air bombardments and strikes on the ground forced Guevara to hide in Fizi-Baraka, where he was cut off from his supply lines.

From Cuba, orders arrived. Guevara was to return to Havana before the whole situation collapsed. He would be replaced and the magnitude of the operation scaled down. The frustrated comandante withdrew, taking a number of his men on four gunboats onto Lake Tanganika. An exile unit in a heavily armed boat intercepted Guevara's fleet. Cuban fought Cuban in a night battle on an African lake. Guevara's boat escaped, but many of his escort died as a vessel sank into the waters of Lake Tanganika.

For more than a dozen years the Castro government refused to acknowledge that Che Guevara had been in the Congo—or that his defeat had been caused, in some measure, by Cuban exiles.

CHAPTER XVI.

FREE TO REBEL

In the summer of 1964 some thirty Cuban insurgents, including Maro Borges and Julio Emilio Carretero, fell into a State Security trap as they attempted to leave the mountains and reach exile in the United States. Twelve guerrillas and several supporters were executed, with dozens imprisoned. The executed, including Carretero and Borges, died singing the Cuban national anthem.[1]

Alberto Delgado, the informant who had set the trap for the guerrillas, was hanged at a farm by one of the few remaining insurgent groups, led by Jose "Cheito" Leon. Soon enough, Leon was cornered by LCB troops near Trinidad. Refusing to surrender, the wounded guerrilla blew himself up with a hand grenade as LCB troops rushed his position.[2]

By 1966, virtually all guerrillas in Cuba had been killed or captured.

* * *

In the exile community, organizations disappeared. The DRE, MRR and MRP—weakened by years of struggle, emptied of resources—gradually disbanded. For many exiles, it was time to establish themselves in a new country, find steady incomes and get on with everyday life.

Alpha 66, the organization created by former anti-Batista guerrillas, suffered fractious rivalries but stubbornly pressed on, refusing to quit the war. Eloy Gutierrez Menoyo, one of its top leaders, was captured during an infiltration mission into Cuba and con-

---

[1] Interviews with Amador Acosta, Miami, 1987–1999
[2] Ibid.

demned to a long prison sentence. Menoyo might have saved himself from a firing squad by appearing on Cuban television, advising exiles to forget the use of arms against Castro. At the Isle of Pines prison he endured a horrible beating in which all his ribs were broken.[3]

Andres Nazario Sargen, a former farmer and ex-comandante of the II Front, became the leader of Alpha 66. Nazario Sargen: "We defined our war as a struggle of the Cuban people. Other groups have lived and died by the CIA's aid or lack of it, but Alpha 66 has always been independent. We always bought our own equipment, weapons and boats. When we had three speedboats, we used all three. When we didn't have any, we dipped into our pockets and bought more. We have been accountable to ourselves and to no one else. Ours has been a grassroots movement."

Independent groups were suffering. Orlando Bosch's MIRR, which had staged a number of air raids on Cuban industrial plants, suffered a grave setback when pilot Gervelio "Mimo" Gutierrez, an Escambray and U.S. Army veteran, disappeared over the ocean after bombing a petrochemical factory on November 13, 1966.[4] Raul Fantony, another U.S. Army veteran, died with Gutierrez.

Former swimming champion Tony Cuesta, leader of Commandos L, had carried out a score of quick strikes against Cuba's harbors, one of which had been photographed by *Life* magazine; but in May 1966 luck went against him.

Tony Cuesta: "We had dropped two men in Havana to make an attempt on Castro's life. Both were killed by a police patrol near the beach. Gunboats chased us and we exchanged gunfire and tried to lose them, but it was impossible. Our weapons could not match theirs. All my men were being killed. Guillermo Alvarez was only seventeen. Roberto Anta also died. Eugenio Zaldivar was wounded. I put a lifesaver on Eugenio and threw him overboard, to save him. Then I took a grenade and threw it inside the engine of my boat to kill myself and sink the vessel. Everything went black. Next thing I knew, someone was pulling me out of the water by my hair. I tried to reach for a pistol, but my hand had disappeared."

Cuesta had lost his eyesight as well as a hand. Captured by Castro's Coast Guard units, Cuesta and Zaldivar would spend a dozen years in jail.

*   *   *

Inside Cuba's prisons, resistance continued. Political prisoners had been issued khaki uniforms with a letter "P" painted on the legs and back. Common criminals were issued

---

[3] Interview with Juan Rodriguez Mesa, Union City, New Jersey, 1987
[4] See the author's *Cuba: The Unfinished Revolution,* p. 128.

blue uniforms. By the mid-sixties, however, no more khaki uniforms were issued.

Enrique Ruano: "The penal authorities said they had run out of khaki uniforms. The real reason was that they wanted to dilute the political prisoners with the criminals to make us all look alike. We were not rapists or thieves. We had been jailed for fighting against a system, and we refused to wear the blue uniform. Many of us ended up naked, dressed only in our underwear, and it was very tough because the nights were very cold in some of those jails."

Roberto Martin Perez: "On cold nights, without blankets, many of us slept back to back, curled up in fetal positions, trying to keep warm."

The penal authorities established a "Reeducation Plan," seeking to divide and conquer the political prisoners. Those willing to join "The Plan," as it was plainly called, were promised better food, better living conditions, shortened sentences, weekend passes, work-release programs and good medical treatment. In exchange, prisoners had to wear the blue uniform, perform work details, attend Marxist indoctrination classes, and sign confessions declaring themselves ashamed of their crimes against the state.

Those who refused to join The Plan came to be called *plantados,* or staunch ones.

Francisco Chappi: "For the plantados, a living hell doubled and tripled in intensity. In order to force us to join The Plan, the guards became more sadistic than ever. We were roused from our beds in the middle of the night, beaten with rifle butts and machetes. Sick plantados were denied medical care, fed bowls of rice crawling with worms, locked up in solitary confinement for disobedience. Men in solitary spent months confined to rooms with little or no light, unable to shower, expected to shit in a small hole in the floor without toilet paper. They slept on the floor without pillows or blankets, and in their own urine. Rather than submit, many died in attempts to retain the last shreds of human dignity. Thousands cracked and joined The Plan. I never blamed them. A human body has its limits, and for many The Plan was an option for early release, for escape."

Blas Hernandez was another prisoner who declined to join The Plan. Hernandez: "Political commissars talked to us, trying to convince us to turn over. One of them said to me: 'How can you defend capitalism? Do you know the roots of communism?' I said I did not, and he said: 'How can you fight against something you don't understand?' And I looked at him and said: 'I know the difference between steak and cornmeal.' "

Enrique Ruano: "They tried to divide us but it didn't work. We understood that some had to join The Plan due to health reasons or family pressures, and we held no ill will. Many men in The Plan helped us by smuggling us food, paper, pencils, medicines. It was a matter of individual choice. My father and I refused to join The Plan. We would not submit mentally; and the tougher they became against us, the tougher we grew."

The late 1960's saw the advent of a plan called "The Progressive," whereby prisoners did so-called volunteer work constructing new jails that would house more Cubans. By the end of the decade, the number of political prisoners had grown so large that the Isle of Pines was closed down and its population distributed to more than one hundred different facilities in Cuba.

The *plantados* organized hunger strikes to demand mail deliveries, better food and less harassment.

Ricardo Vazquez: "The hunger strikes were a political weapon. The guards tried to divide us; the hunger strikes gave us a united front against authority. They played games with us. They brought in good food—not the garbage we were used to eating—and placed it near us. We were hungry, starving, and we would smell that food and still refuse it."

Rigo Acosta, an Escambray veteran, took part in more than twenty hunger strikes during his prison years. Acosta: "The first two or three days, you get really bad headaches until the body starts feeding on itself, eating the fat and even muscle tissue, and you don't feel hungry anymore. You dry up slowly. I did a strike where I went down to seventy-eight pounds and my thighs disappeared, leaving only bone and skin. I lost all my teeth. Losing a tooth is common in a hunger strike. The stink of our bodies and breath was horrible. There is no smell worse than a body feeding on itself. Parasites in your body just died. I went twenty-eight days without a bowel movement. The feces formed stones in the intestines. Some had to have the stones scraped out, that is how hard they were.... More than anything, the strike was a mental process. The body asked for food and you tried to fool the body. I drank water and tried to pretend I was drinking soup. No matter how ill I felt, I kept telling myself I would rather die than surrender. To die fighting back is to die a free man. I really believe that as long as I was free to rebel I was a free man. The moment I surrendered, I would be giving up my soul, my dignity.... I walked out of prison with my head high."

Apart from the political prisons, Castro's regime created a new penal plan called the Military Units of Assistance to Production (UMAP). The UMAP units, rather than having anything to do with the army, were camps that housed "antisocial" prisoners doing slave labor in Cuban farm fields. Official statements misleadingly implied that the only inhabitants of UMAP camps were homosexuals (whom the Castro government fiercely persecuted). In fact the camps also housed Jehovah's Witnesses, political detainees, dissident intellectuals and youths who had refused to serve in the armed forces.[5]

---

[5] Descriptions of these camps are abundant in the writings of Cuban novelist Reinaldo Arenas.

Journalist Pablo Alfonso described the UMAP camps in these terms: "Thousands of youths and adults were locked in true concentration camps and forced to work twelve to fourteen hours a day in the fields under the worst conditions. The nutrition was dismal. The confinement—in small barracks housing more than two hundred people each—was inhumane. The camp was surrounded, in true Nazi style, by electrified, barbed-wire fences, soldiers in watchtowers, and trained dogs."[6]

The stark realities of the UMAP camps, which operated from 1965 to 1967, can be seen in these figures: 72 men died from beating or torture; 186 committed suicide; and 507 were hospitalized for psychiatric treatment.[7]

[6] Alfonso, *Cuba, Castro y los catolicos*, p. 151
[7] Ibid., pp. 151–52

CHAPTER XVII.

MARTYRS

Cuba's year of 1968 saw more than one hundred acts of sabotage against the Castro regime. Dozens of arsons were reported in educational centers, apparently the work of student rebels. Large coffee and clothing warehouses were burned in Guantanamo and Camaguey.[1] Two executions were announced publicly, as were the arrests of eighteen alleged "CIA agents" and more than five hundred "antisocial" elements.[2] Yet no event was mentioned more often than the so-called "Micro-Faction" conspiracy.

While charges and arrests were common, those accused in the "Micro-Faction" conspiracy represented a new type of person so marked. They included powerful people in the government structure, high-ranking officers of State Security, and others who had served the regime in prestigious positions. Raul Castro himself had fingered them.

Anibal Escalante, the PSP veteran who had once been the KGB's man in the parallel government, formed a central pretext for Raul's accusations. The alleged conspirators, most of whom had worked with Anibal, faced charges of having plotted with Soviet officials in Cuba to bring about Fidel's exit from power.[3] Three dozen men and women were convicted of conspiracy and sentenced to long prison terms. Ricardo Bofill, a PSP member and an instructor in political economy at the University of Havana, was one of the condemned.

Ricardo Bofill: "I could brag and make up a story about a great conspiracy, but the fact is that there was no conspiracy. There was a purge, a punishment, but no conspiracy. It was all a government invention to create an image. Many of us did not even know each

[1] Halperin, *The Taming of Fidel Castro*, pp. 286–87
[2] *The Baltimore Sun*, November 17, 1968
[3] Bethel, *The Losers*, p. 348

other. Some had raised some questions about economic and social conditions. Anibal Escalante had been powerful in a silent way. He had controlled intelligence operations in Cuba in the early sixties, and friction had developed between Fidel and him in 1962. By 1967, Anibal had long been gone from power and the KGB no longer competed internally— but then came revenge, a purge, and a warning to any and all inside the power structure."

* * *

In the meantime, without significant resources or help from any government, exiles formed a series of movements to keep fighting against the regime. Orlando Bosch created Cuban Power, a secret organization that went in for radical tactics. Arrested on half a dozen occasions between 1960 and 1968, Bosch served time in an Atlanta penitentiary after being convicted of firing a recoilless rifle at a Polish merchant vessel on Dodge Island, Miami. The Polish cargo ship had been on its way to Cuba. Another group was Cuban Representation in Exile (RECE), a small, well-organized movement whose leadership included a labor activist, Amancio Mosquera, and two Brigade 2506 veterans, Tony Calatayud and Jorge Mas Canosa.

During the Escambray war, Castro's government had taken measures to insure that guerrilla activity would henceforth be an unfeasible proposition. Several highways had been built into the mountain regions to allow easy access by motorized units. The regime's expropriations and the formation of cooperatives had pretty much wiped out the small, independent farmers, thereby cancelling many sources of support for insurgents. The lack of consumer goods and strict rationing made support from the remaining population very difficult. Many of the guerrillas' supporters were moved to relocation camps, the "captive cities," away from the hill regions. Castro's military forces were well armed with AK-47 automatic rifles, were well-coordinated via radio communications, and had become proficient with helicopters.

The exiles had to work under dismal conditions. Every weapon was bought illegally; ammunition and explosives were procured with donations from blue-collar workers, through fundraisers among exile clubs and associations. Fighters got their training on Florida farms owned by exiles, but the FBI and local police departments often confiscated their weapons before they could launch their missions on borrowed boats.

Amancio Mosquera, a.k.a. "Comandante Yarey," led RECE's infiltration unit and was a veteran of several missions to Cuba. Tony Calatayud, one of RECE's leaders, recalled a 1969 operation.

Calatayud: "Yarey returned from a mission to Cuba, in which he had spent weeks escaping from pursuing forces. His hair was long and he was full of enthusiasm. He wanted to start guerrilla warfare and coordinate a large uprising in Oriente province. We were initially against it but he insisted he had many contacts in the area, including some in the military. We worked on a plan, seriously limited because we lacked resources; we did not have help from the U.S. and we were acting without approval from the U.S. The idea was to drop off ten men who would form two teams of five. These were seasoned men. Yarey would command one team and Tico Herrera, who had been a captain in the Rebel Army, would command the second. Each of the ten had the experience to lead a small unit. They would carry twenty-five extra weapons into Cuba. We obtained M-14 and M-16 rifles, German machine guns and British Stens. They had more than one hundred grenades, three hundred pounds of explosives and thousands of rounds of ammunition. Much of this equipment was packaged for burial and subsequent retrieval so the men could travel light, but luck was against us. The landing beach in southern Cuba, typically abandoned, that day had a couple romancing in the sand. They spotted the landing and warned the militia. From the time the teams landed they were pursued by hundreds of militia forces. They could not settle in an area or make contacts. Since they had a lot of firepower and grenades, they inflicted heavy casualties on Castro's forces. Finally, however, they were pinned down. Soviet-made helicopters strafed them and fired incendiary rockets. Ground troops swept the area. Bienvenido Fuentes and Justo Leyva died in combat. Yarey was wounded. At the end Tito Pardo and Tico Herrera were alone. Several militia troops approached their position and Tico opened fire with a pistol. Then Tico lifted his head to the heavens, put the barrel of the pistol to the right side of his head and pulled the trigger. Of those who survived the battle, four, including Yarey, were executed and three others sent to prison."[4]

Alpha 66 had a military commander willing to go into the mountains of Oriente. Vicente Mendez was a strapping thirty-nine-year-old farmer from Las Villas. In 1958 he had joined the rebel guerrillas fighting Batista, becoming a lieutenant in the army of bearded warriors. Then he joined the anti-Castro guerrillas in 1960 as second-in-command of a unit of about thirty men. Pursued by militia forces in the Escambray, he managed to break through the troop rings and escape Cuba in a CIA boat in March 1961.

Arriving in the United States wounded and infected, Mendez vowed to return to the battle. He and a dozen men armed with M-16 automatic rifles entered Oriente province on April 17, 1970. The night of their landing they encountered a militia patrol, killing five

---

[4] Miami newspapers reported in January 2003 that Calatayud, a Miami pharmacy-owner, had been arrested on charges of Medicaid fraud. As of this writing, the case is unresolved.

and wounding five others. Chased by hundreds of border guards and militia units, the small group fought several skirmishes. Within a week, the force had been defeated and Vicente Mendez killed in combat. Just one of the thirteen survived. That was Mario Bello, a teenager who had been moved by Mendez's dedication.

Mario Bello: "He knew he was going to die. He understood his plan was almost suicidal. He saw his mission as a way of uplifting the morale of the Cubans. As he traveled through the U.S. and Puerto Rico, pleading for donations from the Cuban community, his speeches inspired those who heard him. A friend of mine was with him in Michigan during a snowstorm. Vicente was wearing a pair of shoes with the soles completely worn out. My friend offered to buy him a pair of shoes. Mendez puffed on a cigar and said: 'Buy some bullets. The only shoes I need are combat boots waiting for me in Miami. I'll be buried in them.' There are those who will tell you he died a foolish death, but I will not be one of them. The man chose his place and time. He awakened the exile community…. Meeting halls became packed once more."

A second Alpha 66 group followed Mendez's team. Jose Rodriguez Perez, a beefy veteran of several infiltration missions, commanded a nine-man unit that entered Cuba in September 1970. Undetected for two days, the group moved fifty kilometers into Cuba, hijacking a truck. They were stopped and pursued by an army jeep on a road near the mountains. Captain Sixto Nicot was a member of the infiltration team.

Sixto Nicot: "We killed two of them at the roadblock. The others sped after us. We exchanged gunfire. Ahead of us was the town of Baire. Police and militia units, hearing the gunfire, had taken up positions. As we tried to speed through town we were caught in crossfire. Rodriguez Perez was the first casualty. A bullet hit him in the forehead. Although he lived for two more weeks, he never regained consciousness. Our men jumped off the truck, firing as they ran, trying to reach the hills beyond the town. I covered their retreat, then jumped off the truck. I ran around buildings and jumped fences, heading for the hills. A bullet hit me above the ankle and a second round hit my thigh. I was captured. I was later told we killed seven and wounded seventeen or eighteen of their men in the several days our battles lasted. Our trial took place in an abandoned farm near Santiago. Five were condemned to death. Two of us, Alberto Kindelan and I, were sentenced to prison. Those condemned to die were told they had a right to appeal. Manuel Artola hugged me and said: 'If you ever see my son, tell him his father did not weaken in his last hours.' Kindelan and I were placed in a Ford vehicle that took us back to State Security. We were only one kilometer away from the house when we heard a salvo of gunfire. The appeal had been rejected. Cuba had five more martyrs."

CHAPTER XVIII.

OUTSIDE THE GAME

The collapse of the guerrilla infiltration teams, for Cuba, marked the end of one era and the beginning of another. With insurrection no longer possible, dissent now took the form of passive resistance and acts of individual sabotage. In May 1971, State Security arrested thirty-two men and women, accusing them of publishing *Testimonio* (Testimony) and *El Militante* (The Militant), clandestine anti-government publications. All were sentenced to prison, with terms ranging from two to twenty years.[1]

Castro's collapsing economy had a big part to play. For a decade, "1970" had been an official byword, with Castro promising that by the early seventies the nation would be fully industrialized and liberated from the one-crop sugar economy. The promise came true in an opposite sense when the "Harvest of Ten Million" failed spectacularly. Industrialization had proven elusive, thanks in great measure to the regime's own policies. By 1971, more than 450,000 Cubans had fled into exile—nearly half of these between 19 and 44 years old. More than one-third were college graduates, skilled tradesmen or technically savvy workers. Fear and repression had drained away a huge part of the country's human resources.[2]

All sectors of society were led, or mismanaged, by Castro's minions, who often lacked training or skill. The government's practice of putting loyalty above ability doomed economic efforts. The regime then made political hay of these failures by blaming them on what it called the "blockade"—the economic embargo the U.S. had imposed on Cuba a decade earlier. In reality the embargo was more symbolic than real, for Cuba could buy anything it needed from other countries, including American products. In 1975 alone,

[1] Alfonso, *Cuba, Castro y los catolicos*, pp. 185–88
[2] Halperin, *The Taming of Fidel Castro*, pp. 169–70

Cuba purchased 90,000 tons of rice from European subsidiaries of U.S. companies.[3]

Cuban workers—forbidden to strike, controlled by the regime's labor bureaus and ineligible for promotions unless they were Castro loyalists—began innumerable silent rebellions. Andres Cuevas was a young electrician in an industrial plant at the start of the seventies.

Andres Cuevas: "We had no incentives. A worker could be stuck in the same job working for a miserable salary, doing overtime without compensation, plus all sorts of 'volunteer' work that was not voluntary at all. We worked more hours than ever and had fewer rights than ever. Promotions and awards were given to those who played politics. Idiots and incompetents were placed in supervisory positions, to spy and report on their fellow workers. Many refused to play the political games. What happened then was a *huelga de brazos caidos*—a strike of fallen arms—as workers slowed down production intentionally. In many cases, workers just didn't show up. Why should you work if you had nothing much worth buying with the money you earned? Shoes, clothing, food, even toothpaste was rationed. Many workers began doing individual sabotage, little arsons, throwing a handful of dirt inside a motor, loosening bolts on machinery. Castro was screwing the Cuban people, but the Cuban people were screwing back."

French Marxist economist René Dumont commented on this proletarian rebellion when he visited Cuba and witnessed the arrival of eighty-four Soviet tractors for farm cooperatives. The Cuban workers, Dumont wrote, removed headlights from the tractors, throwing the parts in canals to avoid being forced to work night shifts.[4]

A parallel crisis had struck in education. At the end of 1970, Education Minister Armando Hart complained that students in Oriente province were neither working nor studying. Guido Garcia Inclan, an official radio spokesman, voiced concern about Cuban youths imitating American hippies, with long hair and rebellious attitudes. Fidel Castro complained in one of his marathon speeches that 81,000 students had failed in their schoolwork.[5] Absenteeism had reached the alarming rate of 15 percent.[6] To arrest the educational and labor crisis, the regime created the "Law Against Vagrancy and Absenteeism."

Luciano Mora was a worker who suffered punishment under the new law. Mora: "In my factory we had to work overtime for free; and the ones that worked the least were the ones being promoted. They worked less but attended all the political discussion groups,

---

[3] Horowitz, *El comunismo cubano 1959–1979*, p. 175
[4] Dumont, *Cuba, ¿es socialista?* p. 184
[5] *The Alternative*, February 1971
[6] Perez, *Cuba: Between Reform and Revolution*, p. 345

prepared signs for pro-Castro rallies and informed on others. So I decided 'The hell with this' and began missing work. I was demoted and sent to work in a broom factory. I missed work there also. Then I was taken to State Security, detained for two days and told that I was very close to spending time on a penal farm. I went to work, but worked very slow. It was at this time that stealing and bartering became the real work of all Cubans. If you worked in a shoe factory you stole a few pairs of shoes. You traded two pairs to someone who was a mechanic and he gave you a battery or a tire for your car. Another pair of shoes went to a butcher who gave you a few steaks, and so on. Since everything was rationed, stealing and bartering became a way of life for all Cubans. Even the ones who were members of the Communist Party did it; for being in the Party was not a guarantee to a better life, unless you were very high in the power structure. Generals and ministers lived like kings, eating steak and lobster, riding in new Lada autos, with air-conditioned homes and swimming pools. The rest of us had to steal shoes if we didn't want to go barefoot, and bartered so our children could eat. Socialism is not a society of equality. Some lived very well and most lived very bad. The capitalist rich had been replaced by the politically corrupt and their control was absolute. Strikes were forbidden, complaints ignored. To protest would brand you a troublemaker. You could not quit a job and look for another. Everyone worked for the same employer, the state, and the state could crush you any time it wanted, for whatever reason—crush you in a total way."

*   *   *

The man who wounded Castro's image at the beginning of the decade was not a protesting worker or a heroic warrior. Poet Heberto Padilla had published a slender volume called *Fuera del juego* ("Outside the Game"), which had won an important prize. Some of his poems—"Cuban Poets Dream No Longer," "Instructions for Entering a New Society," "To Write in the Scrapbook of a Tyrant"—were clearly critical of the system. On March 20, 1971, Padilla and his wife, writer Belkis Cuza Male, were arrested by State Security.

Slapped around and quickly intimidated, Padilla emerged from the dungeons of State Security to make a public recantation, admitting his "sin" of having betrayed the revolution. The terrified writer appeared at a public meeting and urged fellow authors to make similar confessions.

Had Padilla refused to sign the confession and faced years of incarceration, he would have simply vanished into the Cuban gulag. By bending to the system, he had inadvertently exposed its bullying nature.

"Castro demanded executions in public, and the masses echoed his cries. Castro admitted he had lied to the people, cynically telling them he had done so for their own welfare—and the masses cheered him. The whole nation became shrouded in a collective shame."

—Jorge Valls, poet and political prisoner

Execution scenes from Cuba in 1959

"I was poor, extremely poor. I had nothing except the hope of some day having something. Then I saw Castro was confiscating properties from those who did have something. Castro was closing the only door I had to improve my life. I had had my hope stolen from me—and I had to fight to try to recapture it."

—Agapito Rivera, farmworker and guerrilla fighter

Guerrillas in the Escambray mountains, early 1960's

"The options for anyone fighting Castro were very limited, and the one that offered the best weaponry and resources was the CIA. We did not feel like mercenaries or employees of the Americans. We did what we did because we were Cubans and we loved our country."

—Jose Basulto, resistance fighter and refugee rescue pilot

Cuban CIA commando unit, early 1960's

Perico Sanchez, a cattleman from Matanzas, had led an insurgent unit for two years. In 1963 two of his sons died in battle, two days apart. Wilfredo Fernandez gave shelter to the guerrilla commander. "I was twenty-three and he hugged me with feeling, saying I reminded him of his sons. He was tall and thin and looked haggard from suffering. He reminded me of Abraham Lincoln without the beard."

Comandante Perico Sanchez, killed a month after losing his sons

In Michigan during a snowstorm, Vicente Mendez was wearing a pair of shoes with the soles worn out. "My friend offered to buy him a pair of shoes. Mendez puffed on a cigar and said: 'Buy some bullets. The only shoes I need are combat boots waiting for me in Miami. I'll be buried in them.'"

Vicente Mendez's guerrilla squad, later wiped out in combat; and Vicente Mendez

On May 24, 1972, Pedro Luis Boitel died in prison after a fifty-six-day hunger strike. Sentenced to forty-two years for political dissent, he had faced his jailers with unflinching determination. A prison comrade later said: "He reminded me of a character in one of André Malraux's works.... I saw him die minute by minute, week by week, and I could not do anything, just sit on my cot and pray."

Pedro Luis Boitel

"The battle started at nine o'clock in the evening and lasted all night. We were surrounded by thousands of the enemy and there were only twenty-six of us.... The enemy fired flares into the sky and the night lit up like daytime. We tried to break through their lines and we were fighting hand to hand. Tomasito broke through and could have escaped, but he returned to help a group of us who were pinned down. A bullet hit him in the head and he died."

Tomas ("Tomasito") San Gil, commander-in-chief of the Escambray guerrillas, as depicted in a "wanted" poster

Porfirio Ramirez had been a captain in the anti-Batista guerrilla forces and president of the University Students Federation in Las Villas. After his capture by Castro's forces, his mother had asked for clemency and Fidel had promised that Porfirio would not be executed. Two demonstrations were organized in the city of Santa Clara on his behalf. One of these had many women dressed in widow's black.

Comandante Porfirio Ramirez, executed October 12, 1960

Father Francisco Lopez, a Spanish priest, became chaplain of the Escambray guerrillas. Following a massive deportation of priests and nuns, church officials in Cuba adapted to circumstances by obeying government mandates. A papal nuncio shocked many by pronouncing Castro "ethically Christian."

Father Francisco Lopez (center) with Escambray guerrillas

In the early sixties, Castro intervened in the Congo by supplying one of the warring factions with arms and technical advisors. The U.S. sent a team of anti-Castro Cuban pilots to fly air strikes against that force. Castro launched a full-scale military operation in the Congo under Che Guevara's personal command—and a replay of the Bay of Pigs battle was set in motion.

Cuban exile pilot Rene Garcia in the Congo

(Left) "What could State Security do? If they arrested us, then the news would be printed in European and American newspapers and it would create static with international human rights groups. It was a good blow to the system. The more public we became, the better our chances of survival."

Ricardo Bofill, pioneer of the human rights movement in Cuba

(Center and Right) In 1999, Oscar Elias Biscet organized a forty-day fast—a day for every year of the regime—in which some eight hundred dissidents across the island took part. Arrested, beaten and burned with lit cigarettes, Biscet was sentenced to three years in jail. In 2003, when Castro's major crackdown occurred, he was condemned to an additional 25 years and placed in solitary confinement.

Oscar Elias Biscet and his wife, Elsa Morejon; Free Biscet poster in international use

The forty-day protest fast at 34 Tamarindo Street, Havana, June 6–July 16, 1999, led European ministries as well as the Catholic Church to raise disturbing questions about human rights in Cuba. Castro's government denounced the fast but made no arrests.

(Above) A group prayer during the fast at 34 Tamarindo Street

The small town of Pedro Betancourt in Matanzas province has been a center of nonviolent resistance. Standing in this family photo, from left, are brothers Guido, Francisco and Miguel Sigler Amaya. When this photo was taken in March 2000, a fourth brother, Ariel, was in jail serving a twenty-year term. Guido was arrested in the March 2003 crackdown and condemned to twenty years. As of this writing Miguel is also in jail, with prosecutors demanding he be sentenced for up to twenty-five years. These brothers have been imprisoned for their activity in the dissident Alternative Option Movement.

Guido, Francisco and Miguel Sigler Amaya, with their mother, Gloria Amaya

HAVANA THEN AND NOW

(Above) San Rafael Street, central Havana, in the pre-Castro 1950's
(Below) Near the capitol building, Havana, 2002

"It is preferable that Cuba sink into the ocean, like Atlantis, before the corrupting forces of capitalism prevail."

> —Raul Castro, Fidel's brother and Cuba's second-
> in-command, in a speech to the nation, 1989

The role of State Security, and the Stalinesque trappings of the affair, were visible the world over. For more than a decade, Cuba's tyrant had been the darling of intellectuals throughout Europe and Latin America. Ironically, a poet who caved in to repressive tactics managed to accomplish what thousands of resistance fighters, risking and losing their lives, had failed to achieve. After the coerced confession, intellectuals from across the globe turned their wrath on the Cuban regime.

Sixty-one noted authors signed an open letter to Fidel Castro. Among the signers were longtime Castro stalwarts like Jean-Paul Sartre, Simone de Beauvoir, Mario Vargas Llosa, Susan Sontag, Alberto Moravia and Pier Paolo Pasolini. The letter, citing "prefabricated trials and witch hunts," received worldwide attention.[7] Castro, enraged, responded by calling the authors "intellectual rats" and CIA agents.

A purge on Cuban writers was unleashed, continuing for several years. Norberto Fuentes, who had authored two books on the Escambray struggle, was packed off to a work farm. While Fuentes had portrayed the guerrillas as bandits, his books also acknowledged the mountain warriors as brave men, "whom we had admired and feared, secretly."[8] Some time later, he was cleared and permitted to write a book on Ernest Hemingway's Cuban experiences.

Reinaldo Arenas, a young writer who had survived the UMAP concentration camps, was arrested in 1975 and condemned to a year's incarceration. Arenas, a homosexual who did not hide his predilections, would later claim with sarcastic humor that even when his books were suppressed, his morale was boosted, since now he had an "eager, even voracious audience: State Security."

Filmmaker Amaro Gomez got eight years in prison for clandestine writing and for owning a book by Aleksandr Solzhenitsyn. Rene Ariza and Raul Arteaga got eight years each for their clandestine writings, while Roberto Ponciano got seven.

Despite the repression, clandestine authors flourished in Cuba. Some works, like the verse of imprisoned poet Angel Cuadra or the play *Prometheus in Chains* by Tomas Fernandez Travieso, had been published in foreign lands to the wrath of the regime. Maximo Tomas, a native of Matanzas province who arrived in Miami as a young writer in 1975, recalled how a dissident movement had taken shape among intellectuals.

Maximo Tomas: "Our group created its own method of publishing. Those who worked in government offices used their paper. We stole typewriter ribbons or used clothing dye for color. After work we spent hours on an old typewriter, pecking away, making copies of

[7] *Madrid*, May 21, 1971
[8] Fuentes, *Cazabandido*, p. 31

poems or short stories or essays about the Cuban situation. These we mailed among each other to all corners of the island."

In time, these groups would become the backbone of a human rights movement.

* * *

As workers in Cuba were stalling production and writers were being jailed, strange activities were bubbling in the exile community.

Alabau Trellez, a former Cuban magistrate, had organized a small group in Miami. In September 1971, dressed in olive green with a bandage on his arm, he announced that commandos under his leadership had briefly occupied the town of Guayabal on Cuba's southern coast. Pointing to photographs, he said the group had destroyed buildings and government vehicles and had inflicted casualties on Castro's forces.

Two days later, Miami newspapers were able to show that the photo of a burning concrete mixer truck was a close-up of a store-bought toy, while the weapons in the photos were plastic replicas. Alabau Trellez became the butt of insults and jokes from a scornful exile community. A few months after the uproar, he died from illness.

Jose Elias De La Torriente, an engineer, had briefly worked with the CIA in the early sixties. Beginning in 1969, he and Guillermo Martinez Marquez, a veteran Cuban journalist, were establishing contacts with various officials throughout Latin America. By the beginning of the seventies, the Torriente organization was raising hundreds of thousands of dollars from Cuban exiles and creating an organizational structure in exile communities throughout the hemisphere.

Juan Manuel Perez-Crespo, a Cuban exile then residing in New York, worked with Martinez Marquez. Perez-Crespo: "As former president of the SIP [The Inter-American Press Society], Martinez Marquez knew a lot of people in South America and we obtained assistance from Brazil and Argentina. The basic plan was to carry out commando raids, create internal conditions for a revolt, and build a military force with equipment donated by friendly governments."

All the while, a new generation of anti-Castro militants was coming of age.

CHAPTER XIX.

THE TORCH IS PASSED

The Cuban Student Federation (FEC), starting in Florida, managed to organize chapters in universities throughout the United States, Puerto Rico and Costa Rica. This confederation of student associations published a monthly newspaper and sponsored activities including two national congresses. It varied in militancy from chapter to chapter, with activities ranging from political meetings to cultural and social events.

Parallel to FEC, the Abdala Student Movement was formed in New York. Abdala, with its name taken from a poem by Jose Marti, began as a small political study group in 1968. By 1970 it had several dozen members who took part in the political activities of the New York–New Jersey exile community. On March 13, 1971, Abdala staged a protest at the headquarters of the United Nations. Pedro Solares, then a young architecture student in New York, was among the demonstrators.

Solares: "We had petitioned the United Nations repeatedly to investigate the tortures and brutalities of Cuban political prisons, and they had ignored us. They didn't even answer our requests. We decided to carry out a protest that would bring attention to our plight. Fourteen men and two women joined tourist groups at the United Nations. When we arrived at the Security Council Chamber, we handcuffed ourselves to the furniture and demanded to see the U.N. Secretary General. We really expected for the protest to be short and for ourselves to be arrested quickly. The security force at the U.N. didn't know what to do. What we were doing had never been done before. They were hesitant to call the New York police, for the city had no jurisdiction inside the U.N. What we had expected to last minutes, stretched to hours. A few of our people were in a park across the street, distributing leaflets, and the security force was afraid they would join us, so they closed down the building, evacuating everyone. It was the first time that the U.N.

had been closed down on a working weekday. The impact was tremendous. By the time we were dragged out of the building by local police, every televison network and press agency had sent a crew to cover the incident. It became front-page news. We were thrilled that we had managed to convey a message of our struggle worldwide. The most important thing to me happened years later. A former political prisoner, who had been jailed in Cuba at the time of our protest, thanked me and told me our protest had filled him with hope that someone remembered them. That moved me deeply."[1]

This accidental PR coup made Abdala's name in the exile community. The movement tripled its membership, with chapters in Miami, Puerto Rico, Washington D.C., Chicago and Spain. A group of FEC members joined Abdala. Rolando Feria, then a young Cuban residing in New York and one of the "Abdala Sixteen," explained the tactics that developed after the protest at the U.N.

Rolando Feria: "We received letters from places we didn't even know Cuban exiles lived: San Francisco, Houston, Detroit. We organized Puerto Rico, Miami, Chicago and Washington really fast and began sending people and propaganda to other places. In the summer of '71 we held a student congress at Manhattan College in New York and more than a hundred delegates showed up. By the end of '71 we had fifteen or sixteen chapters and several hundred active members. For some time we had been such a small group that we thought we were a rarity. Suddenly, we realized that many young exiles wanted to get involved. The event at the U.N. had turned out so well, we decided to use variations of the same protest. In '71 we had more than fifty of our members arrested. It was a badge of honor, a status symbol of sorts, and every time we were arrested we made headlines and more young exiles wrote to us from different parts of the world."

During the early seventies, young pro-Castro Americans formed an organization called the Venceremos Brigade. Brigade members journeyed to Cuba and cut sugar cane in harvests; they then returned to spread pro-Castro stories in academic centers. Fittingly, this group had a part in the growth of Abdala.

Tony Garcia was an engineering student in Illinois. Garcia: "The Venceremos Brigade sponsored a 'Cuba Week' on our campus. The Cuban exile students in our university were enraged. Where political activism had been nonexistent, now fifteen or twenty of our people joined together to fight. Abdala sent a man from New York with printed information on Cuba. We debated the Venceremos Brigade on radio. We held vigils at the Student Union, where we read the names of Cubans executed by Castro. The Venceremos Brigade gave us a real enemy, close by, that we could confront."

[1] For more on Pedro Solares, see the author's *Cuba: The Unfinished Revolution*.

On May 24, 1972, Pedro Luis Boitel, the well-known Cuban political prisoner, died after a fifty-six-day hunger strike. As a university student, Boitel had fought against Batista from exile in Venezuela. Returning to Cuba in 1959, he had run against Castro's hand-picked candidate for the presidency of Cuba's powerful student federation, arguing for university autonomy from the new regime. Arrested for resistance activities, he was sentenced to forty-two years in jail.

At the Isle of Pines, El Principe and La Cabana Fortress, Boitel spearheaded protests and hunger strikes. He faced his jailers with unflinching determination, becoming a symbol of rebellion within Castro's dungeons.

Poet Jorge Valls was in prison with Boitel. Valls: "He reminded me of a character in one of André Malraux's works, a man who saw war as his individual quest. Boitel fit the anarchist mold, although he never defined himself as such. The struggle was a very personal thing for him. He fought without worrying about strategic considerations. He refused to eat. I saw him die minute by minute, week by week, and I could not do anything, just sit on my cot and pray. After a certain amount of time he was in a state of stupor, as if dozing. We asked the penal authorities to feed him intravenously, but they refused. After the body had fed on itself, it attacked the central nervous system. Boitel did not sleep; he only lay on his cot, unmoving, staring, without uttering a sound. A few hours before he died, the prison authorities took him away on a stretcher. He was a shrunken shell of bones and dried skin. His skin was the color of wax on a candle. From my neck I took a religious medal of the Sacred Heart and placed it on his pillow. He died stoically."

On receiving news of Boitel's death, Abdala's leaders gathered in a New York apartment.

Pedro Solares: "We could not allow his death to go unnoticed. We decided to take over the Statue of Liberty, which was the perfect landmark from which to tell the world about the freedom fighter. It was not to protest against the U.S. in any way.... We picked fourteen Abdala members, eleven men and three women.... The news of Boitel and what he meant to the Cuban people was reported in many newspapers and on TV."

By 1972, the organization expanded from being a student movement and opened its membership to all exiles. Abdala was by now a well-structured organization, broadcasting radio programming to Cuba, publishing a monthly newspaper, organizing conferences, and joining a new wave of armed struggle that was then taking shape.

CHAPTER XX.

RATIONS FOR CANARIES

While the Torriente Plan and Abdala organized in the exile community, Cubans on the island showed no apparent resistance.

Luciano Mora: "Sabotage continued on an individual level. Machinery was damaged, tires on government vehicles were punctured, small fires were set in warehouses. The government did not publish anything about sabotages or acts of defiance. They didn't announce executions, although the firing squads kept killing Cubans—not by the thousands, as had happened a decade earlier, but executions continued. I know of three people who were executed in 1972. Media censorship gave a false sense of stability. Every Cuban knew about the scores of political prisons on the island: La Cabana, TacoTaco, Kilo Siete, Boniato, San Severino, Guanajay. Yet nothing was heard about political prisons, and no one knew how many thousands were jailed."

Andres Cuevas: "Ironically, the best saboteur in Cuba was the government itself. A worker could damage a piece of machinery; but the government was so incompetent, it did more damage than any clandestine group could. When an epidemic killed half a million pigs, the media blamed it on CIA chemical warfare. Most of us realized that it was actually a problem created by health mismanagement among agricultural planners. One of the stories we heard was that Fidel had ordered all rice fields in Camaguey equipped with huge lights, like the ones used in baseball fields. His idea was that since light makes rice grow, twenty-four hours of light would make rice grow faster. It didn't. What it did do was to burn all the crops."

Luciano Mora: "Repression was tremendous. It is difficult to explain the psychological manipulation, the power unleashed on the people. Television programs dealt with the efficiency of State Security. There were soap operas whose heroes were State Security agents infiltrating counter-revolutionary groups. Castro's opponents were portrayed as sadistic psychopaths, homosexuals and criminals. Radio programs constantly reinforced Castro's dictum that within the revolution everything was possible, while outside the revolution nothing was possible. Meetings in the workplace drove home the idea that employees who did not follow the 'correct' political path could find themselves fired, jailed, or in other serious trouble. This constant hammering on the senses crushed many. And then of course one had the struggle of daily living: standing in line for hours with ration cards to obtain a shirt, a pound of beans, a bit of meat. People had to spend hours working and more hours scrounging with a ration card or trying to buy something in the black market. It was crushing to the spirit."

Gilberto Canto, a translator at Cuba Tobacco, was arrested in the resort town of Soroa, some forty miles from Havana, after having a conversation with a European tourist. State Security never questioned the foreigner, but Canto spent thirty-two days in jail and was placed under probation for five years.

Gilberto Canto: "It was incredible. All I said to the man was that in Cuba, a large producer of tobacco products in the world market, cigarettes were rationed—and I did not even mention some of the more outrageous levels of rationing. One of my neighbors, who owned a canary, was forced to obtain a ration card for the bird. He was told that in order for him to buy birdseed, the canary should have a ration card. It might sound funny but it was true. When I was taken to court at Pinar del Rio, I saw the trial of a young man who had been attempting to buy a small outboard motor in the black market. To State Security, that indicated he was attempting to prepare a boat to flee into exile. For the crime of seeking an outboard motor, the prosecution requested a three-year sentence."

The general desperation was reflected in the methods by which people attempted to flee the island. Improvised rafts, rowboats and flotation devices of all kinds were used in efforts to escape. One group used a trailer-truck to ram its way past army roadblocks and enter the U.S. naval station at Guantanamo under a hail of gunfire. Others swam Guantanamo Bay at night, hoping they would not meet Castro's gunboats or hungry sharks.

A young man named Socarras Ramirez resorted to a most improbable expedient. Hiding with a friend in the landing-gear compartment of an Iberia airliner headed for Spain, he suffered hours of hypothermia while the plane cruised toward Europe at 30,000 feet. His friend perished; but Ramirez, almost frozen to death, managed to survive the journey.[1]

---

[1] Socarras's journey is noted in the *Guinness Book of Records*.

* * *

The Cuban government gave out little information about its penal system, and small wonder. Officials, it seems, did not want to invite the inevitable comparisons between Castro's jails and those of Stalin or Hitler.

Prisoners were mistreated, tortured and killed. At Manacas Prison, Lieutenant Abraham Claro ordered his troops to fire on unarmed prisoners. Oriol Acosta, a political prisoner, died on that August day of 1971.[2] A number of prisoners, including Carmelo Cuadra, Enrique Garcia Cuevas and Reinaldo Cordero, died in hunger strikes during the early seventies. Others, like Ibrahim Torres, Esteban Ramos Kessel and Jose Castillo, died of illnesses caused by malnutrition and lack of medical attention.

Torture techniques were applied to prisoners in the spirit of experimenting with laboratory animals. The regime was looking for ways to break the rebellious will of political prisoners.

Renan Llanes was a *plantado* serving a lengthy term for having helped supply the Escambray guerrillas. Llanes: "They devised a torture method and tried it out on certain men and if they cracked, then more would go through it. This was a war of wills. When a political prisoner was subjected to torture, he knew it involved not just himself but all of us. If he could resist, then they would give up using that method, or they would use it infrequently."

Prisoners were locked in solitary confinement for months, in sealed rooms without light or sanitary facilities. They slept in their own excrement and urine, on stone floors, without blankets. Dressed only in their underwear, they suffered from heat during the day and cold at night. They were denied medical assistance and were constantly harassed by prison guards. Some of the prison cells were built with low ceilings so men could not stand up erect, and were forced to spend months kneeling or crouching. Other units were so small that men could not stretch out on the floor to sleep. When their time in solitary was over, prisoners emerged from darkened cells looking like wounded animals.

Ramon Ramos: "As a guerrilla I have been in many firefights and I have seen men die. I know fear and I have felt it many times. Almost anyone who tells you he has never felt fear in battle is a liar, or just crazy. Yet in political prison we had many men, particularly those in rebellion, for whom fear had disappeared. The conditions, the lifestyle, the harassment, interrogations, tortures, bad food and disease made men forget fear. Death meant rest. I once told an interrogator he could put me in front of a firing squad because

---

[2] Carreno, *Cincuenta testimonios urgentes,* pp. 65–66

I didn't care if he killed me. They never interrogated me after that. I think they figured I had reached the breaking point and gone beyond it. I really did not care at that moment if they killed me or not."

Roberto Martin Perez: "I have seen men come out of punishment looking pale as ghosts, and so thin you could see the bones in their faces. Beards covered their faces and their long hair, down to their shoulders, was crusted with excrement and filth. Some were so weak they had to be carried out on stretchers; and still they held firm. Many of us cried when we saw them in such a condition; and still we felt proud. Castro could kill us but we did not bend to his will."

CHAPTER XXI.

GUERRILLAS IN EXILE

On a clear afternoon of April 1972, twenty-seven-year-old Juan Felipe De La Cruz arrived in Montreal with a suitcase full of plastic explosives. A radio announcer and community figure in the Miami area, he had fought as a teenager in the DRE's underground force. The day after reaching Montreal, De La Cruz placed an explosive charge on the roof of the Cuban Commerce Affairs building. The explosion of April 4 killed Cuban diplomat Sergio Lopez. Shrapnel wounded seven other members of the Cuban diplomatic corps.

This attack marked the beginning of a more extreme approach on the part of Cuban exiles. Such tactics were not entirely new. Eight years earlier, Canada had seen an attack on the *Maria Teresa,* a Cuban cargo freighter. A few weeks later, Julio Perez and brothers Guillermo and Ignacio Novo were arrested in New York, accused of aiming a bazooka at Che Guevara, who had arrived to speak on Castro's behalf at a U.N. meeting.

Veterans of the fight were feeling bitter frustration. Humberto Lopez had served in the anti-Castro resistance, in the U.S. Army and in CIA-sponsored commando raids to Cuba.

Humberto Lopez: "The Americans had trained us in the use of explosives, navigation, weapons; then one fine day they decided they no longer needed us, and closed down our operation. The things we had done in 1963, with the approval of the CIA, were now considered crimes."

Ramon Saul Sanchez was a teenager who participated in paramilitary operations while barely out of high school. Sanchez: "For years the exiles had been trained and helped by the U.S. government. Suddenly, without our having any say, our destinies had been sealed by the superpowers. Could we turn off our feelings as one turns off a spigot? No, of course not. Would George Washington have quit if the French had denied him support in the war against Britain? No, of course not."[1]

At the beginning of the seventies, independent operations launched against Castro had led U.S. officials to crack down on exile activities, confiscating materials and prosecuting some of the same men they had trained and sponsored a few years before. Exile leaders Orlando Bosch, Ramiro De La Fe and Guillermo Novo were doing time in federal penitentiaries. Felipe Rivero was on parole, and Andres Nazario Sargen of Alpha 66 faced charges of illegally possessing automatic weapons and explosives. (These charges were later dropped.)

Exiles' anguish over the thousands killed or suffering in Castro's dungeons was now compounded by bitterness against indifference and active prosecution on the part of the U.S. government. The few remaining exile groups were severely limited in their resources. Without help from any sovereign power, they raised funds through raffles, membership dues and social dances. The pittances they managed to gather went to buy weapons and boats; but U.S. authorities confiscated many of those before they could be put to use against Castro. The price of conventional war had become prohibitive. A single commando operation would cost perhaps fifty thousand dollars, would put at risk the lives of fifteen men, and would involve the use of weapons and boats that were likely to be seized by the U.S. before they could be put into action. On the other hand, a Cuban government office could be demolished with little advance planning, a far smaller risk of detection, expenses of well under ten thousand dollars and just two or three operatives.

These circumstances led various anti-Castro organizations to channel their efforts into what they called a "War on the Roads of the World"—a commitment to strike when they could, as they could. One of those who pioneered the concept of attacking Cuban government targets beyond the borders of the island was Miguel San Pedro, an exiled lawyer who belonged to the Cuban Nationalist Movement or MNC. Led by Bay of Pigs veteran Felipe Rivero, the MNC was not a large group by comparison to the MRR, the MRP or the 30th of November Movement in earlier years; but what it lacked in numbers, it compensated with an aggressive strategy.

Many observers would paint MNC's and similar activities as "terrorism." Another possible term would be the one that Castro's regime had virtually made into a trademark for itself. With equal justice, one could say that Castro's enemies were now waging a guerrilla war from exile.

---

[1] The full texts of interviews with Humberto Lopez and Ramon Saul Sanchez are given in the author's *Cuba: The Unfinished Revolution*.

*   *   *

In exile, one could find political agitprop groups like Abdala, the Brigade 2506 Association and the Cuban Nationalist Movement. Such groups worked in information campaigns, fundraising, lobbying, publishing and community affairs. These organizations had their hidden counterparts, with key men and women from the public groups working at a secret, military level. Clandestine organizations included the National Front of Cuban Liberation (FLNC), Omega Seven, Cuban Secret Government, Cuban Action, and others geared to carry out commando or paramilitary strikes.

Abdala, with its hundreds of activists on college campuses, represented a vital force in the exile community. Some of its members were veterans of resistance activities on the island, which they had joined as teenagers. Other Abdala members, like Cesar Sanchez and Leonardo Viota, had served as U.S. soldiers in Vietnam. Abdala's large membership generated funds to support clandestine operations.

In 1972, Abdala leaders met secretly at Hallandale Beach, Florida, with Brigade 2506 veterans and a few former CIA commandos. From this meeting the National Front of Cuban Liberation, or FLNC, was born. A joint command was set up, with Abdala providing financial and logistic support as well as young men and women to take part in the missions. Parallel to the birth of the FLNC, Orlando Bosch, having been released from a federal penitentiary in Atlanta, gathered a group of veterans and created Accion Cubana (Cuban Action). The Cuban Nationalist Movement (MNC) came to life with the release of Guillermo and Ignacio Novo from federal prisons.

In the same month as the bombing in Montreal, another bomb rocked the offices of the Cuban embassy in Paris and an incendiary device in New York damaged the car of Ricardo Alarcon, Cuba's delegate to the United Nations. In October 1972, naval commandos of the FLNC sank two Cuban vessels near the northern shores of the island. Before the end of the year, more bombs exploded in New York, Montreal and Miami, at offices of businesses that shipped packages to Cuba. On January 28, 1973, FLNC commandos destroyed a Cuban vessel. Before summer 1973, eleven more targets had been struck, including Cuban government travel offices, Cuban diplomatic vehicles and freight companies that did business with Cuba.

In the summer of 1973, Juan Felipe De La Cruz traveled to Spain and crossed the border to France, carrying a load of plastic explosives in a suitcase. His mission was to assassinate Ramiro Valdes, a leading Castro enforcer who was on an official trip to France. On August 3, 1973, having lodged in a hotel in Avrainville, near Paris, De La Cruz was preparing a bomb for the attempt when the device exploded in his hands. More than two thousand Cubans marched behind the coffin carrying his remains to a Miami cemetery.

On October 3, 1973, FLNC commandos at sea north of Cuba attacked a factory ship and a fishing vessel of the Cuban fleet. Juan Robles (nom de guerre), a veteran of U.S. forces in Vietnam, was one of the commandos in the raid. "About sixteen of us boarded two rafts, leaving just a couple of men on the mother ship. I grabbed a rope in my left hand, holding a shotgun in my right. No one talked as we moved through the water toward the vessels. As the ship loomed near, we heard explosions and saw flashes of gunfire. We fired back. Boarding the ship was tough. We went up a nylon rope jammed against each other. On deck I stepped over a body. Later I found out it had been the political commissar of the factory ship. We dumped the body overboard and set the ship on fire. The captured crew was placed on a small island near the Bahamas, where they could be rescued. We sank the fishing vessel with a couple of rounds from our recoilless rifle."[2]

* * *

Even as the FLNC and others were under investigation by the FBI and Florida law enforcement units, the U.S. government, strangely enough, had sponsored an armed action by another exile group. At the end of 1971, with weapons and logistical support from U.S. officials, the Torriente organization attacked the northern coast of Oriente province. Juan Luis Cosculluela, a veteran of the Bay of Pigs and CIA naval operations, was in the raid.

Cosculluela: "We had Thompson submachine guns, some Belgian FN assault rifles and 4.2 millimeter French mortars. I was in the naval end of the operation. We dropped off eighteen commandos in two boats and they entered Sama, to attack a border guard outpost. They met stiff resistance and could not take the position. They did take the port area, and then retreated before morning under intense enemy fire. They killed three men: the guards' commanding officer, a militiaman and a man from State Security. Sadly, three civilians were wounded and a little girl from the village lost a foot. This happened while our men were retreating. One of the mortar shells fell short and hit a home in the village. It was a bitter accident of war. When we returned, we were reprimanded, and we were informed that no further military activities would be permitted by the FBI."

By 1972, as more militant groups gained prominence, the once-popular Torriente group was withering away. Torriente himself was accused of diverting political funds to his personal construction business, and many Miami Cubans withdrew their support.

---

[2] For more on this matter, see the author's *Cuba: The Unfinished Revolution.*

Juan Manuel Perez-Crespo: "What people failed to understand was that the real estate development was a front. The men in the commando units were paid salaries through the construction firm, to feed their families. The problem once more was with the U.S. government. Kissinger [Henry A. Kissinger, President Nixon's advisor for national security] intervened with Latin American governments and all doors closed against us. Even the hundreds of weapons we had stashed in Nicaragua were lost. It was all over for the Torriente group after that."

Torriente's organization was disbanded in 1973—and its leader killed by a sniper at his home in Coral Gables, Florida, on April 12, 1974. The murder was said to be the work of Cubans who blamed Torriente for having been a tool of U.S. political manipulations.

* * *

During 1973 and 1974 the FBI conducted investigations of exile activities. Jorge Chappi was in Abdala and the FLNC.

Chappi: "Years later an FBI agent admitted to us that the agency had been unable to infiltrate Abdala. It was due to our structure. We were a public group, composed mostly of students but very difficult to penetrate. Many of us had arrived in the U.S. as children or just out of our teens. We recruited among relatives, high-school and college friends, and people we had known from the resistance in Cuba. We checked up on anyone who had come from out of the blue wanting to join; and not everyone in Abdala was in the FLNC. Everyone helped indirectly with funding, but many didn't know about the secret structure. Anyone could join Abdala, but if we didn't know him, if he was not related, if we tried to look into him and came up with sketchy information, we placed him in a position where he could not damage us."

In January and February of 1974 the FLNC bombed the Cuban embassy in Mexico City, while Cuban Action sent letter bombs to Cuban diplomats in Lima, Madrid, Buenos Aires and Ottawa. Three embassy personnel were wounded.

Humberto Lopez—the former commando, resistance fighter and instructor in the MRR camps in Central America—had joined the FLNC. Luis Crespo, a former U.S. Army soldier and crewman of the CIA naval units, was another member of the secret organization. On March 22, 1974, they met at the house of Alfredo Sayuz, another FLNC member, to prepare a bomb in the garage.

Humberto Lopez: "In my hands I held the security system while Luis placed the batteries. It was then that a short circuit triggered the detonator. I felt my body being hurled backward. For a few seconds everything was black. The side of my face, the left side, felt heavy, as if a weight were pressing against it. Someone took me by the hand and I was moved inside the house. A woman screamed. I sat on the floor. I saw that three fingers of my left hand had been destroyed, the skin blistered like cooked sausages, the white bones showing. I didn't know it yet, but part of the left side of my face had been ripped away. My left eye was dangling out of its socket, staring at the floor. Luis was brought in. His body was covered with black soot. His face was slashed open. I could see teeth and gums right through his cheek. Half of his right arm was gone; all that remained was a bloody stump starting at the elbow. Luis was hallucinating. He said to me: 'If I die, you must continue the struggle.' He said this twice.... We woke up in a hospital chained to our beds, facing a maximum of 102 years in prison. A lot of pressure was put on me to turn informant, but I refused."

Luis Crespo: "When they tried to force us to become informants, we both told the authorities we would rather spend the rest of our lives in jail, among common criminals, than testify against a single exile fighting for Cuba's freedom."

Lopez and Crespo served time in U.S. federal prisons as the FLNC continued operating. Two days after the Miami accident, an FLNC team placed a dynamite charge in the Cuban Airlines offices in Mexico City. The front of the building was demolished. Next day an explosion rocked the Cuban embassy in Kingston, Jamaica. Less than two weeks after that, an FLNC team set off a charge in the Cuban embassy in Madrid, destroying an entire floor. The FBI and local law enforcement agencies assigned dozens of agents to investigate anti-Castro groups in the United States.

The U.S.-Cuban alliance against Castro, never very effective and often quite bitter, had decisively collapsed.

CHAPTER XXII.

RULE BY FEAR

By the mid-seventies, resistance on the island had withered to insignificant levels.

Aramis Coego was a high-school student in Havana. Coego: "The system seemed so solid, unchangeable. We lived in a hermetically sealed society apart from the rest of the world. Rock music was considered subversive. Students with long hair were arrested and given forced haircuts. Misery was our common denominator and the only ones living well were those in the very upper levels of the power structure. Cuba was sending troops to Africa and the government asked for volunteers to fight in Angola. Some volunteered because they were bored and wanted to leave Cuba, at least for a while. Others refused, and many were jailed. I remember a televised trial of a young soldier who refused to go to Angola. He was executed. At first they executed a few, but then it seemed the resisters were so numerous they started putting them in military prisons."

On April 15, 1975, six young Cubans launched a guerrilla uprising in the Rio Frio area of Las Villas province. The organizer was Manuel Morales, the son of a former Escambray guerrilla. At age seventeen, Morales had been drafted into the Youth Labor Army (EJT), units of young people sent to help harvest crops.

Manuel Morales: "We started by doing small sabotages. We stole paint and wrote signs that said 'Down with Fidel.' It drove the authorities crazy. Young people were against the system. The eagle was said to be a symbol of freedom, and I saw young men tattooing huge eagles on their backs. Others refused to work or wear uniforms, and they were arrested. We decided to start a guerrilla unit, but we only had a few weapons, some hunting rifles and a .45 caliber pistol. We went to the hills. First we destroyed an observation tower and were pursued by many troops. We spent a week being chased. Twice they surrounded us. The first time, we broke through the ring and escaped. The second time, they caught us in a tight trap between four hills. I was kicked around, and Rene Diaz Almeida was badly beaten by State Security. All six of us were sentenced to twenty years in prison."

Roberto Martin Perez, then serving time in prison, encountered another group of young rebels. Martin Perez: "In the mid-seventies State Security arrested a group of young students and workers from Oriente province, accusing them of clandestine organizing. Their weapons had been improvised. They used candles and matches, rags soaked in fluid and ignited; they attacked rubber tires with nails and boards. Even without much equipment they did a lot of damage. The leader was a mulatto named Diego Aroche, about nineteen or twenty. He was executed by a firing squad."

Although the government seldom published details of trials or executions, a few facts indicate the extent of rebellion among young Cubans. In 1973 the government announced that sixteen-year-olds would be treated as adults and severely punished for "crimes against the national economy." Twenty reformatories were filled with young Cubans, many accused of political crimes.[1]

Aramis Coego: "Organized conspiracy was almost impossible. It wasn't a society where you walked into a gun shop and bought a pistol. The few cars up for sale were outrageously priced. A Cuban worker made less than two hundred pesos a month and an old vehicle could cost fifteen thousand or more. One couldn't hide anywhere, for the neighborhood spy groups, the CDR, reported everything to State Security. Phone lines were tapped. For years, the television, radio, teachers in school, commissars in the army, political teachers at the workplace had been telling us, 'No one gets away, we know everything.' And a lot of people were very scared. The government had used the firing wall as a psychological weapon. In sixteen years they had murdered thousands. I have no idea how many; but every Cuban knew the firing wall was there, and if they wanted, if they felt you were dangerous, they would kill you without remorse. They ground that fear into many. It was rule by fear."

* * *

In Cuba's political prisons, the flame of rebellion still burned brightly. Despite torture and murder, hundreds of prisoners still wore their tattered underclothes in punishment cells, refusing rehabilitation.

Laureano Valdez, a *plantado* at Boniato prison, suffered from a gum infection and

---

[1] American University, Foreign Area Studies, *Cuba: A Country Study*, p. 448

decaying teeth due to lack of dental care. Having been denied medical treatment unless he accepted rehabilitation, he tried to extract two rotting teeth with a sharpened spoon. The pain was so intense that Valdez screamed and banged his head against the metal door of his cell.

More than eighty *plantados* threatened to launch a hunger strike unless the penal authorities gave treatment to Valdez. Instead of providing medical assistance, the warden ordered squads of armed guards positioned around the building. At an order, soldiers fired AK-47 assault rifles at the barred windows.

Roberto Martin Perez: "Bullets came in, ricocheting off walls and metal doors. Some of us managed to bust open our doors and make it to the hallway. We grabbed stones, pieces of furniture, anything we could to defend ourselves. A guard appeared at the end of the hallway, firing at us. I was pushed and fell into an open cell. I felt a pain in my crotch and realized a bullet had destroyed one of my testicles. Gerardo Gonzalez, a religious man we called 'The Brother of Faith,' was in the hallway, his face and chest crushed by bullets. He made gurgling sounds and died."

Sixteen other prisoners lay wounded.

Just as the shooting ended, guards entered the prison wing with clubs and beat the unarmed prisoners. Some, unconscious, were dragged out to the courtyard by their feet, their nearly naked bodies dragged over shards of broken glass, their heads bouncing on the concrete steps of a stairwell.[2]

Roberto Martin Perez: "We were taken to the military hospital in Santiago—about twenty of us, dressed only in our underwear, covered with blood. A military doctor, Colonel Granados, came out, looked at us and said, 'I don't take care of *plantados*. Anyone who wants medical treatment has to wear the uniform of the rehabilitated prisoner.' Were we supposed to rehabilitate after being shot? We went back to Boniato as we were. I cured my testicle wound by cauterizing it with a hot spoon."

[2] Interview with Roberto Martin Perez, Miami, 1992

CHAPTER XXIII.

TRAGEDY AND REBIRTH

Abdala broke with FLNC at the end of 1974, citing strategic differences over control of the FLNC power structure. Abdala's leadership also asserted that the attacks outside Cuba were not making any impact inside.

Meanwhile, Orlando Bosch had brought various groups to a meeting in the Dominican Republic and founded the Coordinated United Revolutionary Organizations (CORU). In a series of quick strikes, CORU—targeting commercial offices of nations trading with Cuba—carried out bombings in Venezuela, the United States, Puerto Rico, Jamaica, Argentina and Mexico. In August 1976, CORU commandos kidnapped and killed two Cuban diplomats in Buenos Aires.

In another incident, apparently the work of another group, the Soviet merchant vessel *Ivan Shepetkov* was bombed while at anchor in Elizabeth, New Jersey.

Meanwhile, tempers flared in the exile community. A few days after the shooting of Jose Elias De La Torriente in Miami, a former member of Cuban Power, Arturo Rodriguez Vives, was killed in his Manhattan apartment. Four months later, in August 1974, Hector Diaz Limonta, a former Brigade 2506 member, was found strangled in his Union City, New Jersey, apartment. Luciano Nieves, a vociferous exile who had begun advocating a dialogue with the Cuban government, was gunned down in the parking lot of a Miami hospital. Ramon Donestevez, a yacht builder who had spoken out in favor of negotiating with Castro, was killed by a shot to the head in his Miami office. Radio commentator Emilio Millian had both his legs destroyed by a car bomb.

Rolando Masferrer was a controversial figure among the exiles. A communist in his early years and a veteran of the Spanish Civil War, Masferrer had been a senator in Cuba and, in the 1950's, had commanded a private army. An expert shot and persuasive speaker, he was a tough man with a nasty reputation and numerous enemies. Masferrer was killed by a car bomb in front of his Miami home.

The internecine violence made for deep divisions in the exile community, as many regretted to see that the struggle for Cuba had turned to blind rage. Though many exiles sympathized with the bombings of Cuban embassies, they abhorred the violence within their own community.

In the early 1960's Rolando Otero had been a hero, a veteran paratrooper of Brigade 2506 at the Bay of Pigs and a commando in several raids on Cuban shores. By 1975, Otero had gone over the edge. He was arrested on charges of bombing FBI offices, police stations and Miami International Airport.

The former hero went to prison, escaped, got involved in drug trafficking and was re-arrested. Released from prison in 1990, he again made headlines when he kidnapped and threatened his former lawyer. Taking flight one more time, he became the epitome of a man traumatized by history.

*   *   *

More than fifty bombings occurred in Miami during the mid-seventies, most aimed at businesses that mailed packages to Cuba. Publicly, the exile groups argued that Fidel Castro's government was raking in millions of dollars from the package trade. The FBI intensified its campaign against the exile groups, deploying scores of agents; but arrests were infrequent, and the secret armies kept pounding away at their targets.

In August 1976, former Chilean minister Orlando Letelier and a companion died when a bomb destroyed their vehicle on a Washington D.C. street. Letelier had served in the government of Chile's socialist president Salvador Allende. His death unleashed one of the largest criminal investigations in U.S. history. Federal prosecutors believed Cuban exiles had taken part in the murder. The prosecution built its case around testimony by Michael Townley, a lanky American who had worked as an electronics and explosives expert for Chile's intelligence services.

Townley claimed to have prepared the fatal bomb. He accused members of the Cuban Nationalist Movement (MNC) of having carried out the assassination in conjunction with DINA, the Chilean intelligence branch. Townley specifically named Guillermo and Ignacio Novo, Jose Dionisio Suarez, Virgilio Paz, Alvin Ross and several other MNC members. Apparently, Chilean intelligence services had ensnared the MNC in its plot and then hung the movement out to dry.

U.S. prosecutors called some two hundred Cuban exiles as witnesses before the grand jury. They placed Suarez under questioning and offered him immunity from self-incrimination. Under this offer, Suarez could not legally refuse to testify. If he did refuse, he could be incarcerated for contempt of court. Suarez was faced with the choice of informing on his fellow conspirators or losing his freedom indefinitely.

Jose Dionisio Suarez, an intense man in his early forties, was no pushover. In the resistance against Batista, he had made lieutenant while still a teenager and had twice been wounded in battle. He had then been among the three dozen Rebel Army officers arrested with Huber Matos. After a short spell as a political prisoner, he had escaped to the United States and become a squad leader in Brigade 2506. He had then taken part in several commando raids on Cuba.

Suarez refused to testify before the grand jury and was jailed in a federal penitentiary, where he served more than one year before his release pending trial. As the trial approached, he vanished. In 1990 he was rearrested in Tampa, where he had found work as a house painter, and sentenced to twelve years.

Virgilio Paz, a young member of the MNC, also vanished until his 1991 arrest in West Palm Beach, where he owned a landscaping business. Paz got a long prison term. Guillermo and Ignacio Novo, as well as Alvin Ross, were in jail for almost two years until they were acquitted in second trials. By the end of the seventies the MNC had lost its entire leadership to jail or to underground life in the United States.

✳   ✳   ✳

Grand juries of the late 1970's and early 1980's destroyed several other exile groups. Numerous Cubans including Pedro Remon, Roberto Infante, Andres Garcia and Ramon Saul Sanchez were incarcerated for possessing explosives or refusing to testify. The OPLC (Organization for the Liberation of Cuba), a movement of young Cubans led by Sanchez, was fractured by U.S. federal authorities when several of its key members were jailed for refusing to speak before grand juries.

Ramon Saul Sanchez was a tall, energetic youth who had been a commando while still in high school. Sanchez: "I knew I would be asked by the grand jury about a failed attempt on the life of Fidel Castro when he visited the U.N. in 1979. I found it hypocritical that the U.S. government would try to prosecute me when this same government, by its own admission, had attempted to eliminate Castro on two dozen occasions. For refusing to testify, I served eighteen months in jail. Later, still refusing, I was condemned to nine years' imprisonment.... In protest I went on a hunger strike. I was placed in a punishment cell, without a blanket or a cot. The cell was like a meat freezer. My nose and mouth were bleeding from the cold. I was dressed only in my underwear. I served four and a half years in U.S. prisons, among criminals; and I received treatment worthy of a Castro dungeon, not a U.S. penitentiary."

✳   ✳   ✳

No event in the exiles' war gained more newsprint or stirred more controversy than the bombing of a Cuban airliner in Barbados on October 6, 1976, which killed seventy-three people.

Passengers on the Havana-bound plane had included military officers, diplomats and a fencing team. The impact on all Cubans was shattering. Not even the hardiest anti-Castro warriors favored the destruction of a civilian airliner in mid-flight.

Andres Cuevas: "I was in Cuba fighting against the system. I was among those who were happy when an embassy was bombed or a commando raid reached Cuban shores; but the Barbados bombing stunned me. I went to the Plaza of the Revolution and I saw a nation crying. It was a senseless act—and Castro's government milked it for political purposes. Within days, there were posters everywhere with the photos of those killed."

Eight days later, Venezuelan authorities arrested Orlando Bosch, Luis Posada Carriles and two Venezuelan nationals, charging them with the crime. Posada Carriles, an explosives and electronics expert, was a veteran of CIA covert operations and commando raids in Cuba. For a decade he had worked in Venezuelan intelligence, leading an anti-terrorist unit against Marxist groups accused of kidnappings and assassinations.[1]

Never convicted of the Barbados bombing, the two men remained jailed in Venezuela, presumably due to pressure from the U.S. and Cuban governments. Tried twice for the same crime, acquitted by civilian and military courts, Bosch served more than eleven years. On his release he traveled to the United States, where federal authorities kept him incarcerated for two more years while trying to deport him to a third country. Posada Carriles, after being acquitted and not released, escaped from a Venezuelan prison and made his way to Central America, where he resurfaced as an intelligence officer during the Iran-Contra affair.

To this day, the crime remains unsolved. The Castro government has fingered Bosch, Posada Carriles and their allies, while the exiles have pointed to evidence that the plot was a trap set by Cuban DGI (intelligence) and Venezuelan officials to smear the anti-Castro opposition.

A key player in the event was Ricardo (Monkey) Morales, who had been a resistance

[1] Posada Carriles, *Los caminos del guerrero*

fighter, a CIA-trained commando, a veteran of the "Wild Geese" Congo force and a police informant in Miami. In 1968 he had delivered Orlando Bosch to federal authorities for firing a recoilless rifle at a Polish ship en route to Cuba. Bosch served a four-year prison term in Atlanta, while Monkey Morales continued working as an informant, surviving a car bomb that nearly ended his life on a Miami street.

By 1976 Bosch was living in Caracas, where, under the name of Carlos Sucre, he carried Venezuelan intelligence identification that allowed him to own weapons.[2] He and Posada Carriles had established a network that reached from Miami's Little Havana to the exile community in Caracas, which was their base for launching attacks against Cuban government properties.

To the surprise of both men, Monkey Morales showed up in Caracas. The former Congo mercenary had been hired by DISIP—Venezuela's intelligence service—and given a big job in counterintelligence.

Luis Posada Carriles: "Morales was not a Venezuelan citizen, which he needed to be in order to hold a high-ranking post in DISIP. Within three months he was granted citizenship by ministerial request, despite regulations that mandate at least two years' residence...."

Monkey Morales traveled to Mexico. According to his own later testimony, he met there with Cuban DGI agents who provided him with $18,000 and outlined a plan to blow up a Cuban airliner—a bombing for which Orlando Bosch would be blamed.[3]

Back in Caracas, Morales met several times with Cuban DGI officers Cuenca Montoto and Eduardo Fuentes.[4] On October 2, 1976, Morales met with Cuenca Montoto and an executive of Cubana Airlines named Lazaro Otero at the Anauca Hilton.[5] Morales asked Venezuelan photographer Hernan Ricardo, an associate of Bosch, to ride the plane from Venezuela to Barbados and photograph North Korean diplomats going to Cuba. Ricardo took a backup photographer, a young man named Freddie Lugo.

After doing their work, the two photographers debarked in Barbados. The plane left for Cuba and exploded over the ocean. Hours later, thanks to an anonymous tip, Ricardo and Lugo were arrested as suspects in the bombing. Ricardo had been traveling with a fake passport provided by DISIP and would be convicted by a Venezuelan court for using false documents issued by that court's own government.[6]

[2] Ibid., p. 258
[3] Ibid., p. 214
[4] Ibid., p. 215
[5] Ibid., p. 216
[6] Ibid., p. 261

Orlando Bosch: "We were arrested and bounced around the system like Ping-Pong balls—from civilian courts to military courts to officials who threatened our extradition to Cuba, where we would face a firing squad. We had many threats on our lives; and we were acquitted only to face new trials."

Monkey Morales left Venezuela and returned to Miami, where he became an enforcer and messenger in the drug business. Arrested in a drug raid, he turned witness for the prosecution. In his Miami trial, Morales declared under oath that he had been involved in the Barbados bombing and had set up Bosch and Posada Carriles; but Venezuelan authorities refused to allow Bosch and Posada to use transcripts of that testimony in their own defense.[7]

Luis Posada Carriles: "Not only was Morales's testimony in the Miami trial not allowed, key witnesses from the Barbados Airport were not made available to the defense. Bosch and I were interrogated without legal representation. Documents by an explosives expert named Eric Newton were not made available to us. Our own attorneys were arrested and harassed with contempt-of-court charges."

In 1991, Osmeiro Carneiro, a high-ranking officer in Venezuelan military intelligence, accused two fellow Venezuelans of planning the crime: Orlando Garcia, former chief of presidential security, and police officer Lazaro Rogelio Ugarte. Carneiro claimed that Garcia and Ugarte had set up the Cuban exiles.[8]

The Barbados bombing put an end to exile violence, for the tragedy had discredited any tactic that remotely resembled it. Meanwhile, a surprising new phase of the anti-Castro war was in embryo.

[7] Ibid., p. 272
[8] *El Nuevo Herald*, July 15, 1991

CHAPTER XXIV.

FROM WORMS TO BUTTERFLIES

Even with the collapse of resistance in Cuba, Castro's regime faced dire problems.

Mario Perez was an official in the Ministry of Industries. Perez: "Sugar and tobacco crops had been damaged by plagues. Raw materials for industry were scarce. Incentives consisted of medals or diplomas. Workers were not motivated and did not produce. Prostitution was being used for barter. Alcoholism was a huge problem. Suicide levels were high. Cuba was a terrible place to live—an island of paradoxes. We had a huge fishing fleet, but we did not eat lobster or shrimp, since those products were for export. We produced the best cigars in the world, but tobacco products were rationed. We ended illiteracy and almost every Cuban could read, but we had many forbidden books and authors. Independent thought was censored. Families were divided, thousands of political prisoners rotted in jail, and the revolution had turned to garbage."

The Cuban government decided to open up Cuba's borders to exiles wishing to visit relatives inside the island, thereby promoting a tourism that could bring hundreds of millions of dollars to the rescue of a gutted economy. Such tourism, however, could not be promoted without political justification. For nearly two decades, Castro and his followers had labelled the exiles *gusanos* or "worms." Now, DGI (Cuban intelligence) agents were holding meetings with willing exiles as preparation for a "Dialogue" between the regime and "the community," as Castro started calling the exiles.

"Commitee of 75" was the name given to the group of exiles who attended a Havana conference with Castro. The group included some apparent DGI agents fronting tiny pro-Castro organizations in Miami; exiles involved in travel agencies hoping to gain profits; some relatives of political prisoners; and community activists who sought freedom for those prisoners. Appearing in a televised spectacle with the group, Castro promised he would allow the exiles to visit Cuba, and he pledged to release political detainees.

The prisoner release was beneficial to Castro. Many resistance and guerrilla fighters jailed in the early sixties were close to finishing their sentences. The Cuban government now preferred to export those prisoners rather than keep them on the island, where they might create new problems.

Castro evidently hoped the Dialogue would split the exile community. Some exile leaders could be counted on to make accusations against those who traveled to Cuba, while others would defend their right to go back and see relatives. Such controversies would be likely to erode support for the militant exile groups.

Roberto Martin Perez: "That was not a dialogue but a monologue. Political prisoners could see it as a maneuver. It was not a negotiation between Castro and the exiles. It was strictly a survival maneuver."

On October 10, 1978, a letter signed by 138 political prisoners in Cuba reached the exile community. It condemned the Dialogue and stated: "No individual or group from the Cuban exile community is authorized by us to make arrangements with the Castro government on our behalf."[1] One of the signers was Luis Zuniga, a young *plantado*.

Zuniga: "We did not want to be used. If Castro released a few hundred or a few thousand prisoners, so what? If he allowed people to visit relatives, so what? Did he expect us to forgive the thousands of executions, the violations of human rights, the repression and misery to which our nation was being subjected? State Security was still there. The prisons were still there. Repression still existed and human rights violations occurred every minute. If Castro wanted to free us, all he had to do was to open up the prison gates, not pretend to make peace with his enemies. We did not accept being used in a PR game."

* * *

Many exile organizations accused the "Committee of 75" of being traitors and Castro stooges. As passions flared, violence resurged; Dialogue proponents in Puerto Rico and New Jersey were gunned down, while others had their homes bombed.

Other groups, publicly criticizing the Dialogue, also used the new channels to establish contacts on the island. Abdala, Alpha 66 and others were planning to set up new resistance movements inside Cuba. Abdala, after breaking with the FLNC, had spent four years trying to create such a network. By 1978 Abdala had published a clandestine leaflet and carried out minor sabotages inside Cuba.

[1] *Of Human Rights*, Spring 1980, pp. 21–22

Jose Chorens: "We considered the Dialogue immoral, but we had to take advantage of any opportunity. We selected a small group of men and women who were not known to the public and who would not arouse suspicion if they traveled to Cuba. They had not attended our rallies or frequented our offices. They had never been mentioned in our publications. Some had even infiltrated pro-Castro groups to increase their credibility. In Cuba this group became clandestine. We also used the mails to send thousands of subversive leaflets into Cuba, and we increased pirate radio transmissions to the island. State Security was going crazy."

Domingo Jorge Delgado, a young lawyer, was active in dissident groups that were starting to form inside Cuba. Delgado: "For a time in Cuba, when a person was arrested for clandestine activities, the first question was: Who recruited you, Abdala or the CIA?"

However efficient and dedicated, Abdala and other exile groups still lacked the resources to challenge the system in a meaningful way. Tourists arriving in Cuba, on the other hand, were creating a serious problem for the regime. Aramis Coego had been opposing the government from inside Cuba.

Aramis Coego: "Fidel had spent decades cursing exiles, calling them 'worms.' Now the worms had turned into butterflies. From one minute to the next, everything changed. Exiles were welcome. We had been told that blacks were persecuted in the United States, that they lived in misery and poverty. The first one to arrive in my town was a black Cuban from New York. The man was well dressed and he brought gifts for his family. They all brought gifts. A number of hard-line communists who had no relatives in the exile community were left out of the goodies. We had a joke: 'I'll trade you three communist uncles for one in exile.' The trips opened many eyes. It wasn't just the consumer goods. The visitors seemed happy, without fear. In Cuba, where we were in constant fear of the government, to see a happy man, a man without fear, was like seeing an alien from another planet. Fidel had invented the Dialogue for his own benefit but it turned into a double-edged razor—and Fidel cut himself."

Reinaldo Puentes was a bartender in one of Cuba's hotels during the first wave of tourist flights. Puentes: "I was used to seeing tourists, but they were European tourists. Suddenly Cuban exiles were all over the place and a lot of people in Cuba began questioning the system—I mean, people who were loyal to the system. When we saw a man from our neighborhood, one of our own, who was there in front of us wearing a European suit and Italian shoes, we wondered: 'Why not me? Why do I have to live in misery standing in lines, hoping to be able to buy underwear or a new pair of socks? What makes us different? We are both Cubans.' I'll tell you what made us different. We lived under a government that totally controlled our lives. It wasn't about European suits or Italian shoes. It was about having options, having a future. It was not only that the government employed you, fired you, decided where you would live. It was beyond that. They decided how much meat you could eat every month, how much soap you were allowed to use each year. Freedom is a great thing, mostly understood when one lives without it."

The impact of Cuban tourists on Castro's Cuba would help create one of the biggest upheavals of the time.

CHAPTER XXV.

EXODUS

It started with a brief incident of violence. On April 4, 1980, a truck carrying six Cubans who wanted asylum in Peru rammed through the gates of the Peruvian embassy in Havana. A policeman trying to stop them was killed, while three in the truck were wounded.

When the Peruvians refused to return the refugees to Cuba for prosecution, an enraged Castro removed all Cuban guards from the embassy. Perhaps the leader was encouraging a mob to create trouble for the Peruvians so the diplomats would give up and hand back the refugees. For once, the wily ruler apparently had no notion of what would ensue.

In prior months, the situation had turned critical. Individual acts of sabotage had increased. A warehouse in Havana storing consumer goods to be traded for tourist dollars had been torched, while a few blocks away, a movie theater had been incinerated by electrical sabotage. In the westernmost province of Pinar del Rio, a cradle of Cuba's vaunted cigar trade, several tobacco storage depots had been damaged by arson.

Ricardo Brown was a Cuban exile who had traveled back to the island as a journalist. Brown: "I saw frustration in the people. I saw anti-Castro slogans painted on walls. The youth of Cuba had become machines of destruction. They carried out acts of vandalism, slicing seats in theaters and buses, breaking things, setting small fires. I could sense a palpable undercurrent of anger and frustration."

Frank Suarez was a student in his last year of high school in Havana. Suarez: "I had lost two friends in Angola and two others were jailed for refusing to serve in the military. The exiles who visited Cuba had opened our eyes to the reality of our misery. We became aware that, only ninety miles from our shores, there lived a world without execution walls, repression or hunger. One thing was to hear stories, and another thing was to see those people. In Cuba the only ones with a future were the children of high-ranking officials. The state decided. If a student was a good communist with good grades and he wanted to study engineering, and the government decided it needed plumbers, then forget engineering—unless, of course, the student had connections in the inner circle of power. Fidel's son can study atomic engineering, but the son of a baker has to do as he's told. We were told that class privileges had ended in Cuba, but it wasn't so. I knew sons of high-ranking party members who had cars and chauffeurs. Where was the equality? That's why a human wave ran for refuge at the Peruvian embassy."

In the space of just forty-eight hours, 10,800 Cubans had squeezed into the embassy grounds, covering every square inch of the building and yard. People were sitting on tree branches, sleeping in a fetal position on the porch, trampling over shrubs and flowers, jammed shoulder to shoulder inside the embassy's rooms. Castro's troops cordoned off the area near the embassy, preventing thousands more from reaching the gates. The incident had become a full-fledged crisis.

*   *   *

In Miami and other exile communities, anti-Castro organizations quickly sent representatives to visit heads of state, requesting intercession on behalf of the trapped refugees. The governments of Peru, the United States, Costa Rica and Spain offered asylum to the nearly eleven thousand Cubans at the diplomatic compound.

For Castro the situation had turned extremely awkward. Allowing the refugees to leave would draw public attention of the worst kind, showcasing popular opposition to the regime. Instead, Castro announced that all "scum" would be permitted to leave Cuba. It turned out to be an ingenious plan. By opening up the port of Mariel, Castro said good riddance to thousands of actual and potential enemies. To discredit the exodus, Castro's officials gathered thousands of criminals and mental patients and mixed them in with the refugees.

Frank Suarez: "The Mariel boatlift undercut internal opposition. One hundred thousand leaving the island meant fewer mouths to feed, more property to share among the elite—and we were labeled criminals, homosexuals, antisocial elements, mentally unstable. By putting those labels on us, Castro turned a moral defeat into a propaganda victory, making it look as if only the wicked and evil were leaving Cuba."

*   *   *

The opening of Mariel harbor occurred so swiftly that it caught the United States by surprise. President Jimmy Carter had no counter to Castro's cunning move. Before any contingency plan could be put in place, hundreds of Florida pleasure-craft were heading toward Cuba to pick up refugees. All the United States could manage was a threat to confiscate the vessels traveling to Cuba—a statement breezily ignored by thousands of exiles who had grasped the opportunity to rescue their families and friends on the island.

Enrique Gonzalez-Pola: "Mariel harbor was packed with every kind of vessel—small boats, large boats, commercial fishing boats and sailboats. Cuban immigration officers went from boat to boat, picking up lists of relatives who were to board. Some boats took relatives. Others were loaded with people who had just been waiting at the docks. Every hour, more people who wanted to get off the island showed up. It was unreal."

Many thousands of Cubans made formal requests to leave the country. In answer, the regime undertook its "Acts of Repudiation."

Gilberto Canto: "A woman who lived next to us had tried to reach the embassy grounds but had been unable to pass by the lines of police. She returned home and asked for permission to join the Mariel boatlift. Within hours, a truck loaded with her co-workers had arrived in front of her home, carrying signs that read: 'Whore, what will you do in the United States? Work as a whore?' The government claimed such acts were spontaneous, but it was not so. Looking from my window, I could see that many who screamed were ashamed at what they were doing. When they went, they left the signs tied to her fence. I was so enraged I went there and took down the signs. The neighborhood spy committee came to see me. They suspected me of having removed the signs. I denied it, but I decided it was time to leave Cuba, so I also applied to leave the country."

Frank Suarez: "We had incidents of people being stoned or beaten. Some were killed by the mobs, and many were wounded. It was a most humiliating time."

Gilberto Canto, a U.S. Navy officer in the Second World War and a former political prisoner in Cuba, easily qualified as an "undesirable element" and a candidate for emigration. Canto: "I was taken to a filthy warehouse in Luyano, a place that had been used to repair trucks. Hundreds of men, women and children were in the place, many sleeping on the floor, all waiting to be transported to Mariel. I was lucky. They took me quickly to a place called The Mosquito, near Mariel. This was a rocky beach baked by a scorching sun. Everyone just sat around on the rocks. We were divided into two groups. On one side of the road they placed criminals and on the other side they placed us."

Frank Suarez: "The criminals were truly frightening. Many were almost naked, covered with tattoos. One of them had a large snake tattooed on his back."

Refugee-processing centers had been hastily set up in Key West and Miami, manned by hundreds of exiles working as volunteers. Grocery stores were donating food by the ton; doctors and nurses from all over South Florida spent free time working at the centers. For three months, wave after wave of humans kept coming. The tally rose to 125,000 people. Of these, 1,774 were considered hardened criminals and several thousand more had served time for minor crimes. About 1,500 had been imprisoned on charges of homosexuality. Three of the new arrivals had leprosy, and some 600 were mentally impaired.[1]

In proportion, the criminal element was not large, but in numbers it was quite enough to make an impact. Due in no small measure to Castro's PR campaign portraying the refugees as "scum," an atmosphere of panic took hold in Florida. Localities were obliged to absorb the shock of mass arrivals into the work force and school systems. Many refugees could not speak English and were unprepared to face the sudden change.

Frank Suarez: "The crime level rose in Miami. Hundreds of the criminals died in gunfights with local police or with each other. Some decent people without work or knowledge wound up joining the criminal ranks. In those first couple of years our image was bad; but then people began to understand that the great number of 'Marielitos' were decent people. The boatlift brought to America many architects, doctors, skilled workmen, artists, painters, writers. In time we gained respect."

*　*　*

The exodus had also brought new recruits to the exile groups. In short order, some refugees were going back to Cuba as part of infiltration teams under sponsorship of Alpha 66.

Andres Nazario Sargen: "The new arrivals were perfect for infiltration. They knew the street language and many had contacts inside the island. We trained them in weapons and sabotage techniques, then sent them in to create resistance groups."

Less than six months after the end of the boatlift, the first team reached Matanzas province.

Alpha 66 had itself been infiltrated by a double agent: Francisco Avila, a former political prisoner working for both Cuban State Security and the FBI. After a tip from Avila, U.S. officials arrested several commandos at Knight's Key and confiscated their weapons. The men went to serve time in U.S. penitentiaries.

Between the end of 1980 and the beginning of 1983, twelve infiltration operations

---

[1] *The Miami Herald,* May 17, 1980

deposited sixty-seven Cubans on the island, resulting in the most active period of para-military activity against Castro since the early sixties.[2] At least five commandos died in gunfights with Castro's military forces. Seventeen were executed by firing squads and several others incarcerated.

A clear link between Alpha 66 and resistance units inside Cuba—indirectly verified by the regime—can be found in the 1983 transcripts of Cuban court proceedings against the "Zapata Group."

Active from 1978 to 1983, this clandestine organization, with its three dozen men and women, was accused of carrying out 170 acts of sabotage against the government. Cuban prosecutors claimed that the Zapata Group had committed 28 acts of arson, damaging crops, factories, electrical lines and government vehicles in three provinces. The group had also printed and distributed anti-Castro propaganda in those provinces, attempting to create a national labor-union movement similar to Poland's Solidarity.[3]

All of the Zapata Group's members went to jail. One of the women, Caridad Pavon, either was murdered or committed suicide in a State Security prison.

[2] Alpha 66 files
[3] Sentencia 9, Causa 77, Tribunal Popular de La Habana

CHAPTER XXVI.

THE EMPEROR FIDEL

From within the regime's own ranks, a few economists and technocrats were still strug-gling to reform the ailing system. Humberto Perez, a high-ranking official in charge of economic planning, developed the "Farmers' Free Markets," a form of free enterprise not allowed since the 1960's. Within a few months the markets had made improvements in rural areas; but soon they were abolished, for their very effectiveness had threatened the system's ideology. Other attempts at reform likewise collided with the regime's dog-matic structure.

Lacking hope for improvement, Cuban society had gone into rapid decay, with alcoholism and suicide rates jumping. In 1977, suicides had been 17.1 per 100,000 inhabitants. By 1981 that number had reached an alarming 27.5, one of the highest levels in the world.[1] The suicides included such prominent revolutionary figures as Haydee Santamaria, a founder of the 26th of July Movement, and Osvaldo Dorticos, who had served for seventeen years as Cuba's president under Castro.

After the months of Mariel, Castro had abruptly re-established the law against emigration, but Cubans were still attempting to flee the island. On February 13, 1981, two families tried to seek asylum in the embassy of Ecuador. Despite the fact that asylum had been granted, State Security officers entered the building, arrested the families and beat them severely. Domingo Jorge Delgado, a lawyer and human rights activist, was related to one of the families. "Owen Delgado, who was just a fifteen-year-old boy, was brutally beaten and died in a hospital. His mother, father and a few others were allowed to attend the funeral. State Security took away the body. Years later they returned some remains to the family. We are not even sure if they were really Owen's."

[1] Carbonell, *And the Russians Stayed,* p. 303

* * *

While Cuba's economy increasingly relied on a huge Soviet subsidy, Castro promoted subversion in many corners of the globe. Indeed, from the moment he gained power, he had supported Marxist guerrilla groups. He had sponsored failed invasions of the Dominican Republic and Panama, backed subversive groups in Venezuela and Colombia, and set up camps in Havana and Pinar del Rio provinces to train terrorists from many Latin countries.[2]

Since the mid-sixties, when Che Guevara had attempted to become a key player in the Congo uprisings, Castro's regime had also been militarily active in Africa. By the mid-seventies, Cuban army advisors were working in several African nations; and the Angolan civil conflict had escalated into a full-fledged war in which thousands of Cuban troops were fighting on the side of the Marxist MPLA. In the early eighties, Castro had also established a military base on the Caribbean island-nation of Grenada, by permission of its Marxist rulers.

By 1983, Grenada had a huge weapons depot guarded by several hundred Cuban troops, most of whom were part of a construction/engineering battalion assigned to build military warehouses and enlarge runways at the airport. These renovations would allow heavier transport planes to fly supplies on and off the tiny island. The military warehouses contained 3,400 automatic and semi-automatic rifles, 200 machine guns, 100 rocket launchers, 12 mortars and artillery pieces, and more than 3,000,000 rounds of varied ammunition.[3]

Following a clash between political factions that threatened the lives of a thousand Americans on Grenada, the administration of President Ronald Reagan sent U.S. soldiers to rout Cuba's force, totaling about seven hundred men, from the island. Despite his bellicose rhetoric, Castro did not really relish the idea of an armed clash with the Americans. When he realized that U.S. warships were sailing toward Grenada, he decided against sending reinforcements to the besieged island. Instead he dispatched a single officer, Colonel Pedro Tortolo, to Grenada with orders to defend the island "to the last drop of Cuban blood."

Castro's media pumped out a flow of narrative describing the Cubans' fierce defense of their installations, perishing heroically in the face of America's lightning attack. In one of its last transmissions, Castro's official Rebel Radio told an emotional tale of a savage

[2] Extended accounts of these activities are given in Benemelis, *Las guerras secretas de Fidel Castro.*

[3] Fontaine, *Terrorism: The Cuban Connection*, p. 88

battle in which the last Cuban troops on Grenada had died "embracing the flag."

Perhaps Castro had hoped for a "Caribbean Alamo" that would rally the Cuban people against the United States; but the truth was that Cuba's forces had yielded unheroically to the U.S. airborne assault. American forces gained total control of the island after a few hours of skirmishing, and Tortolo surrendered with more than six hundred men. About twenty U.S. soldiers and thirty Cubans had died in brief fighting.

Tortolo and the prisoners were released, then returned to Havana to be greeted by Castro. Photos of the wounded were published in Cuban newspapers to back up the official reports of hard fighting. In private, Castro expressed rage at the lack of enthusiasm that Cuban troops had shown. Colonel Tortolo was broken to private and shipped off to fight with a line unit in Angola. Other officers were demoted and punished.[4]

General Rafael Del Pino, then a ranking officer in the Cuban Air Force, would write years later: "Men fight to the last ditch and are prepared to die when they are convinced that they are giving up their lives for a just cause. When they are in combat to keep one group in power or to flatter delusions of grandeur in others, they simply do not fight—and that is what happened in Grenada."[5]

* * *

Cubans, having first gone to Angola as military advisors, became a full-fledged occupation force numbering in the thousands. Their support of the MPLA government went beyond direct combat assistance to include supervision of police units, work with mass organizations, and numerous facets of political control.

Ernesto Quintero was a corporal in a Cuban infantry unit stationed in Angola during the early 1980's. Quintero: "Most of us didn't want to be there. Some thought it would enhance their careers to be internationalist heroes, but when they returned to Cuba they were given lousy jobs and faced a housing shortage. One cannot eat a medal when one is hungry. Angola was a tough war for the soldiers in the field. The rebels sniped at our columns by day and attacked small outposts at night. They shot down our helicopters and ambushed our patrols. We controlled the roads and they controlled the bush. They controlled hundreds of kilometers of territory and dozens of small villages. There were a lot of rebels, thousands. Pretty soon I was asking myself: What the hell am I doing here? This is just a civil war and we are an army of occupation and most of the people, including the ones we are supposed to be helping, do not even like us."

[4] Del Pino, *Proa a la libertad,* pp. 25–26
[5] Fermoselle, *The Evolution of the Cuban Military, 1492–1986,* p. 442

Cuba's part in Angola stemmed from Castro's enormous economic debt to the Soviet Union. Castro was using Cubans as a mercenary force on behalf of Soviet interests. In another sense, the mission was a source of economic gain for Castro. Angola's government paid all salaries of the Cuban force, totaling 600 Kwanzas a month for privates, 900 for officers and 1,200 for members of the high command.[6] Then, too, Castro was clearly enchanted by the notion of 'his' Cuba fielding an army on a faraway continent—a fact that promised to turn him from a head of state into a head of empire.

Meanwhile, Cuba was sharpening its troops, creating cadres of battle-seasoned veterans and keeping thousands of youths away from the island, living and eating at another nation's expense. And it was not only in Angola that Cuban troops were stationed. By 1984, Cuba's forces were dispersed throughout nearly thirty countries in Africa and the Middle East—a total of 71,645 military and civilian support units in such areas as Mozambique, Ethiopia and Yemen, many active in wars of repression against nationalist insurgents.[7]

Cuba's imperial policy took its toll. Although the Cuban government has placed the number of its combat dead at less than three thousand, figures vary. General Rafael Del Pino, commander of Cuban Air Force units in Angola, has estimated that as many as 10,000 Cubans were killed or mutilated in the war. Ezzedine Mestiri, an African historian, stated that in the early months of the intense conflict, Cuban casualties could have been as high as 2,000 killed and 3,000 wounded. The rebel UNITA has claimed 5,000 Cuban troops killed and 11,000 wounded up to 1985, with 300 casualties per annum in years following.[8]

The impact of yearly casualties by the hundreds in Africa had an effect in Cuba, even with the government publishing little about the war.

Ernesto Quintero: "Most Cubans who died in Angola were buried there and remained there for several years until the early nineties, when the war was over. Only then were a lot of them sent back to be buried in Cuba. While the war was on, unless the dead was a very high-ranking officer, or a relation of someone in power, burial was in Angola. Some of the badly wounded were sent to hospitals in East Germany. I think it was due to Castro's not wanting young men without arms or legs on the streets of Havana. When I went back to Cuba, I found out that one of my cousins was in a military prison for refusing to serve in the army; and he was not alone. Cuba's military prisons were jammed with young soldiers and draftees refusing to fight."

[6] Del Pino, *Proa a la libertad*, p. 13
[7] Benemelis, *Castro, subversion y terrorismo en Africa*, p. 563
[8] Ibid., p. 575

Thousands of draftees and officers were incarcerated in military prisons such as El Pitirre, Ganusa and Melena Dos (also called Guira de Melena). In effect these were concentration camps. According to General Rafael Del Pino, the number of desertions and absences without leave in the Cuban armed forces reached a spectacular number: 56,000 incidents in a three-year period.[9] In Angola, a few Cuban soldiers, like Sergeant Miguel Garcia Enamorado, deserted and joined UNITA to fight alongside rebel forces.[10] The many Cubans imprisoned in military camps included Roberto Del Risco and Frank Benitez Ferrer.

Roberto Del Risco: "At El Pitirre we had two or three thousand men. I spent three years there. We were beaten and tortured. A garrison captain named Raul Rosales Del Peral kicked me in the face, chipping a tooth and knocking out two others. I spent forty-four days in a punishment cell, naked. I was not allowed visitors or mail. We were allowed to bathe once every twenty-eight days. We had to run through a long line of showers, soaping and rinsing while they screamed orders and sometimes hit us with clubs. About two hundred of the prisoners were officers. Most were there for refusing to participate in the war. Some were there for having sold weapons to the rebels in Angola. I met one who claimed to have sold a helicopter, another an armored car. Some had sold grenades and bullets to the rebels."

Frank Benitez Ferrer: "I was a sub-lieutenant. My father is a colonel in the Ministry of the Interior. I was accused of 'ideological deviation' and insubordination and sent to prison for two years and a month. At Guira de Melena we had 2,500 or 2,600 men; about 180 or 200 were officers. We were forced to drill in the hot sun until we dropped from the heat. The food was usually a plate of dried noodles and sometimes we were fed a foul-smelling fish that was hard to digest. I saw men with scabs on their bodies from poor hygiene. We were beaten constantly. Almost all of us were young. Most of us had been conceived under the revolution."

In Cuba, another generation had come of age. Young men, yet unborn when the Escambray guerrillas and urban rebels had fought Castro, had become resisters and filled military prisons rather than serve the wishes of the regime.

---

[9] Del Pino, *Proa a la libertad*, p. 32
[10] Benemelis, *Castro, subversion y terrorismo en Africa*, p. 359

CHAPTER XXVII.

FROM MY WHEELCHAIR

Time had been taking its toll on the exile communities. Groups perished from internal strife, lack of funds, or simple exhaustion after years in the fray. By the early 1980's, Abdala was gone.

Jose Chorens: "We were mentally tired. Abdala had been a dynamic movement. It absorbed us totally. We worked more hours at Abdala functions than at our own jobs. After ten years of sleepless nights, constant meetings, divorces, travel, planning, and paying out of our own pockets, we were spent. Almost all of us kept in touch, but we went our separate ways."

Pedro Solares: "We had been ahead of our time. We had talked about lobbying and establishing a base of political power in the exile community ten years before it began to happen. We had predicted a perestroika-style process in the Soviet Union and the collapse of the Soviet economy when no one else was considering such concepts; but because of our youth and limited resources, we couldn't do all we knew had to be done. We had an impact in our time, and our members have had an impact since. From Abdala emerged a U.S. congressman, a mayor in South Florida, two judges, top writers and journalists, a movie director, and scores of lawyers, doctors, college professors, professionals and community leaders, almost all of whom remain leaders in the Cuban cause."

Another young movement to vanish was the OPLC (Organization for the Liberation of Cuba), led by Ramon Saul Sanchez and Lino Gonzalez. Sanchez was serving time in a U.S. federal prison for refusing to testify against other exiles before grand juries. Lino Gonzalez, a veteran of resistance fighting inside Cuba and a former political prisoner, died of leukemia at age thirty-three.

Orlando Gutierrez: "We had more than thirty members arrested in 1981. Four of our people were sentenced to serve between nine and forty years in U.S. jails. It was a hard blow for such a young organization."

As these movements dissolved, others formed. Huber Matos, the former Rebel Army commander who had spent twenty years in Castro's prisons, arrived in Miami, where he created CID, or Independent and Democratic Cuba. CID fielded clandestine units inside the island while broadcasting radio programs from Miami. Matos's movement survived early problems, including strife among its leadership, to build a base of support in the exile community.

Individual passions were as strong as ever. At Miami International Airport, a Cuban Airlines plane was waiting to refuel when an exile airport worker, Aquilino Carrodeguas, drove a trailer-truck onto the tarmac with supplies for a departing flight. In a moment of rage on seeing the Cuban plane, Carrodeguas aimed his large truck toward the airliner, stepped on the gas and rammed the nose of the aircraft, causing thousands of dollars in damage. After his arrest, Carrodeguas was applauded by many in the exile community and treated to legal assistance by OPLC.

These years also witnessed a broadening crisis in Central America, where America and Castro confronted each other through Nicaragua's civil war. Washington backed the anti-Sandinista rebels, or "Contras," while Castro supported the ruling Sandinistas—a leadership cadre that had enjoyed, for decades before taking power, a unique degree of friendship with Castro's regime. Cuban exiles went to fight in this war and joined the Contras.

Ramon Cala was among the veteran commandos who saw action in Central America. Cala: "I was not a mercenary. A mercenary fights for money. I fought for my convictions. I never accepted money, nor did I expect to be paid. I even helped acquire thousands of dollars in equipment and medicines to help the cause. This was not a picnic. The newspapers may at times have given the impression that the Contras were a well-trained, heavily funded, CIA-backed organization. Perhaps it was so with some groups; but where I was, with Comandante Chamorro, we were strictly self-funded. We were poorly equipped and poorly fed. Wild fruits, some rice and an occasional roasted monkey made up our diet. I saw 'mountain leprosy'—tiny worms eating the skin, making festering holes in a matter of hours. A man might wake up and find a hole the size of a quarter on his wrist. We used to pour gasoline in the holes, hoping to kill the worms and clean the wounds. Sometimes it worked and sometimes it didn't. I saw a Contra with a hole in his back big enough to put a fist in. I saw another whose face was rotting away."

In Miami, a young Cuban exile doctor named Manuel Alzugaray created an organization called the Miami Medical Team. The team, joined by exile doctors, nurses and therapists, used their free time to travel to Angola and Nicaragua, where they worked with rebel factions, gave care, performed medical operations and contributed medical supplies.

✳ ✳ ✳

By the early 1980's, more than two decades of exile had seen the refugee community in the United States reach more than a million strong. The exiles had developed significant economic power and the potential for political influence. A new organization, the Cuban American National Foundation (CANF), began to exploit this political potential.

The key figure in the CANF was Jorge Mas Canosa, a man with an extensive background in the anti-Castro movements of the early sixties. By 1981, when he and a group of friends created the organization, Mas Canosa was one of Miami's wealthiest exiles.

Jorge Mas Canosa had left his native Cuba in 1960. The former university student from Oriente joined Brigade 2506 and was assigned to a unit that did not disembark during the April 1961 invasion. Back in Miami, he worked as a milkman while becoming one of the leaders of RECE, an organization that sponsored several raids into Cuba, including the guerrilla missions of Comandante Yarey. By the early seventies, Mas Canosa had become a small contractor installing fiber-optic cable for Southern Bell. Within a decade the company was a multimillion-dollar corporation, and Jorge Mas a wealthy entrepreneur.

Mas determined to create a communications and lobbying entity that would work in Washington to counter Castro's enormous, and enormously successful, publicity machine. Along with two other wealthy exiles—real estate investor Carlos Salman and banker Raul Masvidal—Mas organized the CANF and hired Frank Calzon as its Washington lobbyist. Calzon, a former Abdala member and head of an organization called "Of Human Rights," was a savvy political operator who knew the intricacies of bureaucracy and legislation. Within months Calzon had established the CANF as a presence in the nation's capital.

Although Salman, Masvidal and Calzon eventually left the CANF, the idea blossomed and the organization grew. Within a few years, it had more than thirty full-time employees in Miami and Washington, with more than fifty thousand members contributing small monthly fees to fund activities. The wealthier contributed their share, with some directors spending as much as $200,000 per year on CANF activities.[1] Along with the attention it attracted, the CANF also begot controversy.

---

[1] Interviews with Roberto Martin Perez, Miami, 1995

Roberto Martin Perez, after serving twenty-eight years in Castro's political prisons, became a CANF director upon arrival in Miami. Martin Perez: "I don't pay attention to those who argue that the foundation is a millionaires' club. Those are the same people who years ago complained that the wealthy exiles did not contribute anything to the cause of Cuba. Now, when wealthy Cubans do something, they still complain. Those who say the CANF is too pro-U.S. have no basis for such complaints. The CANF has used the American legal and political system to damage the Castro regime, to lobby on behalf of the anti-Castro struggle, to aid refugees, to help anti-Communist guerrillas in Angola. Years ago, when we lacked economic wealth and political power, we were used. Now we have a voice, and we use it."

The Cuban American National Foundation became the principal public vehicle for anti-Castro activity. It was instrumental in lobbying for Jonas Savimbi's UNITA and in obtaining help for Angola's rebels. Later, perhaps more crucially, it succeeded in instigating anti-Castro legislation in the United States.

* * *

Other anti-Castro Cubans gained prominence in the eighties, including former political prisoner Armando Valladares and exiled writer Carlos Alberto Montaner. Valladares, imprisoned in Cuba, had managed to send books of poetry to his wife in exile, and she distributed them. The poet, claiming to be paralyzed, gave one of his works the title "From My Wheelchair." Cuban authorities insisted Valladares was faking his illness in order to gain sympathy.

Carlos Alberto Montaner, from his home in Spain, launched a campaign on behalf of Valladares by working with the Christian Democratic Movement and a number of other exiles including human rights pioneer Humberto Medrano. The campaign struck roots. Spanish playwright Fernando Arrabal lobbied French President François Mitterrand, while actress Liv Ullmann created a pro-Valladares committee in Oslo.[2] The poet was released from prison and arrived in Paris, walking without difficulty. He claimed that he had been paralyzed for some time, and that in response to political pressure the regime had provided medication, a better diet and therapy to cure him before his release.

Valladares published a prison memoir, *Against All Hope,* which became an international bestseller, with translations in a dozen languages. The English edition sold more than one hundred thousand copies and was touted by President Ronald Reagan. Within

[2] Valladares, *Against All Hope,* pp. 373–75

two years after leaving prison, Armando Valladares was designated U.S. ambassador to the Human Rights Commission at the United Nations.

In the larger world, communism was hurrying to its demise; and on the island a new kind of resistance was taking shape.

CHAPTER XXVIII.

WAR WITHOUT BULLETS

If the Cuban resistance of the sixties and seventies had been waged with armed struggle and exile violence, the opposition of the eighties and nineties would express itself as a campaign for human rights, critically assisted by modern telecommunications.

Clandestine literary and political dissident groups had existed in Cuba since the early 1970's. One such group was accustomed to meet at a park in the Vedado section of Havana.[1] A key figure to emerge from that small association was Ricardo Bofill, a former political economist at the University of Havana.

A wiry man with a gift for rhetoric, Bofill had roots in the Socialist Youth branch of the old PSP. He had lived in the Soviet Union, worked with Anibal Escalante, and then served time in Castro's prisons following the "Micro-Faction" purge of the late sixties. His knowledge of Marxist methods became a weapon that he was able to turn against State Security. As Bofill became prominent, he was vehemently denounced by the Castro regime, and also for different reasons by many exiles.

Ricardo Bofill: "I was never a Castro follower. I was never a member of the militia. I was a member of the Left, of the Socialist Youth; but I had been confronting the system since the early sixties. I have been arrested and incarcerated many times."

Even as Cuba seemed to stand still, the world kept rotating and changing. With advanced telecommunications and fax machines, the global village imagined by Marshall McLuhan was becoming a reality. Within the socialist world, founding concepts of equality and income redistribution had long since given way to a Marxist brand of feudal, aristocratic rulers—Milovan Djilas had called them "the new class"—yet more oppressive and more decadent than the rulers they had replaced.

[1] *The Miami Herald,* August 25, 1990

Dissident movements had risen to challenge these hard-fisted regimes. In Poland, Lech Walesa became a legend in the shipyards of Gdansk. In Czechoslovakia, an imprisoned poet named Vaclav Havel dared to question the organized Reign of Terror. From the U.S.S.R. itself, Aleksandr Solzhenitsyn and Andrei Sakharov were able to touch the conscience of the world with their defiance.

Communist regimes facing economic and technological bankruptcy had to choose between joining the West or falling hopelessly behind it. The ineffectiveness of those regimes was shown most nakedly in a telecommunications gap. Rather than by ideology, the Iron Curtain had been unhinged by the telephone, the computer and the fax machine.

While Castro resisted change with all his might, the new winds could not be contained. Young Cubans who had studied in the Soviet Union, Poland, Hungary and other nations returned to the island influenced by new concepts. Cuba's own bureaucracy was filled with young technocrats for whom Castro was no dashing hero of the mountains. Rather, they saw him as an outdated figurehead clinging to a vision in which no one believed.

With this new perspective—evolutionary rather than revolutionary, international instead of parochial—Cuban human rights activists began their work, meeting quietly at first, developing contacts that could protect them from the wrath of State Security. Enrique Hernandez and Domingo Jorge Delgado were among Cuba's first human rights dissidents.

Enrique Hernandez: "In order to function, we needed the world to be aware of our existence, so that when State Security came calling we could have an international human rights group intercede on our behalf."

Domingo Jorge Delgado: "A factor for our survival was that we could shelter ourselves under the U.N.'s Universal Declaration of Human Rights. We read the U.N. documents and understood that what we were attempting to do was legal. In this way we could petition international civil and human rights groups and demand that they help protect us from repression."

Ricardo Bofill: "In 1979 and 1980, when we started coming out of the shadows, our first international contacts were with Amnesty International and UNESCO. At first, State Security did not arrest us because they were waiting to prosecute us for bigger offenses than information gathering. I knew how they worked, how they planned operations and how they thought. I had spent five years in prison with the man who created State Security, Anibal Escalante. Among those of us jailed during the 'Micro-Faction,' fourteen had been high-ranking officers and instructors in State Security. I spent five years learning their methods, and when the human rights movement began I knew how to fool them. We used to prepare a meeting at one place and switch to another place at the last minute. We fed misinformation to people we knew were informants. We fooled State Security often and confused them and they didn't crush us when they had the chance. They waited too long."

*   *   *

A tremendous boon to the growing human rights movement inside Cuba was the creation of Radio Marti. The Cuban American National Foundation (CANF) had lobbied the Reagan administration to create a federally funded radio station, like Radio Free Europe, to broadcast to Cubans inside the island.

From the time of its invention, radio had played an important role in Cuban politics. After Castro's takeover, Miami-based radio stations, whose signals could be heard in Cuba, broadcast strong messages against the regime. Some radio commentators—Agustin Tamargo, Armando Perez Roura, Tomas Garcia Fuste—wielded as much influence in the exile community as any politician, and could rally thousands of exiles to a demonstration with their microphones. Anti-Castro organizations had also utilized radio. Abdala transmitted eight hundred programs during the second half of the seventies; by the mideighties, Huber Matos's CID was broadcasting daily; and Alpha 66 also dispatched hundreds of anti-Castro programs that told potential saboteurs on the island how to make explosives in their own homes.

Many of these programs were in direct violation of Federal Communications Commission (FCC) laws, and many of the radio stations were unlicensed. Alpha 66 broadcaster Diego Medina was arrested and his equipment confiscated; but Alpha 66 got new equipment and kept sending programs.

Pedro Solares had made broadcasts for Abdala during the seventies. Solares: "About ten of us worked on the radio team. We spent hours researching, writing, editing and preparing the weekly programs that had a mix of news, interviews, commentaries and an editorial. We rehearsed once and then taped the shows. Three half-hour programs were done every week. We felt that the FCC, like most regulatory agencies, was probably understaffed and that if we could avoid actual complaints, they would probably leave us alone. We placed our transmitter on a farm in rural Dade County. Including the drive, it took about four hours to put a half-hour program on the air. Most of the time no one lived at the farm and it was pitch dark, with all kinds of farm animals roaming around the shed from which we transmitted. More than once an inquisitive goat poked its head in the door."

Radio Marti began broadcasting in May 1985. At first the broadcasts were rather neutral, with lots of music and cultural programming and not so much hostility to Castro's government. A program on the "Canimar Massacre" broke the ice and made an impact on clandestine listeners. This was a story about Cuban border guards machine-gunning a boat with men, women and children attempting to flee the island.[2] Within months, Cubans across the island, including many Castro supporters, were tuned in to the station.

Ivan Ortega was one of the early listeners. "I listened from the first day. After a few months, you could walk down almost any street in any city in Cuba and hear a radio program from Radio Marti. You heard a phrase as you passed one window, another phrase as you passed the next window, and so on. I think even Fidel tuned in Radio Marti. Some people were arrested for listening and others were fired from jobs, but the time came when so many were tuned in, State Security could do little. Even radio jamming didn't work. People still listened. I think of those early years of Radio Marti. The station did a lot to damage the system. It opened up many eyes."

Radio Marti's broadcasts on human rights activity inside Cuba allowed the groups to grow; for State Security hesitated, knowing that reports of their attacks on such groups could be broadcast to the Cuban people. Radio Marti became a source of information that tied internal dissident groups to others in Cuba and the rest of the world.

Reinaldo Bragado, a writer who had served time in Castro's prisons for attempting to leave Cuba, found out about Ricardo Bofill's Cuban Committee for Human Rights (CCPDH) in a surprising way.

Bragado: "I wanted to leave Cuba. Then one day I heard on Radio Marti about Bofill and his committee for human rights and I said to myself, I'm not leaving now. I figured if this group was active, then I had a reason for staying. I knew a painter who knew Adolfo Rivero Caro, who was one of the key people with Bofill. I met Bofill that way. It became a very happy time in my life. We were often arrested and hassled; but we had a purpose in our lives. Bofill created a very good network, and we received a lot of information from all over Cuba. Many of the people who joined the human rights groups were former political prisoners; and we even had connections to a prison grapevine, sending and receiving messages from jails all over Cuba. We sent a lot of information to the United Nations, to Amnesty International, to Radio Marti, to newspapers and magazines in different countries. We fought a war without bullets."

On December 10, 1987, six human rights activists, including Bofill and Bragado, met at a house in Havana, taped a conference on human rights violations in Cuba and smuggled the tape to the United States. The conference was aired by Radio Marti—the first time

[2] Radio Marti, Report of Advisory Board, 1989

that an anti-Castro meeting of its kind had been broadcast in Cuba while its participants were still on the island.

Ricardo Bofill: "What could State Security do? If they arrested us, then the news would be printed in European and American newspapers and it would create static with international human rights groups. It was a good blow to the system. The more public we became, the better our chances of survival."

Reinaldo Bragado: "Some people in my neighborhood avoided me like leprosy. If they saw me walking down the street, they moved across the road to avoid talking to me, for they felt I was a marked man, a target for State Security. One day I heard a knock on my door. It was a man I knew by sight, a guy from the neighborhood. He said: 'I've been told you are one of the people who spoke on Radio Marti. Is it true?' I nodded my head and he said: 'Well, here, this is for you.' He gave me a bag full of groceries, which are very valuable in Cuba."

Bofill established contact with Armando Valladares, who was in Geneva as America's ambassador to the U.N. Commission on Human Rights. Valladares was trying to obtain a condemnation of Castro's regime by the world body. In this effort, he had the help of writer Carlos Alberto Montaner, journalist Humberto Medrano, the CANF, the MDC and several other exile groups that were busily documenting human rights violations inside Cuba.

Domingo Jorge Delgado: "The amount of work our group did inside the island was massive. We provided Valladares and the exile organizations with hundreds of files, documenting beatings, tortures, illegal arrests and discrimination against dissidents. Huber Jerez and I met with members of the U.N. delegation to Cuba. It was a very emotional moment."

￼   *   *   *

In time the human rights movement on the island had grown from a tiny meeting in a Havana park to more than one hundred organizations with four to five thousand active members. Problems arose—the product of clashing egos, of distrust or paranoia, and of infiltration and manipulation by State Security.

A rift developed between Bofill and Elizardo Sanchez, another well-known activist. Sanchez then created his own organization, the Commission of Human Rights and National Reconciliation. Some exiles expressed doubts about Sanchez's movement, for it demanded that Castro initiate political changes—an idea many considered implausible.

Fractiousness was not the only problem facing the human rights organizations. Tania Diaz Castro, a former journalist turned activist, was arrested, mentally broken and put on Cuban television, where she accused dissidents of being funded and controlled by the CIA.

One of the best-known dissidents was the writer Roberto Luque Escalona, who published in Mexico while still living in Cuba. His critical and bitingly sarcastic work gained the attention of State Security, and thereafter the author was frequently arrested.

Dissident groups continued to organize. Among the many new movements were the MCL or Christian Liberation Movement, led by a young man named Oswaldo Paya; Liberty and Faith; Cuban Triangle; Association Pro Free Art; the Maceista Movement for Dignity; and dozens of others. Many activists were arrested and sentenced to prison for distributing "enemy propaganda" or being "dangerous" to public safety. At the same time, Castro faced mounting challenges from within his own ranks.

CHAPTER XXIX.

8 - A

On May 28, 1987, a twin-engine plane landed at Boca Chica Naval Station in Key West. On board was General Rafael Del Pino, former head of the Cuban Air Force, and his family, seeking political asylum.

A former guerrilla fighter against Batista, Del Pino had been a combat pilot at the Bay of Pigs, destroying two Brigade 2506 aircraft. He had served as the Cuban Air Force commander in Angola, where he had personally flown missions. Del Pino was considered a member of Castro's inner circle; his defection garnered headlines in the world press.

In Washington, Del Pino was embraced by Erneido Oliva, the former Bay of Pigs veteran who was now a brigadier general in the U.S. Army. In Miami his former foes, the pilots of Brigade 2506, welcomed him to the exile community.

Del Pino's radio and TV interviews contained stunning revelations—going far beyond the exiles' harsh accusations—of the decadence and corruption in which Cuban leaders indulged. According to Del Pino, Castro had dozens of homes for his personal use, including a highly guarded mansion that occupied the whole island of Cayo Piedra. The residences were equipped with widescreen televisions, satellite dishes, electronic amenities of all kinds, heated swimming pools, private gyms, tennis courts and bowling alleys purchased in Japan.[1]

Castro, in these accounts, lived like a maharajah. Military helicopters flew over fields on the Castro brothers' private domains, scaring birds and animals from their hideouts so that the Castros could shoot them. Del Pino described how Fidel drank twenty-one-year-old Scotch and dined on gourmet meals while the Cuban people lived in misery. The former general also detailed the lifestyles of high-ranking Communist Party members.

[1] Del Pino, *Proa a la libertad,* p. 44

The powerful in Cuba, according to Del Pino, lived in mansions equipped with central air conditioning; they had drivers, chefs and servants at their disposal, well-stocked refrigerators, wet bars and automobiles ranging from Mercedez-Benzes to Ladas, according to rank. Many had private swimming pools. One general even had a wood-paneled cockfighting center. Those in the upper echelons and their families enjoyed access to Cuba's finest hospital, which exclusively served Castro and his close associates.[2]

Del Pino's interviews, particularly those transmitted by Radio Marti, made a deep impression on Cubans inside the island. Felix Vega, a factory foreman in Havana, heard Del Pino on radio. Vega: "We all knew in Cuba that the high-ranking lived well, but one thing is to imagine it and another thing is to hear it from one of them. It makes you aware that in most countries there are several different kinds of people: poor, rich, middle-class. In Cuba there are two kinds of people: those who starve and suffer, and the elite who crush us. Even being a communist is not enough. I know communists who go hungry and scrape to find necessities like everyone else; but the elite has it all. The rest, the workers, the ordinary citizens, go to bed hungry, in dilapidated housing, without hope for a better future."

Del Pino also predicted that perestroika, the new wave of political change then sweeping the Soviet Bloc, would lead to conspiracies and purges within Cuba's nomenklatura.

* * *

General Arnaldo Ochoa was Cuba's most famous warrior. He had joined the 26th of July guerrillas in the struggle against Batista and had made first lieutenant while still a teenager. As a young field officer, he had led a combat unit at the Bay of Pigs and had hunted guerrillas in the Escambray. Sent to Frunze Military Academy in the Soviet Union, Ochoa became fluent in Russian and graduated with honors. In the late sixties he went to Venezuela as a military advisor to assist guerrilla units sponsored by Castro. In 1971 he served in Vietnam with Vo Nguyen Giap. In 1973, as Castro's military envoy, he fought in the Yom Kippur War. Authors Juan Benemelis and Melvin Manon wrote:

"Leading Syrian artillery units, reinforced with Cuban tank officers and North Korean fighter pilots, Arnaldo Ochoa achieved what had not been achieved and would not again be achieved: stopping the ferocious attack of the legendary and invincible First Armored Unit of Israel."[3]

[2] Ibid., p. 48
[3] *Juicio a Fidel*, p. 43

The tall, thin Ochoa was an ideal commander, preferring the company of his troops to the perks of Havana. He seldom discussed politics, and had spent most of his adult life away from Cuba in military theaters.

When Castro sent him to Ethiopia, the general launched a series of swift tank strikes, destroying the Somali army and consolidating the regime of Soviet dictator Mengistu Mariam. In Nicaragua, Ochoa was the military advisor who transformed the Sandinista army from a guerrilla unit into a cohesive force that could face the U.S.-backed Contras. In Angola he commanded 37,000 Cuban troops. As war escalated, Ochoa organized the defense of Cuito Cuanavale, managing to halt the advance of the South African army and UNITA's guerrilla units in a fierce battle that gave the Cuban force a strategic victory.

Arnaldo Ochoa was decorated by Castro and proclaimed a national hero; yet not all was well. The victory at Cuito had been gained by Ochoa's personal talents, without regard for orders from the Ministry of the Armed Forces or from the commander-in-chief. Indeed, Castro had written to Ochoa: "I don't understand the things that are being done in Cuito. Many times you do not even bother explaining the reasons for which these things are being done.... We are bitter about what is happening."[4]

Upon his return to Havana from Angola, the general was also upset. Apart from Castro's meddling in the most insignificant details of the African operation, Ochoa resented the fact that returning veterans did not get adequate housing or employment. Conditions had worsened in a society ruled by political priorities rather than human needs. In 1980, the annual housing deficit had reached the point where the government needed to construct 300,000 units just to reach a level of normalcy.[5] By 1989, the problem had worsened because the population had grown, while the government had become more and more inefficient.

Ochoa and Raul Castro had several meetings in Havana. The talks turned into shouting matches as Ochoa complained about how returning veterans were being treated, and about problems in the military. Ochoa further stated he was a proponent of perestroika, a notion dreaded by the Castro brothers.[6]

Ochoa had been away from Cuba too long; for apparently he had forgotten the basic rule of survival in a totalitarian state—or perhaps he believed his credentials as a warrior gave him the right to defy Raul Castro. As a result of the dispute, Ochoa was denied the command of Cuba's Western Army, a post to which he had already been assigned. Then,

[4] *Granma,* July 12, 1989
[5] Clark, *Cuba: mito y realidad,* p. 307
[6] Oppenheimer, *Castro's Final Hour,* p. 91

out of fear that Ochoa would defect or even plot against Castro, Raul ordered his personal guard to arrest the general.[7]

*   *   *

An embarrassing, dangerous matter was looming on the horizon. Since 1963, U.S. federal agents had suspected Cuba's government of narco-trafficking. By the 1980's they believed Castro was working with international drug lords—among them Colombians Jaime Guillot-Lara and Pablo Escobar, as well as Cuban exiles Jose Alvero Cruz and Osiris Santi—allowing them to use Cuba as a refuge and refueling area.[8]

Cuba's part in this business would have been handled by Colonel Tony De La Guardia and a special unit in the Cuban Ministry of the Interior (MININT). De La Guardia was the twin brother of General Patricio De La Guardia, head of Cuba's Special Forces. He was also a close friend of Ochoa and son-in-law of Diocles Torralba—the latter a minister in Castro's cabinet, a close friend of Ochoa's and a discreet proponent of perestroika.

Mounting evidence in U.S. intelligence agencies of Cuba's drug connections, including DEA infiltration of a drug network and videos of drug planes flying into Cuban territory, posed a serious problem for Castro. On top of that, the Cubans had links with Noriega's drug-dealing government in Panama—another potential embarrassment. All of this would create a scandal if the illicit commerce were verified.

Once again, Castro needed scapegoats. The De La Guardia brothers, Diocles Torralba and members of their staffs were incarcerated by State Security and their fate bundled with Ochoa's. All would be charged with treason, fiscal corruption or narco-trafficking.

*   *   *

Explaining the matter to the Cuban public, Raul Castro sent mixed signals in a rambling discourse. He accused Ochoa of "independent thought ... betrayal against the morality, the principles and prestige of our revolution ... that type of betrayal which leads, sooner or later, to political betrayal.... It is preferable that Cuba sink into the ocean, like Atlantis, before the corrupting forces of capitalism prevail."[9] Raul's allusions to betrayal and the forces of capitalism made some listeners wonder whether Ochoa had been involved in a conspiracy to bring political change to Cuba.

[7] Ibid., p. 93
[8] Benemelis and Manon, *Juicio a Fidel,* p. 110
[9] *Granma,* July 6, 1989

This view seemed to gain plausibility as Jose Ramon Balaguer of the Central Committee, speaking on Cuban TV, hinted of "penetration and attempts to assassinate Fidel." Carlos Rafael Rodriguez, a wily old PSP veteran ever cautious in his pronouncements, publicly asserted that the situation had "threatened the existence of Fidel."[10]

The trial itself, on June 27 and 28, 1989, recalled the Stalinist show trials of the mid-century. Defendants accused themselves and praised the leader, while prosecutors delivered indignant discourses. Ochoa was stripped of his rank, his titles, his medals, and dishonorably discharged from military service. He was even deprived of the right to wear his uniform, and had to finish the trial in civilian clothes. In the streets, the slogan "8-A" (meaning "Ocho-A" in Spanish) appeared in graffiti—an apparent show of support for the general.

Ochoa was condemned to die before a firing squad. Also stripped of rank and condemned to die were Colonel Tony De La Guardia, his assistant Major Amado Padron, and Ochoa's aide Captain Jorge Martinez. Six men, including General Patricio De La Guardia, were condemned to thirty-year prison sentences, while four others received terms of five to twenty years. Diocles Torralba, convicted of fiscal corruption in a separate trial, got a twenty-year sentence.

There was more to come. Three ministers and nine vice-ministers were chucked out of their positions. Eleven generals and a score of colonels and lieutenant colonels were demoted or forced to retire from the military. Hundreds of junior officers in the MININT were reassigned or placed under virtual house arrest until the government decided their fate. A few were eventually reassigned to State Security, while many others were shifted to work in civilian life, often in menial jobs.

The most surprising of demotions was that of Interior Minister Jose Abrahantes. A man responsible for thousands of deaths and executions, and a former chief of Castro's personal escort, Abrahantes was one of the tyrant's most trusted officials and one of Cuba's most reviled men. Sentenced to twenty years' incarceration, the former minister would die in prison less than two years later. The government stated that the cause of his death was a stroke, but foul play was naturally suspected.

The purge wreaked havoc even among the most loyal members of the regime. And outside Cuba, the Soviet Bloc fell apart with astonishing speed.

---

[10] Benemelis and Manon, *Juicio a Fidel,* pp. 32–35

CHAPTER XXX.

EXILE POWER

In the last months of the eighties, the world seemed to change every minute.

The Berlin Wall, symbol of the world's division, crumbled under the hammers of a people impelled by dreams of freedom. From dungeons and concentration camps, poets and writers emerged to lead nations. In Romania, a tyrant's own army executed him. The Soviet Union dissolved under pressure from internal strife, a bankrupt economy and ungovernable forces of change. Even in the People's Republic of China, Mao's legacy was on the verge of crumbling as thousands of young people crowded Tiananmen Square and made their stand for liberty, until army troops mowed them down.

On March 15, 1990, a young Afro-Cuban publicly declared that "Communism is a utopia" and said, "Cuba requires the same changes as have occurred in Eastern Europe." For so speaking, Jorge Luis Garcia Perez, also called Antunez, was convicted of "hostile propaganda" and put in prison, where he remains as of this writing.

* * *

The growing dissident movements in Cuba attempted a new strategy.

When human rights leader Ricardo Bofill went into exile, Gustavo Arcos, a veteran of Castro's campaign against Batista, replaced Bofill as the movement's chief organizer. Arcos, in a meeting with foreign reporters, demanded a new dialogue with the Castro regime. Exile leaders Tony Varona and Armando Valladares criticized this initiative, calling it a "betrayal." For many exiles, and for some opposition groups inside Cuba, a dialogue could only be possible with the departure of the Castro brothers and their chief collaborators.

To others, the demand for dialogue looked like a smart maneuver. Should Castro accept a dialogue, he would legitimize the Cuban human rights movement. A refusal to negotiate would confirm Castro as an unbending tyrant and open his regime to worldwide criticism. In this view, the move had everything to win and nothing to lose. Meanwhile, however, a real rift had opened up between some exiles in Miami and activists in Cuba.

Reinaldo Bragado: "Valladares did not have to share our outlook, but he didn't have to be so vehement in the way he attacked Arcos. Our committee had worked very hard to provide him with information on hundreds of human rights violations."

Ricardo Bofill: "Our people inside Cuba were facing heavy repression. Gustavo and Sebastian Arcos were arrested many times. Their houses were surrounded by State Security-sponsored mobs. Their lives were threatened. The walls of their homes were painted with government graffiti. Hundreds of human rights activists were detained, threatened, jailed for ridiculous reasons. The government tried to crush us. It's a miracle we survived."

At about the same time, an exile group—led by writer Reinaldo Arenas and filmmakers Nestor Almendros and Jorge Ulla—demanded a plebiscite in Cuba. Their "Open Letter to Fidel Castro" gained international publicity, having been signed by Nobel laureates, movie actors, and literary personalities including poet Allen Ginsberg and novelists Saul Bellow, Camilo Jose Cela and Mario Vargas Llosa. Arenas, who had served time in Cuba's prisons for his political convictions and sexual preferences, declared: "The objective is to ask precisely what [Castro] cannot give, because it would mean his downfall."[1] Indeed, Castro's government attacked the letter as malicious.

*   *   *

With the loss of Cuba's principal donor, the island's economy—which had otherwise depended on low-profit agricultural products and bargain-rate tourism—took a nosedive.

Enrique Callejas was a teacher in Havana during the early nineties. Callejas: "In the years after the collapse of the Soviet Union, Cuba changed dramatically. Many loyal Party members, from the high echelons to the lowest levels, were disconcerted. They did not understand what had happened. Then came the slogans that said we must survive as a socialist nation at all costs, even if we reached 'Option Zero.' This meant total poverty, hunger and bankruptcy. From Castro, in his speeches, came warnings that the nation faced the bleakest moment in its history. Of course he never considered resigning. Abdi-

[1] *The Washington Post*, December 28, 1988

cation from power for the common good was unthinkable.... Spare parts were not received from Europe because a lot of countries demanded payments and limited credit lines. Machinery broke down. Raw materials for manufacturing were not available. Transportation was so poor that ox carts replaced buses in many places. Cubans could not survive on their salaries. Robbery, black-marketeering and prostitution for the tourist trade had become a way of life. Castro, who denounced Batista for allowing prostitution in Havana, had turned Cuba into the biggest bordello in the hemisphere."

For a time, Cuban officials hoped that the old Communist Party would regain power in the Soviet Union and renew its bond with Castro. Those hopes were dashed in August 1991, when a coup against Gorbachev failed and Boris Yeltsin emerged as a new hero of Russian reform. Hundreds of Cuban officials abroad—diplomats, journalists, scientists, even members of DGI—requested asylum in foreign countries. During a three-month period at the end of 1990, thirty-two Cuban government officials requested political asylum in Spain alone, during flight layovers. Twelve of those were technicians assigned to the Chernobyl-type nuclear plant being built at Juragua, in central Cuba.[2] Thousands of other Cubans, unable to leave the nation or find asylum in embassies, set out to sea in rafts made of inner tubes and rope. In 1993, the U.S. Coast Guard would tally 3,656 new arrivals, while speculating that thousands more had perished in the desperate journey.[3]

Cuban rafters even showed up in the Cayman Islands and Mexico. When the Mexican government returned a group of refugees to Cuba, exiles in the U.S. organized demonstrations and obtained through diplomatic pressure what in an earlier day would have been impossible. Castro's government released the imprisoned rafters, all of whom reached the United States via Mexico. It was a display of political clout that showed Cuban exile influence working beyond U.S. borders.

Exile groups joined together under umbrella movements to coordinate anti-Castro activities. An organization called Cuban Unity was formed under the leadership of radio commentator Armando Perez Roura. Two of the protests it helped organize exceeded one hundred thousand participants.

Castro, who for decades had been damning the United States, was now trying hard to find a way of reestablishing some level of relations that, without loosening his hold on power, would ease the embargo and allow Cuba a larger line of credit. Through contacts at the United Nations and other forums, Cuban diplomats hammered out condemnations of the embargo, looking for openings that would not compromise the country's

[2] Radio Marti, December 5, 1990
[3] *The Miami Herald,* May 3, 1995

political structure. Former Costa Rican President and Nobel laureate Oscar Arias, France's President François Mitterrand and Spanish Prime Minister Felipe Gonzalez were among many world leaders who urged the United States to move away from the embargo policy, at the same time asking Castro to institute democratic reforms. The U.S., however, held to the position that the embargo would not let up as long as Castro refused to moderate his regime.

Enrique Callejas: "If Cuba needs computers or cars, it can buy them from Japan or Germany. Cuba has trade with Canada; it buys oil from Mexico and Venezuela. Cuba is bankrupt and it has lost credit lines since the Soviet collapse. Tobacco is a Cuban product and it is rationed. Malangas, avocados and yuccas are grown in Cuba, they do not come from Ohio or Idaho, yet they are rationed. Why? Because the Cuban government is a shambles, and the anti-embargo campaign is an excuse to justify its failures. At the same time, lifting the embargo would provide Castro with a moral triumph. He could gather his followers and say, 'See, I was right, I defeated the United States.' To end the embargo would allow Castro to go to the World Bank, to international lenders and say, 'See, I have made peace with the capitalists'—and he would be able to borrow hundreds of millions of dollars to keep his repressive machinery...."

*   *   *

By the early nineties, Cuban exiles in the United States had gained some real clout.

In 1970 there had not been a single Cuban candidate running for the Florida Legislature. In 1971 there were only about 20,000 registered Cuban-American voters in Dade County; by 1975 the number had more than doubled, to 48,445.[4] In 1982 there were three elected Cuban-Americans in the Florida Legislature. Two years later they numbered seven.[5]

By 1993, the exiles had three of their own number in the U.S. Congress: Florida Republicans Lincoln Diaz-Balart and Ileana Ros-Lehtinen, and New Jersey Democrat Bob Menendez. In the Florida Legislature, exiles had three senators and five representatives. In Dade County they had five commissioners and four city mayors, also controlling an impressive number of key positions at county and municipal levels. The exile vote, predominantly Republican, numbered more than two hundred thousand in Florida. While Florida's Hispanics represented only 7 percent of the vote in the state, their finances

[4] Leyva De Varona, *Cuban-Mexican Relations During the Castro Era*, pp. 73–77
[5] Ibid., pp. 87–88

made up 15 percent of Florida's contributions for national political campaigns.[6]

In analyzing the exiles' political power, Adolfo Leyva De Varona wrote: "The political impact of Cuban-Americans in South Florida is not limited to their growing number of voters or the influence of their elected officials. It is also felt in the influence exerted by interest groups, mostly emanating from the powerful economic enclave that Cubans have created."[7]

The economic power of the exile community was significant. Of the seventy-five wealthiest Hispanics in the United States, twenty-seven were Cuban exiles—a percentage far above their place in the Hispanic population.[8] Cuban exiles in South Florida owned or managed half a dozen radio stations, and they controlled a good portion of the import-export market. They were prominent in ownership of multimillion-dollar corporations including liquor, cigar, textile and soft-drink manufacturers. Dade and Broward Counties in Florida, and Bergen and Hudson Counties in New Jersey, had thousands of small Cuban-owned companies and corporations—retail outlets, service contractors, restaurants and other businesses.

Cubans had penetrated the mainstream economy. The president of Coca-Cola was a Cuban exile. Cubans owned car dealerships and fast-food franchises. More than four hundred banking executives in South Florida were of Cuban birth or descent. Some two thousand exiles were doctors; many sat on the boards of Florida hospitals, or owned clinics or medical centers. Seven hundred exiles were practicing law in South Florida. Cuban exiles controlled fully a quarter of the large building industry, whether as developers, supply distributors, architects, engineers, contractors or tradesmen. By 1996 there were 7,949 Cuban-exile-owned firms in South Florida, with sales and receipts totaling more than seven billion dollars a year.[9]

With growing political and economic influence came newfound means to wage the anti-Castro struggle. The exiles who had worked under U.S. orders at the Bay of Pigs were now in a position to lobby the U.S. government. Congressman Robert Torricelli, a New Jersey Democrat backed in the Senate by former Florida Governor (and fellow Democrat) Bob Graham, proposed an amendment stipulating that U.S. corporate subsidiaries in foreign countries no longer be allowed to trade with the Castro regime.

Many U.S. corporations had legally sold goods to Cuba through foreign subsidiaries. Advocates of the proposed measure argued that it would interfere with Castro's ability

---

[6] *The Wall Street Journal,* October 16, 1992
[7] Leyva De Varona, *Cuban-Mexican Relations During the Castro Era,* p. 96
[8] *Hispanic Business,* March 1996, p. 18
[9] *The Miami Herald,* August 26, 1996

to do business by causing the cancellation of numerous contracts and depriving Castro of millions in revenues. Opponents argued that it would mortgage Cuba's future to the United States without significantly hindering the Castro government.

Passage of the Graham/Torricelli amendment, under the name of the Cuban Democracy Act, was an undoubted coup. Cubans, mostly registered as Republicans, had achieved the legislation by relying on two Democrats. Indeed, presidential candidate Bill Clinton had supported the bill before President Bush did, thereby picking up $275,000 in campaign donations from Miami Cubans.[10]

"Surprisingly," Adolfo Leyva De Varona wrote, "it was ... Clinton who was perhaps most responsible for passing the bill. During his campaign in September 1992, Jerry Berlin, a prominent Miami fundraiser ... arranged an introduction between Mas Canosa and Clinton at a restaurant in Miami. Bush was not very pleased with the bill because, through it, Congress would tie the Executive's hands in managing U.S. foreign policy toward Cuba.... It thus appeared that the bill was destined to die. It was at this moment that Clinton arrived on the scene and saved the bill by telephoning several key Democrats and lobbying for their support.... The president of the Cuban American National Foundation then called Jerry Berlin and offered to credit Clinton for his efforts.... President Bush, afraid that Clinton was making dangerous inroads into the Republicans' traditional turf within the Cuban community, quickly decided to sign the bill in a public ceremony in Miami."[11]

Jorge Mas Canosa: "This is not a Republican or Democratic issue. I am a friend of George Bush and I shall vote for Bush but I am grateful to the Democrats. Torricelli is a Democrat. Bob Graham is a Democrat. And both are friends of the Cuban cause."

The Cuban Democracy Act would prove difficult to enforce. Some countries—like Canada, which had $125 million in trade with Cuba in 1991—passed their own laws attempting to block the American measure, calling it an interference in their national sovereignty.

While Castro complained about the U.S. embargo, exiles were active in international campaigns against the regime. Tony Varona traveled to Moscow, meeting with officials of the new Russia. Huber Matos's CID established an office in Poland. The CANF set up a press office in Moscow, while Mas Canosa and other CANF directors helped Cuban students in Russia to seek asylum in the United States and attempted to influence Russian relations with Cuba.

[10] *The Wall Street Journal,* October 16, 1992
[11] Leyva De Varona, *Cuban-Mexican Relations During the Castro Era,* pp. 457–58

As soon as the CANF gained power, it attracted the attention of journalists. Given Castro's popularity in American media, coverage of the CANF was not destined to be friendly. *The New Republic* would be obliged to pay $100,000 rather than face judgment as to whether it had defamed Mas Canosa in a controversial 1994 headline;[12] and the energetic CANF leader was often at loggerheads with media. Meanwhile, the situation of Cubans on the island was growing ever more grave.

[12] *The Miami Herald,* July 16, 1998

CHAPTER XXXI.

AIR FORCE WITHOUT BOMBS

As the situation in Cuba worsened, thousands fled the island in rafts made of inner tubes, wooden planks or anything that floated. One intrepid traveler arrived in a windsurfer after sixteen hours of perilous travel. Many did not make it. Dead bodies of rafters frequently washed up on Florida shores.

Jose Basulto and Billy Schuss—pilots who had served in infiltration teams of the early 1960's—formed Brothers to the Rescue, a volunteer air force that would overfly Caribbean waters in search of rafters. At first the planes went out three times a week. Then they flew every day, dropping supplies to those in need, deploying color dyes to mark locations and radioing information to the U.S. Coast Guard. The group was funded by monthly donations from individual supporters.

Rescue flights were dangerous operations. In order to spot rafters, pilots had to fly low, as close as three hundred feet above the waves. One plane belonging to Basulto crashed into the ocean. Another was destroyed in the Everglades, and pilot Coqui Lares was seriously injured.

Jose Basulto: "We started with Cuban exiles but it became an international organization. We have Argentine, Nicaraguan, Peruvian, French, Swedish, Venezuelan, American pilots and even a Russian. We have young pilots and old pilots. One of our best pilots is a woman who leaves her children with a baby-sitter to fly missions. We have the support of thousands of exiles who send in small donations, two dollars, five dollars. It is an emotionally draining task. We feel elated when we arrive in time to save lives, but we feel crushed when we spot an empty raft and wonder if we could have saved another life. Brothers to the Rescue is a labor of love. It is an air force without bombs."

Ramon Martinez: "I was rescued after three days at sea. There were two of us. The sun was cooking our skin even though we wore long-sleeved shirts. We had little food and were running low on water. We had about a gallon left and then this plane came flying right over our heads, circled above us, and I knew we were saved.... Seeing that plane above us was the sweetest thing."

Between the summer of 1991 and the end of 1994, Brothers to the Rescue—according to Jose Basulto—saved upwards of four thousand lives.[1] Similar groups, including the Puerto Rico–based Rescue Legion and the Cuban Pilots Association, also launched significant rescue operations.

Arturo Cobo, a Brigade 2506 veteran residing in Key West, created "The Transit Home for Cuban Refugees," a nonprofit operation to help rafters once they had arrived on U.S. shores. With the aid of two dozen local volunteers and funding from supporters, Cobo refurbished an old house on nearby Stock Island. As soon as the U.S. Coast Guard released rafters, the volunteers took over. Refugees were provided with hot meals, medical check-ups, clean clothing and beds to sleep for a number of days, until relatives picked them up or charitable organizations helped resettle them in new lives.

Arturo Cobo: "What we provided more than anything was human warmth. Cubans arrived, wet and scared after days at sea. They were in a strange country, and their own people were there to help. At any hour they came in, three or four in the morning, someone was there to greet them. We gave them soap, towels and shaving gear. They showered and we provided them with clothing. We cooked a hot meal even if it was at four in the morning. In the first months of our operation we gave away more than a thousand pairs of shoes, a thousand toothbrushes, and it was all done by exiles, without the help of governments."

Ramon Martinez: "I had grown up hearing how exiles were greedy and cruel and did not love Cuba and then I was in this shelter and these people I didn't even know were cooking steaks and rice and beans for us. They were giving us new sneakers, jeans, socks, underwear. I showered with scented soap, I shaved with a brand new razor and these people were telling me, 'Don't worry, you are among Cubans. We love you. We will help you. Your nightmare is over.' They had this house that was clean and full of bunk beds, and they even had toys for the little children who arrived in rafts. I had never dreamt that such people existed. This was what being Cuban was all about—not the lies that I had grown up with."

*   *   *

In Cuba the situation became more desperate by the day. A number of human rights

[1] Interview with Jose Basulto, Miami, 1998

opposition leaders, including Huber Jerez, Hiram Abi Cobas and Elizardo Sanchez, were
jailed and condemned to prison terms. Another dissident, Angel Galvan, was killed by a
policeman in a street confrontation.[2]

In 1991 a number of street protests against the government took place in the towns
of Aguacate, Jaruco, Bejucal, Santiago de las Vegas and Cardenas, with dozens of citizens
arrested. Other incidents occurred in Havana, Cienfuegos and Holguin, where police
beat protesting women. Three university students in Santa Clara were sentenced to prison
after being accused of belonging to a resistance movement called "New Lights of Liberty." In October 1991 six men were arrested in Matanzas on charges of burning sugar
cane fields; they got sentences ranging from five to eighteen years in political prison
camps.[3]

An especially defiant act was the announcement of a demonstration to take place
at Villa Marista, the State Security headquarters in Havana. The Liberty and Peace
Movement—led by brothers Daniel and Tomas Aspillaga, joined by Omar Del Pozo and
other human rights activists—called the protest for September 6, 1991, by phoning
Miami radio stations and saying they intended to picket State Security headquarters.
Omar Lopez Montenegro was one of the human rights activists in Cuba who took part.

Omar Lopez Montenegro: "I slept at a friend's house the night before the protest....
On that morning many human rights activists were detained by State Security before
they could leave their homes. Even with the arrests, we managed to get together two
groups of about fifteen people each. One group began moving down San Miguel Street
and the second group down Mayia. As we approached the State Security compound we
saw hundreds of agents waiting for us. It was an impressive display. I look back on it now
and I realize they were the ones who were afraid of us. They could not conceive of what
was happening. Some reporters from the foreign press were there, and State Security
could not crush us without endangering their public image; so they tried to intimidate us,
to scare us into quitting. Omar Del Pozo told them that they were wasting their time, we
refused to be intimidated. We began screaming anti-Castro slogans, demanding freedom
for political prisoners. An old man joined us.... They finally closed in on us. Basilio Alexis
Lopez, Daniel Aspillaga, Raul Dimas and Tomas Aspillaga were beaten by State Security
agents. All four were arrested at once. It is hard to describe how important that moment
became for the opposition in Cuba. We showed we were not afraid of facing the system.
We went from being idealists who verbally demanded changes to idealist activists who

[2] *El Nuevo Herald*, October 4, 1990
[3] *The Miami Herald*, October 24, 1991

physically demanded changes. I was arrested eleven times in the next seven months."

Before the end of 1991, seven clandestine members of Huber Matos's CID and twenty-eight other members of resistance movements had been arrested in the eastern city of Holguin.[4] In Matanzas three exiles were arrested after entering the island with weapons and explosives. One was executed, while the other two received prison sentences.

During 1992, hundreds of Cubans were imprisoned on charges of spreading "enemy propaganda." Two human rights activists, Rogelio Carbonell and Juan Novoa, were gunned down by police officers. Sebastian Arcos was sentenced to four years' imprisonment. Despite the repression, dozens of opposition groups inside Cuba, boasting several thousand members, were active at year's end.

* * *

Miami exiles, in defiance of U.S. authorities, were still launching armed operations on Cuban shores. Tony Cuesta, the one-time swimming champion who had been on two dozen raids to Cuba in the early sixties—losing his eyesight, an arm, and years of his life in Cuban jails—was dying of hepatitis. He spent his final weeks organizing a group of hard-core fighters to make one more attack.

Given that much of Cuba's income derived from tourist resorts owned by Spanish corporations, Cuesta targeted a hotel where only tourists were allowed and where Cubans were denied admission. Late on a summer night in 1992, a rubber raft with four commandos swept past the Melia Hotel in Varadero Beach, machine-gunning the resort with more than two hundred rounds of automatic rifle fire. No tourists were injured; but after news of the attack had been published in the European press, numerous vacation cancellations were received.

Meanwhile, the Castro government was taking harsh actions against refugees. In mid-1993, U.S. officials charged that Cuban marine patrols, using grenades, snipers and gaff hooks, had killed several people who were swimming toward America's naval base at Guantanamo. In May 1994, Cuban officials arrested attorney Francisco Chaviano, who was working to document abuses against refugees. Despite being a civilian, Chaviano was tried by a military tribunal for violating state secrecy and given a fifteen-year sentence. He remains in jail as of this writing.

[4] *The Miami Herald*, December 21, 1991

CHAPTER XXXII.

A VAST HUMAN CRISIS

After several hijackings of ferryboats and passenger vessels in Havana, Castro's officials were bound and determined to stop any further mass escapes. On July 13, 1994, seventy-two Cubans attempting to flee the island boarded an old tugboat called *Trece de Marzo*. Many of the conspirators were traveling in complete families, and the group included a good number of children.

As the slow-moving tugboat left Havana harbor, Cuban authorities reacted with fury. Seven miles out to sea, they turned high-pressure water hoses on the vessel. Many refugees were swept off the deck by the force of the water. People scrambled for shelter inside the boat's cabin. Castro's vessels rammed the craft. Crushed by steel hulls, the tugboat sank, and dead bodies floated on the water. Of the seventy-two Cubans who had boarded the craft, forty-one perished in the massacre, including at least nine children.[1]

The regime tried to conceal the incident. For years, people had heard that Castro's helicopters dropped sandbags on rafters, and that Cuban gunboats rammed rafts on open seas. The sinking of the tugboat had taken place very close to Havana, with many dozens of people involved. The survivors were placed under arrest and told to keep silent; but within hours, human rights activists in Havana were gathering information about the massacre, phoning Miami and setting up clandestine interviews with foreign journalists.

When the news came out, Castro's government tried to play it down by arguing that it had been caused by the refugees' recklessness. A number of survivors went on Cuban television to blame themselves and others in the group for the tragedy.

*   *   *

[1] *The Miami Herald,* July 21, 1994

Three weeks later, on August 5, 1994, large crowds gathered on Havana's oceanfront in response to rumors that exile vessels would be arriving to take refugees. Within hours, the crowds had turned into a riotous mob. Carlos Trellez, a mechanic, was one of those present.

Trellez: "I was working on a truck and a mob turned the corner. There were hundreds of people, young and old, black and white, men and women screaming anti-Castro slogans, crying, 'Freedom! Freedom!' A chill went up my spine. I had dreamt of this happening. I locked up my tools and walked down the street, following the crowd. I saw young boys throwing rocks at store windows. The sidewalk was full of shattered glass. Near Luz Street a police car was on fire. When another police car drove by the mob chased it, throwing rocks and anything they could find. A few minutes later I saw a line of cops advancing on a group of rioters. The rioters threw rocks and the police moved back, waiting for reinforcements. Later, a dozen trucks brought hundreds of officers that advanced on the mob. The crowds broke up on Luz Street, with people running into buildings, jumping fences. I ran across to another street. Clusters of students and young workers were fighting with officers. One policeman had to be carried away, his face covered with blood. A young man was on the ground bleeding, and a policeman was handcuffing him. It was like that on several different streets. I saw a police car driving down a street, and four young boys up on a roof throwing bricks at it. One of the bricks dented the roof of the car, which turned a corner and disappeared. The whole thing lasted a couple of hours and I was told that several officers had died in the street fighting, but I don't know if that's true. I heard reports on Radio Marti that as many as thirty thousand people were involved in the incidents, but I don't know how anyone could figure out how many people were involved. It was not a single riot but a lot of incidents in many different streets in a section of the city. Some streets were quiet and others were packed with screaming protesters. Whenever police showed up in force, the mob dispersed and then regrouped a couple of blocks away. I went back home after being chased by police and State Security agents. From the balcony of my house I could see police cars forming roadblocks. They arrested a lot of people, hundreds or maybe thousands. I saw two officers armed with nightsticks hitting a woman. I saw a young boy being chased by police but they couldn't catch him. That kid ran like a bullet.... The police were able to contain the riots before nightfall. If the riots had lasted a few more hours and spread to other sections of Havana, it would have been the end for Castro."

Enrique Callejas: "In areas of Havana where nothing happened, you saw a lot of police activity. A neighbor of mine, a member of a human rights group, was picked up by State Security. They held him for several days until they were sure the riots had calmed down and the situation was under control. Hundreds were arrested in the aftermath of August 5. It was a day on which the Castro government trembled."

In days following, the regime reverted to an old strategy of defusing an explosive situation by letting people off the island—and thousands fled on makeshift rafts.

Enrique Callejas: "One day the frontier guards were arresting rafters, and the next day they were standing by, watching people build rafts out in the open. It was incredible. Many saw it as an opportunity. We didn't know how long it would last, for in Cuba the situation changes by the day. People were breaking their furniture and the walls in their houses to get wood and materials for rafts. In less than a week, thousands had set out to sea and thousands more were building vessels."

Abruptly, the Clinton administration was facing a refugee crisis on the scale of the Mariel boatlift. With America's general mood being anti-immigration, Clinton could not afford to allow many thousands of refugees to enter the United States on a carte-blanche basis.

On August 19, the President announced that any refugees intercepted at sea would be sent to the U.S. naval base at Guantanamo, there to be placed in internment camps. On August 22 and 23, the U.S. Coast Guard picked up 5,224 rafters.[2]

Once more, a vast human crisis was turned into a game of political extortion. Clinton had vowed that Castro would not dictate the immigration policy of the United States; but Castro managed to do so by causing Clinton to act against the refugees. The favored status that Cuban exiles had enjoyed in fleeing from Castro suddenly vanished as internment camps were set up at Guantanamo. The exiles were stunned. To them, the internment of refugees was a betrayal of principles, tantamount to punishing the victim instead of the blackmailer.

Some exile leaders attempted to salvage what they could from a losing situation. Jorge Mas Canosa of the CANF and several other Florida power brokers met with Clinton at the White House. Enraged, the exile leaders argued that the administration was violating the Cuban Adjustment Act of 1966, which allowed refugees to apply for permanent residency in the U.S. a year and a day after arriving in the country. In an apparent effort at placation, the White House increased restrictions on travel to Cuba and limited the amounts of money exiles could send to their families on the island, thereby cutting the income that the Castro government could realize from these transactions.

On August 27, the United States announced it would resume immigration talks with the Castro government. The talks, many exiles asserted, might presage an effort by

[2] *The Miami Herald,* May 3, 1995

Cuban diplomats to obtain a lifting of the embargo—while the U.S. administration, fearing a bigger wave of refugees, might give up the embargo in exchange for political calm.

Within weeks, the number of refugees in the Guantanamo internment camps had reached 31,000 men, women and children. Carlos Trellez and Enrique Callejas were among the thousands who had left Cuba in rafts and ended up in the detention centers.

Enrique Callejas: "I left with two others and was picked up within hours after leaving Cuba. But although many thousands were rescued, thousands more probably died at sea. I saw two bodies floating in the water, both young males. One of the men with me saw a body that washed up at Guanabo Beach the day before we set out."

Carlos Trellez: "I spent a day and a half in a small rowboat with a cousin. We saw debris from several rafts. One raft was all torn up and had stains that looked like dried blood."

Enrique Callejas: "When I arrived at Guantanamo, they were setting up a tent city. It was horrible, very depressing and hot. The ground there is very dusty and dust was everywhere. Some of the soldiers were very kind but others were rude and screamed at us. I was stunned. I had risked my life to escape from hell, and I found myself in a concentration camp. I know the Americans say it was not a concentration camp, but it was—barbed wire, horrible living conditions, poor sanitation. We were not allowed to receive letters from our relatives in Miami or newspapers from the outside world. We didn't know if we were going to be there for a month or ten years."

Carlos Trellez: "Every day more arrived. Most were very decent people. We had doctors, engineers, teachers in our compound; but there was desperation. We couldn't understand what was happening, why we were not allowed to go to Miami…. There was frustration and resentment; we had some fights and several suicides. It was a time of my life I want to forget. In Cuba we had no hope, no freedom, no future. So we had left Cuba and then found ourselves back in a corner of our own country, living behind barbed wire, guarded by American soldiers, denied news of the outside world, not even being told what the future held for us. It was like being badly wounded and then being wounded again by doctors and nurses in the hospital where one is supposed to be cured."

By September, Cuban and U.S. diplomats had reached an agreement. Fidel Castro would re-close Cuba's borders and prosecute people who attempted to flee the country, while the United States would accept up to twenty thousand immigrants from Cuba per year. Once again Castro's guards were patrolling the Cuban coast, arresting all those who were caught trying to flee the island.

For months, the situation at Guantanamo remained in limbo. A few hundred refugees were allowed entry into the U.S. with humanitarian visas. Brothers to the Rescue attempted to make personal deliveries of humanitarian aid to the interned refugees, but were denied permission. In May 1995, after meetings with Cuban diplomats, U.S. officials announced that they would allow the Guantanamo refugees to enter the States, agreeing at the same time to return all future rafters to Cuba.

Exiles showed more anger than ever. They expressed bewilderment at the idea that the U.S. Coast Guard, which had saved thousands of rafters throughout the years, would now intercept fleeing Cubans and return them to the dungeon isle.

"The immigration question is only part of our objection to the deal," wrote Congressman Lincoln Diaz-Balart. "It involves deep frustration that is caused by seeing the same administration in Washington negotiate secret deals with the Cuban tyrant while subjecting other Caribbean tyrants to total blockades. Cuban-Americans are not demanding that 20,000 Cubans leave the island. They seek a quota of only two: the Castro brothers."[3]

Jeane Kirkpatrick, former U.S. representative to the United Nations, seconded these views. "When the U.S. intercepts and returns Cuban refugees," she wrote, "the U.S. Coast Guard makes itself an arm of Fidel's tyranny. The administration made no demands and secured no concessions.… The president should not make agreements which violate fundamental American principles."[4]

Jorge Mas Canosa and the Cuban American National Foundation, which had pledged millions of dollars to help resettle the Guantanamo refugees, now withdrew the offer. "They made this policy alone," Mas Canosa said. "Let them solve the problems of Guantanamo alone."[5]

Several exile organizations, joined by thousands of others, created massive protests in Miami the likes of which had rarely, if ever, occurred in an American city. Cars full of exiles blocked tollbooths on a Miami expressway, allowing only ambulances to pass, backing traffic up for miles. Two days later, cars blocked exit ramps on expressway entrances and exits, causing more gigantic traffic jams.

Lightning protests became the order of the day. Organizations pooled their membership to stage sit-ins at busy intersections and downtown areas. Hundreds of Miami businesses closed for fifteen minutes as owners and employees moved into the streets and paralyzed traffic. A night vigil in a public park drew four thousand exiles with candles. In other places from Puerto Rico to California, exile groups rallied and picketed at immigration offices and other federal buildings.

[3] *The Miami Herald,* May 21, 1995
[4] *International Herald Tribune,* May 24, 1995
[5] *The Miami Herald,* May 3, 1995

The Miami demonstrations caused much controversy, for daily confrontations were affecting the tourism industry as well as the lives of millions.

Jose Basulto: "What are we supposed to do? Stand by while our people are detained in international waters and then turned over to Castro? We have to make a point, to make it clear to the administration that the exile community is enraged with this violation of human rights and of international rights. We are not burning down buildings, destroying neighborhoods or looting. We are protesting in a way that will show our anger and our unity as a people."[6]

Ramon Saul Sanchez had served time in federal penitentiaries during the eighties for his paramilitary activities against the Castro government. Now leading the Cuban National Commission, he was also masterminding the protest activities.

"The audience that Sanchez is playing to," according to commentator Tom Fiedler, "is not in the White House, but rather in Cuba. He hopes that the Cuban people who hear of the protests on Radio Marti, read of them in the controlled press or learn of them in phone calls from Miami relatives, will use them as models for their own protests sometime in the future."[7]

U.S. Attorney General Janet Reno, for whom many Cuban-Americans had expressed dislike due to her defense of Clinton's policies, requested a meeting with exile leaders. Remarkably, political and community leaders in a major U.S. city refused to meet with America's chief law enforcement official.

[6] Radio Mambi, Miami, May 15, 1995
[7] *The Miami Herald*, May 21, 1995

CHAPTER XXXIII.

GRUMBLING DISPLEASURE

Political and diplomatic efforts of the Cuban government now focused on pressing the United States to ease the embargo. It seemed that not a United Nations or other diplomatic meeting could go by without Cuba's delegation calling on the U.S. to change its policy. An unlikely ally came from the ranks of the anti-Castro groups.

Eloy Gutierrez Menoyo was a Spanish-born, Cuban-raised former comandante in the struggle against Batista. Soon after Castro had seized power, Menoyo turned coat on an anti-Castro conspiracy and helped the regime arrest more than a hundred rebels. Then he fled into exile. In Miami he led Alpha 66, launched commando raids on Cuba and was captured during an infiltration. After expressing remorse in a Cuban TV interview, Menoyo spent twenty-two years in Castro's dungeons and survived brutal beatings in which his hearing was damaged and his ribs broken. After leaving Cuba, he retired to Spain and made statements only rarely. A couple of years later, he returned to Miami and showed himself changed from the tough warrior he had once been.

Menoyo declared that confrontation between Cubans must end, and that an opening to the future lay in negotiation with Fidel Castro. He created Cambio Cubano (Cuban Change), a small organization that called for an end to the embargo, for the establishment of a legal opposition party in Cuba, and for the continuation of Castro's regime if, in exchange, it offered some form of political compromise to the exile community. In his interviews, the controversial Spaniard was seldom critical of Castro's system; but he did speak bitterly against the Cuban American National Foundation, against exile journalists and paramilitary groups.

Many exile leaders returned the fire. They accused him of being in the pay of the Spanish government, an agent of Castro's intelligence, or just plain foolish to imagine he could negotiate with a tyrant. For the pro-dialogue groups, Menoyo was a godsend. He did not have the challenging approach to a dialogue with Castro that people like Carlos Alberto Montaner were presenting. Gutierrez Menoyo did not seem to demand much. He was willing to lobby against the embargo; and his name still had the luster of his warrior's prestige.

Castro played the political card that had offered itself. During a visit to Cuba by Gutierrez Menoyo, the dictator met with the former political prisoner. A handshake was photographed, and the two remained in each other's company for three hours. Upon returning to Miami, Menoyo was brusque with members of the exile press and gave few details about the meeting. Agustin Tamargo, an exile journalist who had been a friend of the former political prisoner, posed his own questions in a radio broadcast.

Agustin Tamargo: "Menoyo owes the Cuban people an explanation of what transpired.... Did Menoyo speak on behalf of the nation? Did he demand that Castro abdicate from power? Did he demand at the very least that the iron gates of all prisons be opened? Menoyo speaks of reconciliation but he turns his back on more than a million exiles, maintains silence and only has harsh words for those who have struggled against Castro for decades.... The old tyrant knows the value of creating an illusion. A handshake, a photograph printed in newspapers in Europe and the United States, and the Cuban government can claim it is now more lenient. This is a mirage, political make-up to portray totalitarianism as embryonic democracy. Has Gutierrez Menoyo lost his senses?"[1]

The Menoyo-Castro handshake apparently had little effect on the Cuban government. Spokesmen averred that, even if they were willing to speak to more "moderate" members of the opposition, the regime would not permit a multiparty system or reforms that would alter its structure. When queried on this point, Menoyo said that the political change he envisioned would take time. In a Havana meeting of "moderate" exiles, which included several owners of travel agencies and charter companies doing business with Cuba, Menoyo challenged the government to bring about change. The regime played this occasion for all it was worth, claiming it had shown the "open policy" of Cuban socialism.

When former U.S. President Jimmy Carter offered to mediate a dialogue between exiles and the Cuban government, Menoyo did not attend the sessions at the Carter Center, stating he had other commitments. He remained the exile's exile, distanced by the regime and distrusted by many of his fellows.

* * *

[1] Radio Mambi, Miami

May 20, 1995, marked the one-hundredth anniversary of Cuba's War of Independence against Spain's colonial rule. As Cubans on both sides of the Florida Straits were celebrating, a Zodiac rubber raft with four passengers approached a Spanish-owned hotel at Cayo Coco on Cuba's northern coast. The raft made a sweep past the pier and patio area, and its riders—commandos of Alpha 66—opened fire with AK-47's and a .50 caliber semi-automatic rifle. They traded gunfire with members of Cuba's Frontier Guard and then hurried back to a temporary base on an uninhabited key of the Bahamas. As FBI agents probed the incident for possible violations of U.S. neutrality laws, Alpha 66, the oldest of all anti-Castro paramilitary groups, vowed to continue its attacks on the Cuban coast.

Andres Nazario Sargen: "Some people doubt these raids are effective, yet the first hotel company to pull out of Cuba was the Guitart corporation, the same one that owns the Cayo Coco resort. Could one of the reasons be that we raided their property on three occasions? Of course."

In December 1995, the FBI in California arrested three Cuban exiles on charges of possessing automatic weapons and military equipment for raids on Cuba. Other exiles, including Rodolfo Frometa and Fausto Marimon, were already serving time in U.S. penitentiaries for illegal possession of explosives.

The arrests did not seem to intimidate various other anti-Castro groups that were still planning raids against the island. As the year closed, at least three training camps on farms bordering the Everglades offered military training to those exiles who favored armed struggle.

*   *   *

Ramon Saul Sanchez was now expounding a strategy of nonviolent resistance. A veteran commando while still in his teens, and a prisoner in the U.S for paramilitary activities, Sanchez had come to the tactics of Gandhi and Martin Luther King in planning the massive exile protests in Miami. Now he proposed an unarmed flotilla of exiles that would enter Cuban waters to challenge the regime. His idea was to stage a demonstration at sea, six miles from Havana, exactly where Cuban authorities had sunk the tugboat of refugees a year before.

The flotilla, announced for July 13, 1995, received ample publicity. The U.S. government warned the exiles they would be courting danger by entering Cuban waters. Cuban authorities threatened to stop the flotilla at any cost. Despite the controversy, thirteen boats packed with more than one hundred people set sail from Key West. The lead boat, from which Sanchez directed the operation, was named *Democracia* (Democracy). Above the flotilla flew planes of the Cuban Rescue Legion and Brothers to the Rescue, carrying film crews from network television stations.

As the boats entered Cuban waters, Castro's gunboats intercepted them. The *Democracia* was rammed by two gunboats that sandwiched the exile craft between steel hulls. Rigo Acosta, a former political prisoner, was on the *Democracia.* Acosta: "When they hit us, all the glass from the cabin window exploded, sending shards everywhere. We had three wounded."

One of those was Dade County commissioner Pedro Reboredo. His foot was smashed, and a toe later had to be amputated. Cuban exile pilots tried to prevent a second ramming by flying dangerously low. Sergio Ramos, a former leader of Abdala, was in one of the planes.

Ramos: "I was flying with Jorge Bringuier of the Cuban Rescue Legion and when the gunboats began closing in on the *Democracia,* Bringuier dipped the plane down and went straight toward the gunboats. We were flying ten or twenty feet above the water, the landing gear almost touching the waves. Bringuier flew in between the two gunboats and made them veer away. It was like a strafing run without machine guns."

After the attack on the exile vessel, Jose Basulto and Billy Schuss of Brothers to the Rescue, each piloting a twin-engine plane, decided to cause a distraction in order to draw attention away from the damaged boat. Both pilots headed their craft into Havana. Cary Roque—the former TV actress and activist, now an exile journalist—was flying with Billy Schuss. Roque: "It was an intense moment. We were flying over Havana! A helicopter was following us but we kept on going, flying for several minutes. We had stickers with the 'Brothers to the Rescue' logo and a slogan that said 'Brothers, Not Comrades!' We dropped thousands of the stickers over Havana."

On shore, police were detaining hundreds of human rights activists and opposition members to prevent their going to the seawall across from the demonstration. Uniformed officers cordoned off areas near the seawall to keep others from assembling. The only civilians in Havana who could witness the events were those living in the tall buildings close to the shore. Laida Arcia Carro was in the flotilla. Arcia Carro: "A former political prisoner in the flotilla used a small mirror to reflect the light of the sun as a way of sending a signal to the people in the buildings along the shoreline. It was a way of saying we were here; and from a couple of different buildings, mirrors flashed back."

The crippled *Democracia* began to take on water and the boats withdrew, their passengers leaving flowers on the waves in front of Havana. The flotilla had an appreciable impact. Images of two Cuban gunboats ramming an unarmed vessel, and of exile planes dropping leaflets over Havana, made newspaper headlines and television features. Sanchez, elated, announced that a second flotilla would stage a protest in front of the tourist hotels at Varadero Beach.

On September 2, some two dozen craft had left Key West; but one of the flotilla sank less than twenty miles offshore. Some forty people floated for an hour in the water while a rescue operation took place; and the boats turned back. Lazaro Gutierrez died of heart failure after being rescued.

Georgette Franco was one of those who clung to debris for an hour. Franco: "The boat went down fast. We were floating in the middle of the ocean, wearing life jackets and hanging on to floating debris. We sang the Cuban national anthem. We watched out for each other. A Channel 10 helicopter filming the flotilla spotted us. It hovered over us for a while. After we were rescued the pilot saw me in Key West and said sharks had been swimming around us; he could see them from above."

Shortly afterward, Sanchez announced that a third flotilla would beam radio and television signals to Cuba from a sea location near the island; but that flotilla had to be cancelled due to inclement weather conditions.

* * *

While some exiles played the friendship card with Castro, and others inconvenienced him with shooting raids or flotillas, the Cuban economy continued on its perpetual downward trajectory. The government announced "economic reforms" including the creation of free-trade zones, agricultural flea markets, legalization of individual journeymen trades and licensing of privately owned small eateries known as *paladares.* Most of these reforms, rather than create new jobs, were intended to control and collect taxes from black-market activities that had been thriving for decades.

By 1995 Cuba was facing its third disastrous sugar crop in a row with a harvest of 3.3 million tons, one of the lowest yields of the century.[2] Tobacco production had decreased considerably, while manufacturing had withered from lack of raw materials and spare parts, as well as from sabotage.

As Castro's diplomats tried convincing the U.S. to relax the embargo, exiles launched a new offensive in Washington by backing legislation that would close the U.S. to foreigners who traded with Cuba. The proposed law—sponsored by North Carolina Senator Jesse Helms and Indiana Congressman Dan Burton, both Republicans—would allow American citizens to sue anyone who had purchased confiscated U.S. property from

[2] *Latin Trade*, August 1995, p. 12

Castro. It would also require the U.S. to withhold aid from countries that traded with
Cuba.

The three Cuban-American congressmen in Washington backed the new legislation.
Lincoln Diaz-Balart, Ileana Ros-Lehtinen and Bob Menendez joined with Robert Torricelli
from New Jersey to lobby for the law's approval. The Cuban American National Foundation also mobilized support for its passage. Even before the Helms-Burton proposal went
up for debate, it was slowing foreign investment in Cuba. The Australian mining company
BHP and a Canadian firm canceled plans to launch business ventures.[3] The Spanish-based
Guitart Hotel chain sold its properties in Cuba, while a French manufacturer with U.S.
holdings also decided not to invest.

In attempting to defuse Helms-Burton, the Clinton administration eased some travel
restrictions to Cuba, even allowing monetary assistance to be provided to human rights
and dissident groups inside the island. Castro's government, meanwhile, kept resisting
change, and Cuba's economic picture remained dismal. Aside from a few hotels and
resorts owned by European companies and a citrus farm owned by Israeli investors,
foreigners held few properties in Cuba. Unlike China, Cuba lacked even the appearance
of an infrastructure that could promise a safe return on investment.

"The difference," a *Wall Street Journal* editorial noted, "is that almost every businessman who visits Cuba comes away with a bad taste, and the sense, as one put it, that
they want your investment, but they don't want you."[4]

While Castro's PR machinery continued to portray Cuba as a "socialist democracy,"
repression increased. Large numbers of dissidents and human rights activists continued
to be detained; many, like Omar Del Pozo, were serving prison terms in Castro's dungeons and penal farms. Other dissidents were fired from their jobs or restricted in their
movements. Independent journalists who sent reports to exile groups were persecuted,
their scant office equipment confiscated or damaged by State Security. These freelance
journalists were confronting the Castro government by publishing articles in the exile and
international press.

In October 1995 a hundred human rights and opposition groups joined together to
form Concilio Cubano (Cuban Council), an umbrella directorate that worked to coordinate a united movement against the system. Some opposition groups in Cuba refused to
join, fearing government infiltration or questioning the motives of its leaders. Within
weeks, a number of groups had broken with the Cuban Council, while several key activists had been arrested or threatened.

[3] Ibid., p. 11
[4] As quoted in *The Miami Herald*, December 13, 1995, p. 19-A

The exile community's reaction to Concilio Cubano was mixed. Agenda Cuba, CID and other organizations supported the council. The Cuban American National Foundation and other groups took a wait-and-see posture, expressing concern that the new movement might be infiltrated or manipulated by State Security, or that it might compromise too much, by accepting cosmetic changes and not pressing for basic reforms.

"We have our agenda," CANF chairman Jorge Mas Canosa said, "and we stick by our agenda. The system has to be dismantled. Cuba needs complete freedom.... One can compromise in matters of procedure, but not on principles."[5]

The nation as a whole lived in grumbling displeasure with the system. Even the old dictator seemed to be aware of truths he publicly denied. When speaking to the National Assembly of Popular Power at an annual review, Castro accused Cuban sugar workers of being responsible for the poor harvest. In place of the customary standing ovation, silence followed this particular speech. Two delegates even challenged Castro. They asserted that the harvest had failed due to lack of fertilizers and equipment, and to poor planning; they added that many cane cutters lacked work boots and gloves, and should not be blamed for the poor production. Castro took the microphone and once more lambasted the sugar workers, also accusing Cuba's construction workers, who had failed to meet their goals by a whopping 40 percent.[6]

* * *

As the regime entered its thirty-seventh year, the new sugar harvest was already committed to repaying old debts. Coffee production was way down and not improving. Tobacco production was expected to be low, much of the crop damaged by bad weather. Some Canadian and European business deals were not consummated. Mexican and Venezuelan oil companies ceased to extend credit and demanded cash. Japanese creditors were also seeking to settle accounts. Although the regime was still profiting from exile dollars carried or sent to the island, the embargo had not been lifted despite tremendous lobbying spearheaded by Castro himself. Inside Cuba, individual sabotage was frequent, theft rampant, and corruption plaguing every level of government. Human rights and opposition groups were more vocal in their defiance. From exile, Cubans kept up their lobbying against the tyranny, while more militant action threatened.

And then, from out of the sky, came another plane of Brothers to the Rescue.

[5] WCMQ Radio, Miami, December 1995
[6] *The Miami Herald,* December 29, 1995

CHAPTER XXXIV.

KILLINGS IN THE AIR

On January 9 and 13, 1996, Brothers to the Rescue planes—flying at high altitude north of Havana and using favorable winds—blanketed the city with leaflets containing the thirty articles of the United Nations Universal Declaration of Human Rights. Cuban authorities denounced the leaflets as "subversive propaganda."[1] A few weeks later, Jose Basulto announced that Brothers to the Rescue would make a donation to Concilio Cubano, the opposition umbrella group on the island.

Castro faced a dual problem. He was being challenged from within by a growing non-violent resistance movement, and by political pressure from without. He understood the need to squelch opposition within his borders; but that was not as easy as in prior decades. The international prestige of Cuba's dissidents and the power of Cuba's exile groups had created an atmosphere that might endanger Castro's government if he unleashed a repressive onslaught.

※　※　※

Two weeks before the planned meeting of Concilio Cubano on February 24, State Security agents imprisoned almost two hundred pro-democracy activists. Several were singled out for speedy trials on trumped-up charges of resisting arrest.[2]

On the afternoon of February 24, 1996, three Cessna Skymasters belonging to Brothers to the Rescue flew north of Cuba searching for rafters. The first aircraft—piloted by Jose Basulto and Arnaldo Iglesias, with activists Jorge and Silvia Iriondo aboard

---

[1] *The Miami Herald,* March 27, 1996
[2] *The Miami Herald,* February 23, 1996

as observers—might have been straddling Cuba's legal airspace; but the other two were several miles distant.

Two Cuban Air Force MiG fighter planes swooped down on the more distant Cessnas. The MiG's fired rockets and the two exile craft—one in full view of a Miami-bound cruise ship—disintegrated. Four pilots were dead.

Armando Alejandre was a six-foot six-inch former U.S. Marine Corps sergeant, a two-tour Vietnam veteran and a well-known activist in Miami. Carlos Costa and Mario De La Pena, sons of Cubans born in the United States, were seasoned rescue pilots in their twenties who had never set foot on Cuban soil. Pablo Morales had been rescued as a rafter by the organization, which he then joined in order to save others.

When Jose Basulto realized they were gone, he turned off his transponder and took cover in the clouds.

Jose Basulto: "It is illegal for the air force of any nation to shoot down an unarmed civilian aircraft. That was premeditated murder. We learned that only a few days before, retired U.S. Admiral Eugene Carroll of the Center for Defense Information had been asked, while visiting Havana, how the U.S. would react if Cuba shot down exile planes."

As Basulto was retreating to Miami, a Castro agent left Miami and went back to Cuba to accuse Basulto's group of being a "paramilitary" organization. Juan Pablo Roque was a beefy bodybuilder and a former Cuban MiG pilot who had gone into exile and joined Brothers to the Rescue, spying for Castro and also selling information on Brothers to the Rescue and other anti-Castro groups to the FBI.

When the Helms-Burton measure came before the House of Representatives, it passed by a vote of 294 to 130. Relations between Cuba and the United States had descended to the cellar. Even more, the European Union made trade with Cuba contingent on reforms, while the U.N. Commission on Human Rights condemned the Castro regime. The shootings also affected the critical tourist industry, with a marked decline in European travel to the island in the following months.

A week after the shootings, nearly seventy thousand people filled the Orange Bowl on a rainy afternoon. The huge crowd had gathered to hold a religious service for the fallen pilots. As a school chorus began the event by singing a hymn, the rain stopped and a shaft of sunlight burst through the gray clouds to illuminate the stage. The crowd gasped. To many believers, it was a sign that God had not forgotten the Cuban people.

CHAPTER XXXV.

THE HOMELAND BELONGS TO EVERYONE

Inside Cuba, Castro stepped up the repression, purging officials who lacked "revolution-ary purity." In like manner, filmmakers, journalists and writers, after being accused of "unpatriotic conduct," were demoted or fired from their jobs.

Global changes continued to reach Cuba despite the repression. The decade of the nineties brought forth a new type of dissident, the "independent journalist," who posed a novel threat to censorship. Independent journalists were dissidents employed by exile radio stations and human rights organizations. Earning a few dollars a week in hard cur-rency, quite enough to subsist in the impoverished country, freelance journalists became the eyes and ears of Cuba, filing reports that ranged from local news to national exposés.

Omar Lopez Montenegro: "The value of the independent press in Cuba has been enormous. For decades the Cuban government had maintained rigid censorship. Sud-denly, with the creation of an independent press, their monopoly on the news was broken. The exile community and the world found out about the sinking of the tugboat *Thirteenth of March* because of independent journalists inside Cuba. The authorities went crazy, accusing independent journalists of being enemy spies and even passing legislation to incarcerate them."

Some independent journalists like Olance Nogueras were constantly apprehended by State Security, harassed into leaving Cuba. Others were allowed to leave the country on tourist visas but were barred from returning, as was the case of Yndamiro Restano in 1995.

Meanwhile, a small entity called the "Dissident Working Group" attracted journalists' attention with a document entitled "La patria es de todos"—"The Homeland Belongs to Everyone." The work first circulated in Cuba, then appeared in the exile press and spread everywhere. Giving a trenchant analysis of the regime's history and its impact on Cuban society, it accused the regime of political corruption, ecological abuse and an imperial foreign policy.

One of the document's four authors, Vladimiro Roca, was the son of Blas Roca, a leader of the Cuban Communist Party and one of the architects of the Marxist "parallel government" established soon after Castro's seizure of power. At one time a political insider, Vladimiro had studied in the Soviet Union and served as a captain in the Cuban Air Force, piloting a MiG fighter.

"Man cannot live on history," the document stated. "There is also a need to be free, to be open. The Cuban government ignores the word 'opposition.' Those of us who do not support the government are considered enemies as the government seeks to give a new meaning to the word homeland, linking it with revolution, socialism and nation. The government ignores the fact that homeland, by definition, is the country in which one is born. We are convinced that the homeland belongs to us all."

Labeling one-party rule as "an old and absurd argument," the document added: "The party insists on unity but forgets that for unity to be real, and not a mere parody, free consensus is necessary. In our country there is no consensus.... The philosophy of the government is not to serve the people but to be their dictator."[1]

Felix Bonne, Rene Gomez and Martha Beatriz Roque signed the paper along with Vladimiro Roca. All four were quickly arrested and held without trial, from the summer of 1997 until June 1999. Then they went before official courts and received sentences for "sedition." The members of the "Dissident Working Group" proved to be a thorn in Castro's side as they repeatedly refused to sign confessions, inform on their fellow dissidents, or choose exile over the squalor of political prison.

※　※　※

In the same months that the four dissidents created news with their controversial document, bombs exploded in Havana hotels. In July, charges were set off at the Capri and the National, followed by another in August at the Spanish-owned Sol Melia. The three bombings were reported by independent journalists and at first denied by Cuban authorities. Rumors spread of further bombings, including one at a government store for tourists in Oriente. Castro's supporters accused the Miami exiles of launching a terrorist campaign against tourism and foreign investment in Cuba.

[1] From the document "La patria es de todos"

In September, three more bombs exploded at the Copacabana, Triton and Chateau Hotels in Havana. A shard of flying glass killed Fabio Di Celmo, an Italian businessman staying at the Copacabana. Within a few days a Cuban tourism office was bombed in the Bahamas. According to an international news agency, eleven bombs were detonated inside Cuba between April and September 1997.[2] Two more were deactivated at tourist centers in October.[3]

State Security initially arrested a German tourist and accused him of setting off a firecracker in a Havana tunnel, then released him after extensive questioning. A Guatemalan named Francisco Cruz Leon was arrested and charged with acts of terrorism. Cruz Leon admitted to having smuggled explosives inside false marker pens and a clock radio. Cuban officials accused Luis Posada of having masterminded the Havana bombings.

Luis Posada Carriles was an exile steeped in war and intrigue. A veteran of the struggles against Batista and Castro, he had served in Venezuelan intelligence and then languished in jail after being accused of involvement in the Barbados bombing. Escaping from prison, he had fled to Central America where, under a false name, he helped run training centers for the Contra guerrillas.

Vanishing after the Iran-Contra disclosures, Posada again made headlines when, in 1990, a team of assassins working for Castro's intelligence ambushed him on a Guatemalan street. The hit team machine-gunned his vehicle, but Posada eluded his assailants and drove himself, wounded, to a hospital. He had been hit by several bullets, one of which had ripped through his face, shattering his tongue. By the time local newspapers had announced the failed assassination and the whereabouts of the mysterious Cuban, Posada had slipped out of the hospital, his face wrapped in bandages.[4]

Luis Posada Carriles underwent plastic surgery at a secret location in Central America, his operation financed by fellow exiles. With a new face and an assortment of new identities, he was back in action with the Havana bombing campaign. In 1998, State Security arrested three more members of his team entering Cuba with explosives.

[2] CNN, November 17, 1997
[3] *20 de Mayo*, September 18, 2000
[4] Author's interview with Posada

CHAPTER XXXVI.

"HOPE HAS NOT MATERIALIZED."

In November 1997 the exile community lost its *de facto* leader.

When Jorge Mas Canosa died of illness, more than twenty thousand mourners attended his funeral. The procession occupied a good chunk of Little Havana as thousands of supporters wept openly or bowed their heads in respect for the fiery little man to whom Cuba had been a "sublime obsession."

In guiding the establishment of the Cuban American National Foundation, Mas had envisioned a lobbying powerhouse that would be patterned after similar organizations of the Jewish-American community. CANF grew to be one of the most influential advocacy groups in the United States, while the former milkman became a world traveler, establishing personal relations with heads of state like Boris Yeltsin, Vaclav Havel, Argentina's Carlos Menem and Portugal's Mario Soares. At home, Jorge Mas befriended Ronald Reagan, George Bush and, briefly, Bill Clinton.

Mas understood the methodology of American politics and used every wedge he could to advance CANF in what he called "The Battle of Washington." He said more than once, "We are playing by the American rules of the game"—and in that game he knew how to reward friends as well as punish enemies.

When Republican Senator Lowell Weicker advocated a dialogue with the Cuban government and a lifting of the embargo, Mas went against him. The Republican National Committee watched in dismay as the CANF put its money behind Weicker's Democratic opponent, Joe Lieberman, in a 1988 campaign. Lieberman won, beginning a Senate career that would lead him to the Democratic nomination for the vice-presidency under Al Gore.

Under Mas Canosa's leadership, the CANF also played important roles in the founding of Radio Marti, TV Marti and the National Endowment for Democracy. One of the CANF's signal achievements was to obtain admission to the United States for nearly ten thousand Cubans exiled in third countries, including the Soviet Union.

Critics of the CANF, particularly those in the pro-dialogue ranks, predicted that the powerful lobby group would disintegrate without Mas to lead it. Indeed, at the time of Mas's death, the CANF was facing manifold difficulties. Several foundation directors were accused of violating neutrality laws by allegedly conspiring to kill Fidel Castro at an Ibero-American summit in Venezuela. The U.S. Coast Guard seized *La Esperanza,* a yacht belonging to CANF director Tony Llama. Two high-powered fifty-caliber rifles having been confiscated on the boat, authorities brought charges against a group of exiles that included CANF directors, former Escambray guerrillas and ex-CIA operatives.

Another public relations problem arose when *The New York Times* published an interview with Luis Posada Carriles in which the former CIA agent allegedly stated that CANF directors, by supporting his activity, had financed the bombings of Cuban hotels. From a hideout in Central America, Posada Carriles denied having said that. He did say he had acknowledged receiving funds from personal friends in the CANF to defray living expenses and to pay for plastic surgery after being wounded in Guatemala.

Although charges of planning assassination attempts against Castro and bombing campaigns in Havana probably damaged the CANF's image internationally, they had an opposite effect among many in the exile community. Some of those who had called the CANF "too political" now cheered the paramilitary operations. As it happened, the seven exiles accused in the anti-Castro plot were acquitted; and *The New York Times* effectively retracted the damaging part of its story about Posada Carriles by regretting "an editing oversight."

The Cuban American National Foundation survived the death of Jorge Mas and accusations of terrorism; but a group of its leaders broke with the organization over political differences and established the Cuban Liberty Council.

✻   ✻   ✻

The relationship between the Catholic Church and the Cuban government had ranged from outright war to cozy coexistence. In the early sixties several churches were used to hide explosives for the resistance. Priests like Father Ismael Teste transported weapons and explosives, while Father Francisco Lopez, a Spaniard, became chaplain of the Escambray guerrillas. Following a massive deportation of priests and nuns, church officials in Cuba adapted to circumstances by obeying government mandates. By the 1970's the political position of the Church had changed to the extent that Monsignor Cesare Zacchi, the papal nuncio in Cuba, declared Fidel Castro to be "ethically Christian," a striking statement that caused an uproar among anti-Castro Cubans.[1]

Roberto Martin Perez, who served almost three decades in Cuban political prisons, recalled an occasion on which the church did not intervene. Martin Perez: "There was a time at which political prisoners were being crushed by forced labor, made to work for hours under a broiling sun without water. Men were passing out from dehydration. A group of us sent out a clandestine letter to church authorities, requesting they intercede on our behalf in regard to the forced labor conditions. What came back was the statement that work makes a man noble. Wasn't that the slogan inscribed on the gates of Nazi concentration camps?"

Omar Lopez Montenegro: "When a group of dissidents was approached by a State Security force we attempted to seek sanctuary in a church, but the priest shut the door in our faces."

In the mid-nineties Castro was hunting for a public relations coup. Under pressure from the European Union, from international human rights organizations and many presidents of the Ibero-American group, the Cuban tyrant wanted to look tolerant to people outside Cuba.

Pope John Paul II's impending visit to Cuba made for mixed feelings at the start of 1998. Although the head of the Church had been instrumental in creating the atmosphere that toppled Marxism in Europe, he had seldom touched on the Cuba matter and had antagonized many when he appointed Jaime Ortega Alamino as Cuba's cardinal. Critics averred that Ortega Alamino had ignored the plight of political prisoners, often making public statements that seemed supportive of the regime. Although he had been imprisoned in the UMAP camps of the mid-sixties, he lacked the stature of Poland's Father Jerzy Popielusko or Hungary's Cardinal Mindszenty. The most outspoken Church official in Cuba was Archbishop Pedro Meurice, who made remarks critical of the government and was quoted, while on a trip to the United States, as complaining about those "who have confused the Fatherland with a single party."

"When the pope visited Cuba," political scientist Juan Lopez wrote, "civil society groups missed the opportunity ... to communicate their demands to the population of Cuba as well as to the international community. This missed opportunity for democratic activists in Cuba may be explained by the enduring disorder of the opposition [stemming from] the government crackdown in February 1996. Some opposition leaders were

[1] *Los Pinos Nuevos*, August 1972

imprisoned for extended periods of time and others were pushed into exile."[2]

To Castro's evident delight, the head of the Catholic Church publicly denounced U.S. embargo policy as "unjust and ethically unacceptable."[3] In other statements, the Pope sent a message that implied a two-way route to resolving tensions. He said: "Do not be afraid. Cuba must open to the world, and the world must open up to Cuba."[4] During a visit to a hospital for lepers and AIDS patients, the Pope called on Cuba to release political prisoners.[5]

"Hope has not materialized," Juan Lopez observed after the visit, "and in an apparent incongruous behavior, the Church hierarchy in Cuba has refused to foster the strengthening of civil society. Cardinal Jaime Ortega, the leader of the Church, and other members of the Catholic hierarchy have adopted a very conciliatory attitude toward the government.... Actually, the Church seeks to distance itself from democratic activists. The Church is not even willing to serve as a channel to send medicines to political prisoners."[6]

The year after the Pope's visit, an editorial in Italy's *La Repubblica* declared: "The Cuba that wanted to open up to the world, so that the world would open to Cuba—as John Paul II had so much hoped—has returned to a police state of the communist nightmare which many thought was now only a memory of the cold war."[7]

[2] Juan Lopez, Department of Political Science, University of Illinois, "Civil Society and Repression," a lecture, p. 4

[3] *The New York Times*, January 26, 1998

[4] Ibid.

[5] Ibid.

[6] "Civil Society and Repression," a lecture, p. 26

[7] *La Repubblica*, March 3–4, 1999

CHAPTER XXXVII.

CASTRO SPIES, THANKSGIVING CHILD

For years, Cuban exiles had been claiming that Castro's spies had infiltrated their community and organizations. Arrests or deportations of intelligence agents had been infrequent, even though defecting Cuban spies had affirmed that hundreds if not thousands of Castro operatives were working within the exile communities.

It came as a surprise, therefore, when the FBI arrested ten alleged Castro spies in Miami on September 8, 1998. The eight men and two women were from the notorious "Wasp Network" of DGI. Still other agents were apparently at large, and three Cuban diplomats were expelled from New York at the end of the year.[1]

The Wasp Network was commanded by Major Luis Medina and Captain Gerardo Hernandez of the Cuban military. Hernandez's cover identity was Manuel Viramontes, a name obtained from Texas birth certificate records. As Viramontes, Hernandez had a Puerto Rico voter-registration identity card, a doctored U.S. passport, a Texas birth certificate and a Mexican driver's license.[2]

During its raid, which capped a four-year investigation, the FBI seized computers, codes and electronic equipment, along with plans to sabotage aircraft hangars. One of the men arrested was Rene Gonzalez, a Brothers to the Rescue pilot. As the spies were brought up on espionage charges, Hernandez was also indicted on four counts of murder and conspiracy in connection with the downing of the Brothers to the Rescue pilots.

According to federal authorities, the main objectives of the spy unit were to collect information on U.S. military installations in Florida and to infiltrate anti-Castro organizations. One of the agents' jobs was that of "sending letters to *[The Miami]* *Herald*

[1] CNN, December 23, 1998
[2] *The Miami Herald,* May 8, 1999

portraying the writers as Cuban-American moderates and attacking community leaders like Jorge Mas Canosa."[3]

As information became public, the spy unit appeared to have been less than efficient. "Paying the rent late and losing a computer containing codes, as the Miami suspects apparently did, are not exactly hallmarks of Cuba's foreign intelligence agency. The ring seemed to have been singularly unsuccessful," *The Miami Herald* reported.[4]

All the arrested agents held full-time jobs as covers for their espionage activities; two were civilian employees at a U.S. military base. Although they could utilize modern devices of America's consumer society, like beepers and cellular phones, the spies were limited in their funding from Cuba and were expected to defray many of their expenses. Their security was apparently lax, as evident from the arrest of so many espionage operatives in a single swoop. Cuba's DGI or intelligence agents, with their training from the KGB and East German Stasi, were reputed to be first-rate professionals in covert operations. It was unusual enough to pin down and arrest even a single spy, nearly unheard-of to dismember a net of ten. And morale among the agents was apparently low; five of them made deals with prosecutors and testified against their fellow agents.[5]

Other arrests followed, including those of a husband-and-wife spy team living in Orlando, a scuba diver in Miami, and Mariano Faget, a mid-level bureaucrat at the U.S. Immigration and Naturalization Service (INS).

The Cuban agents' inefficiency might have had roots in the events of the prior decade. The Ochoa–De La Guardia prosecutions of 1989 had critically weakened Cuba's intelligence structure. After General Arnaldo Ochoa and Colonel Tony De La Guardia had been executed, Castro launched a massive purge at all levels of government with special emphasis on the Ministry of the Interior, where the De La Guardia brothers had enjoyed a major share of influence. Hundreds of officers and agents were reassigned, demoted or subjected to a form of house arrest called "The Pajama Plan." With many high-caliber intelligence agents ousted, those positions were taken over by regular armed forces personnel. The soldiers, accustomed to working in straightforward kinds of military operations, lacked the skills to be effective in the shadow world of espionage. Years later, the effects of the purge bore fruit when the FBI managed to "sting" the Wasp Network.

❖ ❖ ❖

[3] *The Miami Herald,* January 29, 2000
[4] *The Miami Herald,* September 17, 1998
[5] Associated Press, May 8, 1999

On Thanksgiving morning 1999, two cousins fishing off the coast of Fort Lauderdale spotted a black inner tube bobbing in the Atlantic. To their surprise, they found a trembling child clutching the tube and plucked little Elian Gonzalez from the sea.

Eleven rafters from Cuba had perished on the journey, including Elian's mother, Elizabet Broton.

The boy had been miraculously rescued from a shark-infested ocean on a day of spirit's gratitude. To a community that cherished its symbols, he quickly became a byword of resiliency, purity, and a nation's anguish.

Placed by the INS in the care of his grand-uncle, Lazaro Gonzalez, Elian might have lived a normal life under different circumstances; but Fidel Castro, with his perennial need for a boost in PR, was not to be ignored.

Lazaro Gonzalez: "When Elian came to the United States, his father, Juan Miguel, told me to take care of his son. Then Fidel got involved, and people were demanding I give up the boy. I always said I would turn the child over to his father, but Juan Miguel should come here and claim him, like any other father. It was not Juan Miguel requesting the return of Elian. It was Fidel."

What might have been a simple case of child custody became a political confrontation that escalated on a daily basis and became a full-fledged media spectacle.

Many exiles, frustrated and scarred by years of struggle against Castro, were ready to throw themselves into a major contest with the Cuban government. They vigorously argued that the child's mother had died seeking freedom for herself and her son, and that returning Elian to Cuba would violate the boy's human rights.

The American President, like many others before him, did not want to hand Castro a victory; but he was a mark for the canny extortionist. Longtime Clinton intimate Dick Morris analyzed the President's position vis-à-vis Castro in an interview with journalist Paula Zahn. According to Morris, Clinton blamed his 1980 Arkansas gubernatorial defeat on riots in Fort Chaffee instigated by Mariel refugees; and Clinton expressed the view that Mariel had cost President Jimmy Carter his re-election bid.

"Bill Clinton," Morris said, "is terrified of Castro. He looks over his shoulder for rafters the way Castro is always looking over his shoulder expecting an invasion of Marines."[6]

When Castro hinted that he might unleash a new wave of refugees if he didn't get his way, he gave the President a solid incentive to trade the child for political comfort. Other parties came vigorously into the play. The Archer Daniels Midland Company (ADM) and

---

[6] Fox TV News, April 23, 2000

its chairman, Dwayne Andreas—desirous of doing trade with Castro—actively supported Elian's return to Cuba. The influential National Council of Churches and its president, popular civil rights leader Andrew Young, joined the fray on Castro's behalf. Young happened also to be an ADM board member.[7]

From Havana, Juan Miguel Gonzalez made statements requesting the boy's return. A good number of eyebrows went up when Elian's father was joined by a legal representative of the highest order. Pleading the case for Juan Miguel and Castro's regime was no less than Washington attorney Gregory Craig, who had argued for Bill Clinton during the President's impeachment. Craig's law firm happened also to do work for ADM. How Gonzalez *père* had obtained, and paid for, the services of such a lawyer was a natural subject of speculation. To many observers, Craig's presence in the case was a sign that powerful interests—perhaps including the White House—had taken Castro's side.[8]

Altogether, the situation seemed a recipe, if not an outright fix, for Castro's success. It was just the kind of platform he relished—standing for the socialist Fatherland against the "Miami Mafia," with Cuba firmly in his grip and with unseen forces in the United States working on his behalf. On January 5, 2000, the INS ruled that the boy's legal guardian was in Cuba. Elian's Miami family was thereby commanded to return him to the INS for deportation.

Lazaro Gonzalez: "The INS [people were] saying that they were concerned for the welfare of the child, for his mental health. Did they ever send a psychologist to talk to him, to counsel him? Never. Yet they had government-paid psychologists saying on national television that Elian was mentally traumatized. How can you diagnose a mental trauma without ever seeing a patient? Long-distance diagnosis is ridiculous, absurd.... Not one psychologist hired by INS ever came to see Elian. We were the ones who looked for professionals to help him after the INS turned him over to us."

The ensuing controversy was a snare for Cuban exiles. The law of the land was against them, and so was the court of public opinion, which tended to dislike refugees. In Miami, thousands of former refugees were crying for justice, while the refugee-maker in Havana used clever arguments and pulled many strings. The worse the situation got, the louder the exiles cried. The louder they cried, the worse they looked and the more their troubles deepened.

Exiles in the hundreds kept up a round-the-clock vigil at Lazaro Gonzalez's modest rented home in northwest Miami. The faceoff drew hordes of journalists and camera

---

[7] See Charley Reese in *The Orlando Sentinel,* April 24, 1999.
[8] Ibid.

crews to the same street in Miami, where a press encampment sprang up across from the Gonzalez home.

Lazaro Gonzalez: "It was twenty-four hours a day, seven days a week. Most members of the press were respectful. There was one time when I became very upset. This camera crew kept shifting their lights and the light would come right into the bedroom. I asked them a couple of times to point their lights another way and they ignored me and I had some harsh words with them.... It was not easy."

As a battery of South Florida lawyers maneuvered in court to delay Elian's removal, ethnic tension flared in Miami: non-Cubans hurled insults and the exiles grew still angrier. Elian's Miami family continued to balk at handing over the boy. In the wee hours of Saturday, April 22, 2000, more than a hundred INS and Border Patrol agents, dressed in combat gear and armed with MP-5 submachine guns, raided Lazaro Gonzalez's home to remove Elian by force. The small crowd in front of the house was gassed with chemicals as agents entered in battle mode, breaking doors, destroying furniture and yelling at the Gonzalez family. An NBC cameraman was maced and kicked, while AP photographer Albert Diaz snapped a picture of a masked agent pointing a weapon at the child. Little Elian, in tears, was snatched from the arms of the same fisherman who had rescued him. Within hours he was at an Air Force base in Washington, where his father waited.

The hand behind the raid was that of U.S. Attorney General Janet Reno, a figure of special contention for Cuban exiles. As thousands protested in the streets of Miami—with several hundred arrested for disturbing the peace and blocking traffic—the image of armed INS agents nabbing a terrified boy shocked America.

In politics, coincidences are scarce. When journalist Paula Zahn asked former Clinton confidant Dick Morris why such a raid might occur between Good Friday and Easter Sunday, Morris asserted that it "had to happen this week." Clinton and Vice President Al Gore, he said, were being questioned by the FBI over illegal campaign funding; and the deadline for the President to answer the Arkansas Supreme Court on the Monica Lewinsky matter was in the same week.

"Bill Clinton did not want this on the front page," Morris explained, averring that Clinton hoped the raid and its aftermath would push his other troubles out of the top headlines. The seizure of Elian, as per Dick Morris, had been the ultimate in spin control.[9]

[9] Fox TV News, April 23, 2000

CHAPTER XXXVIII.

THE CONSTANT STRUGGLE

While Cuba-watchers focused on Elian Gonzalez, repression increased in Cuba. Between November 1999 and February 2000, at least 592 opposition members were detained or restricted by State Security.[1]

In spite of arrests and harassment, internal opposition had grown. Exile groups—including relative newcomers like the Helena Amos Foundation, Mothers Against Repression (MAR), Agenda Cuba and the Cuban Democratic Revolutionary Directorate—had forged links with nonviolent resisters and civic organizations on the island, sending money and books, as well as smuggling in fax machines and computers.

Alongside independent journalist groups and outlets like Cubanet News, Nueva Prensa Cubana and Cuba Press, the 1990's gave birth to another form of free expression: the independent libraries. While boasting of Cuba's high literacy rate and education system, the regime had also banned the writings of Milan Kundera, Mario Vargas Llosa, Octavio Paz, Boris Pasternak and many Cuban exiles. Castro asserted the problem wasn't censorship, only a lack of funds. Dissidents Ramon Colas and Berta Mexidor challenged that statement by opening their private libraries to the public. Colas was arrested on several occasions and some of his books were confiscated, but the concept caught on. By summer 2000, fifty-five independent libraries were flourishing across Cuba. Rafael Aguirre, a lawyer, college professor and author in Miami, worked with the independent library groups by sending books and information.

Rafael Aguirre: "It is bizarre, almost surreal that a government would arrest a human being for owning and lending books. Not only that, the Cuban authorities even arrest

[1] *Pasos a la libertad: Fe en la victoria 2000* (yearly analysis booklet of the Cuban Committee for Human Rights)

those who visit the independent libraries, whether they are Cuban or not. Belgian tourist Dirk Van Der Broeck was detained by State Security and accused of 'collaboration with the enemy' because he had befriended independent librarians. The factor that has helped independent libraries survive has been that the Castro government is afraid of economic and political sanctions from the European Union, which has pressured Cuba to maintain some standard of respect for human rights."

The existence of independent journalists and librarians gave a strong impulse to non-violent resistance groups. Acccording to one analysis of opposition movements in Cuba—a yearly report by the Miami-based staff of the Directorio Revolucionario Democratico Cubano (Cuban Democratic Revolutionary Directorate)—acts of civil disobedience numbered 40 in 1997, 100 in 1998 and 227 in 1999.[2] Tactics included marches, hunger strikes and individual protests. One man, Henry Martini, was arrested by State Security for wearing a "Down with Castro" T-shirt in public.[3]

Some acts of defiance attracted sizable numbers of protesters. In November 1999 about one hundred dissidents carried out a public meeting at the grave of Pedro Luis Boitel, the political prisoner who had died in a hunger strike in 1972. A few weeks later, protesters marched through the township of Parraga, demanding freedom for political prisoners. In January 2000 more than a hundred activists demonstrated in Pinar del Rio, where independent journalist Victor Rolando Arroyo was on trial.[4]

Key figures in the internal nonviolent resistance were the four signers of "The Fatherland Belongs to Everyone," as well as Maritza Lugo and Oscar Elias Biscet. Maritza Lugo, in the political wing of the 30th of November Movement, was frequently arrested and eventually exiled, while her husband was condemned to a lengthy prison term.

Oscar Elias Biscet, an Afro-Cuban doctor, was the leader of the Lawton Foundation for Human Rights. In 1999 he masterminded a forty-day fast—a day for every year of the regime—in which some eight hundred people across the island took part. Biscet also pioneered a seminar called the School for Nonviolent Civic Struggle. Arrested, beaten and burned with lit cigarettes, he was sentenced to three years in jail.

Biscet and Lugo were among the best-known opponents of the system, but not the only ones. Cuba by the year 2000 had dozens of nonviolent civic resistance groups. These included Cuban Youth Movement for Democracy, Democratic Action Group, Alternative Option Movement, Civic Brotherhood, Unitary Council of Cuban Workers, 13th of July Movement, National Union of Opponents, Cuban Feminist Unity, Christian Move-

[2] Ibid.
[3] Ibid.
[4] Ibid.

ment Love and Peace, Democratic Solidarity Party, National Council for Civil Rights in Cuba and many others. Those people active in civic resistance movements apparently included several thousand, a number especially impressive under a dictatorship.

The human rights and nonviolent civic resistance groups that had started with discreet meetings in Havana parks during the seventies blossomed by the end of the nineties. What had begun as small pockets of dissidents had evolved into a large movement throughout Cuba. Most of the movement's leaders were "children of the revolution" born during Castro's forty-year reign, and many were women.[5]

* * *

In November 2000, a more familiar ritual of the anti-Castro struggle unfolded in Panama. Police detectives of that country arrested Luis Posada Carriles, Guillermo Novo, Pedro Remon and Gaspar Jimenez, all of whom Castro accused of plotting to take his life.

Castro, in Panama's capital for the opening of an Ibero-American summit, stated that the four exiles, "financed and led from the United States ... have been sent to Panama with the aim of eliminating me....They are now in this city, and have brought in arms and explosives."[6]

According to wire reports, the four men were planning to pack an automobile with plastic explosives and detonate it as Castro's motorcade passed. Panamanian authorities, however, had a difficult prosecution because "the links between the accused plotters and the only significant physical evidence in the case—a briefcase full of plastic explosives found in a rental car they were using—are too weak to win a conviction."[7]

Posada and his companions would endure a long and tedious process of motions, postponements and political maneuvers. The Panamanian government stated that Posada would not be extradited to Cuba; but, as earlier in Venezuela, the old exile faced the prospect of years behind bars in Panama while the case played out.

* * *

The new millennium brought war to America in the form of passenger airliners used as missiles against the World Trade Center and other targets.

Ten days after the September 11 attacks, the FBI arrested a high-ranking U.S. intel-

[5] Ibid.
[6] ABC News, November 17, 2000
[7] Glenn Garvin in *The Miami Herald*, January 13, 2001

ligence official on charges of spying for Cuba. Ana Belen Montes of the Defense Intelligence Agency (DIA) was the Pentagon's senior analyst for Cuban issues, a position she had apparently used to influence policy as well as pass information to another government.

The forty-five-year-old Belen Montes, of Puerto Rican descent, pled guilty to one count of conspiracy to commit espionage, agreeing to a twenty-five-year term in exchange for telling FBI and other investigators all she knew about DGI activities.

Among other things, Belen Montes had provided the Castro regime with the names of four U.S. "covert intelligence officers" working in Cuba. She had informed Castro's officials about a "special access program related to the national defense of the United States." Belen Montes had also told her Cuban masters that the U.S. knew the locations of several Cuban military installations.

Castro's PR machine, while beating the drums for five of Cuba's imprisoned spies in America, never mentioned Ana Belen Montes or eight other Cuban spies who had negotiated plea agreements with U.S. prosecutors.

Many media, owing to preoccupation with 9/11, missed the story on Belen Montes; but at least one analyst, Martin Arostegui, wondered about its broader implications:

"As Russia and the United States try to close ranks against the common threat posed by Muslim terrorist networks in Central Asia, say intelligence insiders, Castro's growing ties with radical Islamic movements have become a source of worry for both governments. During his recent tour of Syria, Libya, Iran, Qatar, the United Arab Emirates and Malaysia, the Cuban dictator told a cheering crowd of Muslim students at the University of Tehran, 'Together we will bring America to its knees.' ...

"There are signs that Castro's new alignment with fundamentalist Islam could go beyond crowd-pleasing declarations.... Exchanges between bin Laden's al-Qaeda network and Cuban intelligence also could involve the provision of weaponized biological strains produced by Cuba's extensive chemical/biological warfare facilities.... Reports smuggled out by Cuban dissident scientists confirm that Castro's research has concentrated on developing undetectable methods of spreading deadly bacteria, including the use of contaminated bird flocks. Cuba, meanwhile, has been engaging in scientific exchanges with Iraq, say these scientists. A year ago, Cuban Vice President Carlos Lage opened a biotechnological research-and-development plant in Iran, paving the way for Castro's visit to that country last May."[8]

[8] Martin Arostegui, "Fidel May Be Part of Terror Campaign," *Insight on the News*, November 9, 2001

CHAPTER XXXIX.

THE VARELA PROJECT

After four-plus decades in power, the Castro regime's balance sheet was clear enough. More than a million Cubans had become exiles, with many thousands of families broken by geography or ideology, distance or death.

A formerly rich country, Cuba floundered in underdevelopment. Once beholden to the United States—a condition Castro had pledged to correct—Cuba was now substantially dependent on the U.S. dollar, which the regime had accepted since 1993 as legal tender. The one-crop economy had become a no-crop economy: the falling price of sugar in the international market, compounded by Castro's inefficiencies, had forced the closing of dozens of sugar mills.

Oswaldo Paya Sardinas, a school teacher and head of the Christian Liberation Movement (MCL), jumped to the forefront of the Cuban opposition when he unfolded the Varela Project, which aimed "to convert into laws rights that are already established in the Constitution of the Republic of Cuba and are not upheld." The initiative was named for Father Felix Varela, the nineteenth-century priest who was a political as well as a religious hero to Cubans.

Paya aimed to challenge the power structure by using loopholes in the 1976 Constitution. Paya argued that Article 88g of the Constitution of the Republic of Cuba provided citizens with the right to carry out petitions. For several months he coordinated various human rights groups that gathered more than 11,000 signatures in support of a referendum. When Paya submitted the signatures with that demand, controversy erupted.

The opposition in Cuba and many in the exile community reacted with mixed feelings. To militant exiles, and to some activists in Cuba, the project seemed politically dubious. They argued that the initiative would not damage Castro but would merely haggle over loopholes in the existing structure—indeed, that it stood for the acceptance of a tyrant's constitution and a willingness to collaborate in the official structure. Further, they argued, Paya's platform did not request pardon for political prisoners who had committed violence.

Paya supporters argued that the Varela Project was a clever way to erode Castro's power base. It utilized the system to destroy the system, and it made a noticeable dent in an absolutist structure. Proponents argued that the project could establish basic freedoms—most notably the right of Cuban citizens to own private companies—and procure an amnesty for almost all political prisoners.

In the face of massive internal dissent, Castro put a pretty face on his reaction. He encouraged a reliable old foe, former U.S. President Jimmy Carter, to visit Cuba. The highlight of the visit was an address by Carter, in Spanish, that Cuban TV carried uncensored. From that speech, many Cubans learned of the Varela Project for the first time. During his tour, the smiling Carter also pleased Castro with sweeping declarations that Cuba did not represent a threat to the United States and that the embargo policy was outdated.

Castro made a more sincere response to the Varela Project when, on June 12, 2002, the regime staged a march of one million Cubans in support of "the revolution." Three days later, 130,000 petition stations opened across Cuba to collect signatures for a constitutional amendment that would declare the existing system "untouchable." Officials claimed that 7.6 million persons—more than 90 percent of the voting population—had signed the measure. The referendum had offered no privacy, nor had it included an option to vote no.

*　*　*

The Varela Project coincided with a tougher policy toward Castro from a U.S. administration that the regime especially loved to hate. President George W. Bush, unlike his predecessor, seemed bent on doing precisely what Castro did not want him to do. Rather than let the embargo loosen, Bush tightened it. One of his administration's first steps was to slap heavy fines on illegal U.S. tourism to Cuba. One newspaper reported that "in sharply increasing numbers, those found to have been in Cuba—usually given away by Cuban cigars, rum or other souvenirs in their luggage—are receiving letters from the Treasury Department threatening them with fines that can reach as high as $55,000, depending on such factors as the length of their stay in Cuba and the amount of money they spent there.... A Treasury spokesman said the department sent out 188 penalty letters last year and 517 through July this year. The average threatened fine was about

$7,500; the department gives people an opportunity to respond and sometimes drops its case based on the explanation."[1]

Besides collecting more than two million dollars in fines, the Bush administration also supported the cause of Cuban human rights in international forums. Worst of all for Castro, the president promised to use his veto power to defeat any bill that would weaken the embargo.

Dislike between the governments was palpable. American diplomats in Havana met with Cuban dissidents as openly as Castro's diplomats in Washington met with Puerto Rican nationalists. Bush's tough policy on terror and terrorist regimes may also have aggravated Castro's well-developed "bunker mentality." The Cuban leader, who suffered fainting spells in public and often rambled incoherently on TV, cannot have been pleased when Oswaldo Paya won the Sakharov Prize of the European Parliament, a coveted human rights award.

Pressured by international opinion—particularly in Europe, where the political Left, after decades of compliance, had started to pose tough questions about Cuba—Castro's officials allowed Paya to travel to Europe to receive the award and then proceed to the United States before re-entering Cuba, an extremely rare concession on the regime's part.

Again, a more sincere official response to Paya might have come in December 2002, when the dissident's home in Havana was heavily vandalized. Castro's media asserted that members of the exile group Alpha 66, opponents of the Varela Project, had done the deed; but Paya said he believed the culprits to be Cuban State Security agents.

---

[1] "New Roadblocks for Travel to Cuba," *The Philadelphia Inquirer,* November 22, 2001

CHAPTER XXXX.

THE END OF THE END?

One of Cuba's most pain-filled years, 2003, opened with a concerted official attack against the nation's "parallel economy," its huge black market.

Cuba's black market had become an immense network in which almost everyone, including many officials, took part. Avoiding state structures, people traded and sold the goods they needed for survival. The government, for its part, wanted to control currency tightly—most of all the U.S. dollars that people passed between each other while disregarding official money centers.

Announcing a dragnet on drug traffic, State Security arrested some street dealers and then quickly proceeded to its real target, the parallel economy, by closing down scores of independent businesses.

Paladares or small private restaurants were shuttered, their modest food inventories confiscated. Self-employed tradesmen—carpenters, leather workers, appliance repairmen—found their operations barred and their tools or goods in the hands of authorities. The scope of the arrests and confiscations is hard to determine, but the crackdown was carried out at a national level and sustained for several weeks. In the small city of Guines alone—close to Havana, with a population of about 46,000—twenty government employees were arrested for involvement in so-called illegal economic activities.[1]

An independent press dispatch from Holguin, in eastern Cuba, stated:

"[T]he morning of February 14, police found Milber Galiano had 15 pounds of fish, presumably with intent to sell. The fish were confiscated and Galiano fined 1,500 pesos.

"Yamile Rodriguez was found to be in possession of 8 boards of cedar, 5 plastic bowls, 8 spoons, 2 forks, 2 teaspoons, 78 cloth napkins, one bag of cement, one plastic thermos,

[1] "Twenty Arrested in Guines," *Cubanet News*, February 21, 2003

one plastic tank containing 20 pounds of sugar, one attaché case containing 20 pounds of sugar, one light bulb, one pair of work-gloves, one length of rope, and one 200-gallon plastic tank; all evidence of home brewing. All goods were confiscated and she was fined 1,500 pesos. Her step father was fined 250 pesos; the 8 wooden boards were his.

"Idania Linares, 35, Yamile's neighbor, was fined 200 pesos for complicity in the sale of whatever was being brewed.... Javier Blanco wasn't home when police called. They broke down the door and found 100 pounds of rice and 60 pounds of beans. He was fined 1,500 pesos....Victor Pajon lost 15 pounds of yams, 11 pounds of tomatoes, and 25 eggs. And the 1,500 peso fine.

" 'This is just abusive,' said Yamile Rodriguez, as she showed the receipt for the bag of cement she had bought at a dollar store. 'They even took my spoons, and the bag of cement. It seems a policeman must have needed it.' "[2]

※　※　※

The next crackdown was aimed at the political enemies: human rights activists, independent librarians and journalists. As of early 2003, the civil resistance and peaceful opposition in Cuba still numbered several thousand activists in about five hundred organizations, including independent news services, ecological groups, independent libraries, artist guilds, human rights organizations, illicit trade unions and unsanctioned political parties.

Politically, Castro was about to make a high-risk choice, for he well knew that crushing the nonviolent opposition would bring heavy international pressure on his nearly unsustainable regime; but he also understood the politics of power, and he saw that the opposition, having grown large and bold, needed to be crushed, even at the price of international rebuke. He had made this choice many times before—and he determined, as before, to justify his repressive wave as a defense against conspiracies by his familiar enemies, the "Miami Mafia" and the U.S. administration.

The sweep began on March 18 and proceeded swiftly. Within three days, close to eighty opposition leaders were behind bars, among them Marta Beatriz Roque ("The Homeland Belongs to Everyone"), poet-journalist Raul Rivero, economist Oscar Espinoza Chepe, journalists Omar Rodriguez Saludes and Victor Rolando Arroyo—the latter having already served a prison term for the offense of distributing toys to poor children during the Christmas holiday. State Security and PNR officers ransacked the journalists' homes,

---

[2] *Cubanet News,* February 24, 2003

confiscating books, radios, typewriters, cameras, computers, files, printers, fax machines and furniture.

Barely two weeks after the arrests, trials began behind closed doors. To the astonishment of the civilized world, prosecutors requested life imprisonment for three members of the opposition and prison terms of between fifteen and thirty years for the rest.

In Castro's Cuba, the death penalty can be applied for any of 112 crimes, including any of 79 political offenses. The regime now chose to utilize two of these: Article 91, stipulating prison or death for those who act against "the independence or the territorial integrity of the State," and Law 88, imposing twenty-year sentences on those who carry out "acts that in agreement with imperialist interests are aimed at subverting the internal order of the Nation and destroy its political, economic, and social system."

The evident purpose behind the summary trials and stiff sentences was to break the backbone of the dissident movement. With conspicuous exceptions like Biscet and Raul Rivero, the regime preferred to leave well-known personalities unarrested, while moving directly against the opposition's mid-level leadership. By early April, seventy-five dissidents had been convicted and sentenced to prison terms of up to 28 years.

Of the 75 dissidents, more than 40 had gathered signatures for the Varela Project. Luis Enrique Ferrer Garcia, twenty-seven years old, had coordinated the project in Camaguey province. He drew the longest sentence of all, 28 years. Luis Enrique's elder brother, thirty-two-year-old Jose Daniel, had worked for the project in the city of Santiago de Cuba. He got 25 years. Both were members of the Christian Liberation Movement.

Oscar Elias Biscet—already in jail when the crackdown started—was sentenced to 25 years and placed in solitary confinement. Marta Beatriz Roque, the only woman among the arrested, was given 20 years. Activist Hector Palacios received 25, Victor Rolando Arroyo 26, Omar Rodriguez Saludes 27 and the ailing economist Oscar Espinoza 20 years. Magazine editor Ricardo Gonzalez, journalist Hector Maseda and journalist-poet Raul Rivero each got 20.

In its international PR, the regime insisted that the condemned had been acting as agents of the U.S. Interests Section in Havana in trying to overthrow the system. To give credence to these claims, a few State Security informants and agents who had infiltrated the anti-Castro groups testified during the trials and accused the imprisoned activists of being paid mercenaries. These agents—notably the "independent journalist" Manuel David Orrio—were portrayed as men serving in dangerous roles, despite the fact that opposition groups had readily accepted members and had not engaged in any form of violence.

Human rights organizations—Amnesty International, Pax Christi, Reporters Without Borders, PEN and others—did not buy Castro's defenses and were quick to condemn the repression. Just as quickly, on April 11, the regime executed three Afro-Cuban men for attempting to hijack a ferry and escape into exile.

An offended world made its repulsion clear. From the halls of the Vatican to the parliaments of Europe and South America, a chorus of voices rose against the repression in Cuba, as the European Union threatened cancellations of planned events involving the Castro government. In the U.S. Congress, even pro-Castro members like Charles Rangel and Jose Serrano voted with the majority to condemn the crackdown.

Among the hundreds of articles written and published about the crackdown, *The New York Times* reproduced an essay by the fifty-seven-year-old Raul Rivero. The essay concluded: "No one can make me feel like a criminal, or an enemy agent, or someone who does not love his country, or make me believe any of the other absurd accusations the government uses to degrade and humiliate. I am only a man who writes. And writes in the country where he was born, and where his great-grandparents were born."[3]

On July 14, well-known dissidents whom the regime had not arrested—Oswaldo Paya, Vladamiro Roca, Felix Bonne, Rene Gomez Manzano, Elizardo Sanchez—accepted invitations from French officials to attend a Bastille Day celebration at the French embassy in Havana. Cuban officials boycotted the event in protest against the tie between diplomats and dissidents.

Cuban exiles organized demonstrations against the Castro regime in Madrid, Rome, Prague and Paris, where Cuban diplomats physically assaulted a group of Reporters Without Borders. Exiles also lobbied the U.N. Human Rights Commission in Geneva, pressed the Bush administration for stiffer sanctions against Cuba, and organized letter-writing campaigns. As the agonizing year of 2003 wore on, Castro's regime issued rapid-fire condemnations of governments—like those of France, Italy and Spain—that had been its friends for decades.

The crackdown had also thrown a mighty wrench into Castro's anti-embargo campaign. Lobby groups that had spent years praising the changed atmosphere in Cuba simply disbanded. The entire board of one such group, the Cuba Policy Foundation of Washington D.C., resigned *en masse* with an acknowledgement that the crackdown had made its efforts futile. Several U.S. trade delegations cancelled their trips to the island—even as other anti-embargo advocates, like Republican Congressman Jeff Flake, held to their views. "We never embarked on this policy as a way to reward the Cuban government for good behavior," Flake said.[4]

[3] Raul Rivero, "A Man Who Writes," *The New York Times,* April 22, 2003
[4] Associated Press, April 22, 2003

As Castro clung to power, the civil resistance movement—even though badly wounded—took heart from the wide-ranging condemnation of Castro's forty-five-year-old regime and from the feeling that, for once, Cubans were not alone in their struggle for liberty.

"The Cuban situation is in its final stage," Vladimiro Roca said. "We are at the end of the chess game and we don't know which move will decide the change, but I am sure that the end is very near."

INDEX OF ORAL SOURCES

BIBLIOGRAPHY

Aguilar Leon, Luis, *Cuba: conciencia y revolucion*. Miami: Ediciones Universal, 1972

Aguilar Leon, Luis, *Reflexiones sobre Cuba y su futuro*. Miami: Ediciones Universal, 1991

Aguilar Leon, Luis, ed., *Operation Zapata: The "Ultrasensitive" Report and Testimony of the Board of Inquiry on the Bay of Pigs*. Frederick, Md.: University Publications of America, 1981

Alfonso, Pablo, *Cuba, Castro y los catolicos*. Miami: Ediciones Hispamerican Books, 1985

American University, Foreign Area Studies, *Cuba: A Country Study*. Washington: U.S. Government Printing Office, 1985

Benemelis, Juan F., *Castro, subversion y terrorismo en Africa*. Madrid: Editorial San Martin, 1984

Benemelis, Juan F., *Las guerras secretas de Fidel Castro*. Miami: Fundacion Elena Mederos, 2002

Benemelis, Juan F., & Melvin Manon, *Juicio a Fidel*. Santo Domingo: Taller, 1990

Bertot, Lillian D., *The Literary Imagination of the Mariel Generation*. Miami: The Endowment for Cuban American Studies, 1995

Bethel, Paul D., *The Losers*. New York: Arlington House Press, 1969

Blasier, Cole, *The Hovering Giant: U.S. Responses to Revolutionary Change in Latin America*. Pittsburgh: University of Pittsburgh Press, 1979

Blazquez, Agustin, dir., *Covering Cuba 3: Elian*. A documentary film, 2002

Blight, James G., & David Welch, *On the Brink: Americans and Soviets Reexamine the Cuban Missile Crisis*. New York: Hill & Wang, 1989

Bonachea, Ramon, & Marta San Martin, *The Cuban Insurrection 1952–1959*. New Brunswick, N.J.:Transaction Books, 1974

Bosch, Adriana D., *Orlando Bosch — el hombre que yo conozco*. Miami: Editorial SIBI, 1988

Calatayud, Antonio, *El testamento de los desheredados*. Miami: Editorial Ponce, 1981

Carbonell, Nestor T., *And the Russians Stayed*. New York: William Morrow & Company, 1989

Carreno, Jose, *Cincuenta testimonios urgentes: denuncias en Ginebra sobre violaciones de los derechos humanos*. Miami: Ediciones Universal, 1989

Castro, Fidel, *La experiencia cubana: informe al primer congreso, 1975, y otros documentos*. Barcelona: Editorial Blume, 1977

Chavez, Clara, & Dulce Medina & Samuel Almohalla, *Giron: biografia de la victoria*. La Habana: Editora Politica, 1986

Clark, Juan, *Cuba: mito y realidad*. Miami: Ediciones Saeta, 1990

Crespo, Francisco Julio, *Bandidismo en el Escambray 1960–1965*. La Habana: Editorial Ciencias Sociales, 1986

Cros Sandoval, Mercedes, *Mariel and Cuban National Identity*. Miami: Editorial SIBI, 1985

Cuesta, Tony, *Plomo y fantasia*. Miami: Editorial SIBI, 1984

Del Aguila, Juan M., *Cuba: Dilemmas of a Revolution*. Boulder & London: Westview Press, 1984

Del Pino, Rafael, *General Del Pino Speaks: An Insight Into Elite Corruption and Military Dissension in Castro's Cuba*. Washington: The Cuban American National Foundation, 1987

Del Pino, Rafael, *Proa a la libertad*. Madrid: Editorial Planeta, 1991

Department of State, *Foreign Relations of the United States, 1958–1960*, Volume VII, *Cuba*. Washington: U.S. Government Printing Office, 1991

Diaz-Balart, Rafael, *Decalogo de un exiliado*. Madrid, 1974

Diaz Rodriguez, Ernesto, *Un testimonio urgente*. Miami: Replica Publishing, 1977

Dinerstein, Herbert, *The Making of a Missile Crisis, October 1962*. Baltimore & London: Johns Hopkins University Press, 1976

Dumont, Rene, *Cuba, ¿es socialista?* Caracas: Editorial Tiempo Nuevo, 1971

Edwards, Jorge, *Persona Non Grata*. New York: Pomerica Press, 1971

Encinosa, Enrique, *Cuba: The Unfinished Revolution*. Austin: Eakin Press, 1988

Encinosa, Enrique, *Escambray: la guerra olvidada*. Miami: Editorial SIBI, 1989

Encinosa, Enrique, *Cuba en guerra*. Miami: Endowment for Cuban American Studies, 1994

Fermoselle, Rafael, *The Evolution of the Cuban Military, 1492–1986*. Miami: Ediciones Universal, 1987

Ferrer, Eduardo, *Operacion Puma*. Miami: International Aviation Consultants, 1975

Fonseca Llorente, Leonardo, *De Angola a Miami*. Miami: Editorial SIBI, 1978

Fontaine, Roger W., *Terrorism: The Cuban Connection*. New York: Crane, Russak & Co., 1988

Franqui, Carlos, *Family Portrait with Fidel*. New York: Random House, 1984

Franqui, Carlos, *Vida, aventuras y desastres de un hombre llamado Castro*. Barcelona: Editorial Planeta, 1988

Fuentes, Norberto, *Cazabandido*. Montevideo: Libro de la Pupila, 1970

Fuentes, Norberto, *Condenados de Condado*. Buenos Aires: Centro Editor de America Latina, 1968

Fuentes, Norberto, *Nos impusieron la violencia*. La Habana: Editorial Letras Cubanas, 1986

Garthoff, Raymond L., *Reflections on the Cuban Missile Crisis*. Washington: The Brookings Institution, 1987

Gonzalez, Reynol, *Y Fidel creo el punto X*. Miami: Saeta Ediciones, 1987

Halperin, Maurice, *The Taming of Fidel Castro*. Berkeley: University of California Press, 1980

Higgins, Trumbull, *The Perfect Failure: Kennedy, Eisenhower and the CIA at the Bay of Pigs*. New York: W.W. Norton & Company, 1987

Horowitz, Irving L., *El comunismo cubano: 1959–1979*. Madrid: Editorial Playor, 1979

Hurt, Henry, *Reasonable Doubt*. New York: Holt, Rinehart & Winston, 1985

Ichaso, Leon, dir., *Bitter Sugar*. A feature film, 1996

James, Daniel, *Cuba: First Soviet Satellite in the Americas*. New York: Avon Books, 1962

Jimenez Leal, Orlando, dir., *8-A*. A documentary film with dramatized footage, 1993

Johnson, Haynes, *The Bay of Pigs*. New York: Dell Publishing, 1964

Kennedy, Robert F., *Thirteen Days: A Memoir of the Cuban Missile Crisis*. New York: W.W. Norton & Company, 1969

Kissinger, Henry A., *The White House Years*. Boston: Little & Brown, 1979

Larzelere, Alex, *The 1980 Cuban Boatlift*. Washington: National Defense University Press, 1988

Lasky, Victor, *JFK: The Man and the Myth*. New Rochelle, N.Y.: Arlington House, 1965

Lazo, Mario, *Dagger in the Heart*. New York: Funk & Wagnalls, 1968

Lewis, Oscar, & Ruth M. Lewis & Susan M. Rigdon, *Four Men Living the Revolution: An Oral History of Contemporary Cuba*. Champaign: University of Illinois Press, 1977

Leyva De Varona, Adolfo, *Cuban-Mexican Relations During the Castro Era*. Ann Arbor: University of Michigan Dissertation Services, 1995

Luque Escalona, Roberto, *Fidel: el juicio de la historia*. Mexico: Editorial Dante, 1990

Lynch, Grayston L., *Decision for Disaster: Betrayal at the Bay of Pigs.* Washington: Brassey's, 1998

Martinet, Giles, *Los cinco comunismos.* Editorial Tiempo Nuevo, Caracas, 1972

Maso, Jose Luis, *Buenos dias.* Miami: New House Publishers, 1971

Medrano, Humberto, *Caminos de papel.* Miami: Editorial AIP, 1977

Medrano, Mignon, *Todo lo dieron por Cuba.* Miami: The Endowment for Cuban American Studies, 1995

Montaner, Carlos Alberto, *Informe secreto sobre la revolucion cubana.* Madrid: Ediciones Sedmay, 1976

Navarro, Antonio, *Tocayo.* Westport, Ct.: Arlington House, 1981

Navarro, Osvaldo, *El caballo de Mayuagara.* La Habana: Editora Politica, 1987

O'Connor, James, *The Origins of Socialism in Cuba.* Ithaca, N.Y.: Cornell University Press, 1970

Oppenheimer, Andres, *Castro's Final Hour.* New York: Simon & Schuster, 1992

Oro, Jose R., *The Poisoning of Paradise: The Environmental Crisis in Cuba.* Miami: The Endowment for Cuban American Studies, 1992

Padilla, Heberto, *La mala memoria.* Barcelona: Plaza y Janes, 1989

Perez, Louis A., *Cuba: Between Reform and Revolution.* New York: Oxford University Press, 1988

Phillipson, Lorrin & Rafael Llerena, *Freedom Flights.* New York: Random House, 1970

Portuondo de Castro, Juan Miguel, *Como se apoderaron los comunistas de la Universidad de La Habana.* Miami: Ediciones del Directorio Magisterial Cubano, 1962

Posada Carriles, Luis, *Los caminos del guerrero.* 1994

Riesgo, Rodolfo, *Cuba: el movimiento obrero y su entorno socio-politico.* Miami & Caracas: Saeta, 1985

Rivero Collado, Carlos, *Los sobrinos del tio Sam.* Madrid: Ediciones Akal, 1977

Rodriguez, Felix, & John Weisman, *Shadow Warrior.* New York: Simon & Schuster, 1989

Ros, Enrique, *Giron: la verdadera historia.* Miami: Ediciones Universal, 1994

Ruiz, Leovigildo, *Diario de una traicion 1959.* Miami: Editorial Lorie, 1965

Ruiz, Leovigildo, *Diario de una traicion 1960.* Miami: Editorial Lorie, 1970

Ruiz, Leovigildo, *Diario de una traicion 1961.* Miami: Editorial Lorie, 1972

Ruiz, Leovigildo, *Diario de una traicion 1968.* Miami: Editorial Lorie, 1970

Sales, Miguel, *Desde las rejas.* Miami: Ediciones Universal, 1976

Schoultz, Lars, *National Security and United States Policy Towards Latin America.* Princeton, N.J.: Princeton University Press, 1987

Silverio Sainz, Nicasio, *En la Cuba de Castro.* Miami: Ediciones Universal, 1967

Suarez, Andres, *Cuba: Castroism and Communism, 1959–1966.* Cambridge, Ma.: MIT Press, 1967

Suarez Amador, Jose, *La lucha contra bandidos en Cuba.* La Habana: Editorial Letras Cubanas, 1981

Suarez Nunez, Jose, *El gran culpable.* Caracas, 1963

Suchlicki, Jaime, *Cuba: From Columbus to Castro.* New York: Charles Scribner's Sons, 1974

Suchlicki, Jaime, *University Students and Revolution in Cuba, 1920–1968.* Coral Gables, Fl.: University of Miami Press, 1969

Szulc, Tad, & Karl Meyer, *The Cuban Invasion: Chronicles of a Disaster.* New York: Frederick A. Praeger, 1962

Taylor, Maxwell, *Swords and Plowshares.* New York: W.W. Norton & Company, 1972

Thomas, Hugh, *Cuba: The Pursuit of Freedom.* New York: Harper & Row, New York

Tricka, Jan F., *Communist Party States: Comparative and International Studies.* New York: Bobbs-Merrill, 1969

Valladares, Armando, *Against All Hope.* New York: Alfred A. Knopf, 1986

Weyl, Nathaniel, *Estrella roja sobre Cuba.* Miami: Editorial La Polilla, 1962

Wise, David, & Thomas B. Ross, *The Invisible Government.* New York: Random House, 1964

Wyden, Peter, *Bay of Pigs: The Untold Story.* New York: Simon & Schuster, 1979

INDEX

(See also Glossary, p. xv)